Roots and Wings

For a complete list of books by Bhagwan Shree Rajneesh
please write to Rajneesh Foundation,
17 Koregaon Park, Poona, 411001, India

Roots and Wings

Talks on Zen

Bhagwan Shree Rajneesh

COMPILATION
Ma Krishna Pria

EDITOR
Swami Krishna Prem

Routledge & Kegan Paul
LONDON, BOSTON AND HENLEY

First published in India in 1975
This edition first published in 1979
by Routledge & Kegan Paul Ltd
39 Store Street, London WC1E 7DD
Broadway House, Newtown Road,
Henley-on-Thames, Oxon RG9 1EN and
9 Park Street, Boston, Mass. 02108, USA

Printed in Great Britain by
Redwood Burn Limited, Trowbridge and Esher

ISBN 0 7100 0420 6

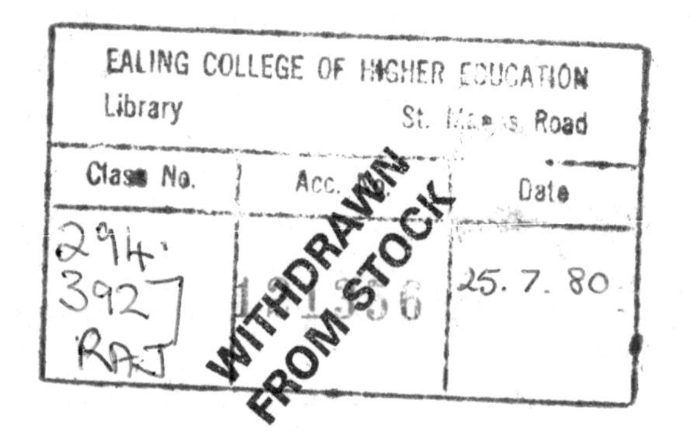

ROOTS AND WINGS

eleven talks
based on Zen stories
and seekers' questions
given by
Bhagwan Shree Rajneesh
from June 10th to June 20th 1974
in Poonah, India

CONTENTS

INTRODUCTION

Love . . .

In Poona, India, there is a fast flowing river with a waterfall pounding over some boulders in a spot near the Rajneesh Ashram at 17, Koregaon Park. I sat there one evening with a friend and tried to think how I could tackle the job of introducing this book, and Bhagwan Shree Rajneesh, to you.

For me, rivers have a way of dissolving mental rubbish and reducing everything to its simplest terms.

Sitting there, listening to the sounds of night-time and the rushing water, looking at a river plant being tussled in all directions by the current, I was reminded of the Zen story of Chiyono. When she became enlightened, she wrote a poem:

This way and that way
I tried to keep the pail together,
hoping the weak bamboo
would never break . . .

and I cried: for me, for Chiyono, for the plant. The river spirit seemed to be changing and broadening my focus about the task.

And I felt a feeling of Bhagwan growing inside, in the sounds, in the wind, in my friend.

I had the sense that my whole life has been an introduction to Bhagwan, to becoming a disciple of his, to everything that I was that moment. It all became necessary, perfect.

I felt how much Bhagwan personifies Zen, how everything about him is like everything else that I know, but none of it is him; how the river, India, is like him, a flow of paradoxes and contradictions, but deeply balanced, deeply right.

It is the most appropriate thing that Bhagwan should speak on Zen, because he feels so Zen-like—incomprehensible, yet totally simple.

And this Zen of his being is not the Zen that many in the

West have adopted intellectually, not the Zen that has often been misinterpreted as the path of least resistence, the way that requires nothing of you, for: "The grass grows by itself"; but a Zen so fast and deep, that it goes beyond all words and concepts.

The word "Zen" comes from the Japanese "Za-zen" which means sitting quietly, doing nothing. And watching Bhagwan speak, one gets the feeling that he also is just sitting, doing nothing. A process that seems unrelated to him is happening. A lecture happens, like a ripple in the river, there is no effort or preparation. It happens all by itself! There is no interference on his part. His being speaks to your being. What is so incredible is that he can do nothing, and continue to do everything as usual, or rather, everything around him happens as it should.

As with every deep teaching, by and by, the key to the door is lost, and we are left with a mere shell of the original experience. And because religion is another way of seeing whatever is, (and I find, a truer way), we take the message and run it through our minds of shallowness and fear, distort it, until the key no longer fits and the door has become a wall. The truth seems to be that we don't have the vaguest idea of what the ancient wise ones were talking about, although we pretend so well.

In this selection of stories, as well as in the spontaneous questions and answers which follow each talk, Bhagwan shows us the incredible liquid versatility of his being. Religion has always been for "wings", renunciation, and against "roots", pleasure, the world.

Bhagwan tells us that wings cannot develop without roots, just as a tree cannot flower independent of its seed, its roots. The growth is a continuum; you can't skip the birth pains, the suffering, the effort, the pushing upwards and begin with the flower, the bliss, the meditation. But that is precisely what we all seem to try to do: ignore our own sickness and pretend to health.

Bhagwan is for both "this", the roots, and "that", the wings. There is no choice to be made, he says. If you accept the roots, explore them deeply and consciously, in other words, be where you are, that is the nourishment that the roots need to blossom into wings.

In *Roots and Wings,* Bhagwan is not explaining Zen stories. If he were, he would only be perpetuating the whole game of spiritual materialism.

What he is doing is taking us deeper into the mystery of these stories. He says that life is not a problem to be solved, but a mystery to be lived. Mysteries can't be solved—H_2O is not a river—but mystery can penetrate you. Often, in the activity of finding out, we are closed to what we seek by the very tension that the search causes.

And for me a secret of understanding Zen, or Bhagwan, is not to try to argue, to solve, to make sense out of it. Zen makes no sense, and if it did, I doubt that it would have any value for transformation. The understanding of Zen, or Bhagwan, is an understanding of the heart, of the deeper layers of being, not of the mind. Which is to say . . .

Nothing can really really be said.

In this book, we are all invited to enter the door, and be mystified unto understanding.

Ma Yoga Sudha

First Talk

10th June 1974

Bhagwan,

The Japanese master Nan-in gave audience
to a professor of philosophy.

Serving tea, Nan-in filled his visitor's cup,
and kept pouring.

The professor watched the overflow
until he could restrain himself no longer:
Stop!
The cup is overfull, no more will go in.

Nan-in said:
Like this cup,
you are full of your own opinions and speculations.
How can I show you Zen
unless you first empty your cup?

You have come
to an even more
dangerous person than Nan-in,
because an empty cup won't do.
The cup has to be broken completely.
Even empty, if you are there, then you are full.
Even emptiness fills you.
If you feel that you are empty,
you are not empty at all, you are there.
Only the name has changed.
Now you call yourself emptiness.
The cup won't do at all.
It has to be broken completely.
Only when you are not
can the tea be poured into you.
Only when you are not
is there no need really to pour the tea into you.
When you are not,
the whole existence begins pouring,
the whole existence becomes a shower
from every dimension, from every direction.
When you are not, the Divine is.

The story is beautiful.
It was bound to happen to a professor of philosophy.
The story says a professor of philosophy
came to Nan-in.

He must have come for the wrong reasons,
because a professor of philosophy, as such,
is always wrong.

Philosophy means
intellect, reasoning, thinking, argumentativeness.
And this is the way to be wrong,
because you cannot be in love with existence
if you are argumentative.
Argument is the barrier.
If you argue, you are closed.
The whole existence closes to you.
Then you are not open,
and existence is not open to you.
When you argue, you assert.
Assertion is violence, aggression,
and the truth cannot be known by an aggressive mind,
the truth cannot be discovered by violence.
You can come to know the truth
only when you are in love.
But love never argues.
There is no argument in love,
because there is no aggression.

And remember,
not only was that man a professor of philosophy,
you are also the same.
Every man carries his own philosophy,
and every man in his own way is a professor,
because you profess your ideas.
You believe in them.
You have opinions, concepts.

And because of opinions and concepts,
your eyes are dull, they cannot see;
your mind is stupid, it cannot know.
Ideas create stupidity
because the more the ideas are there,
the more the mind is burdened.
And how can a burdened mind know?
The more ideas are there,

the more it becomes just like dust
which has gathered on a mirror.
How can the mirror mirror?
How can the mirror reflect?
Your intelligence is just covered
by opinions, the dust,
and everyone who is opinionated
is bound to be stupid and dull.

That's why professors of philosophy
are almost always stupid.
They know too much to know at all.
They are burdened too much.
They cannot fly in the sky;
they can't have wings.
And they are so much in the mind,
they can't have roots in the earth.
They are not grounded in the earth,
and they are not free to fly into the sky.

And remember, you are all the same.
There may be differences of quantity,
but every mind is qualitatively the same,
because mind thinks, argues,
collects and gathers knowledge and becomes dull.
Only children are intelligent.
And if you can retain your childhood,
if you continuously reclaim your childhood,
you will remain innocent and intelligent.
If you gather dust, childhood is lost,
innocence is no more,
the mind has become dull and stupid.
Now you can have philosophies.
The more philosophies you have,
the more you are far away from the Divine.

A religious mind is a non-philosophical mind.
A religious mind is an innocent, intelligent mind.
The mirror is clear; the dust has not been gathered.
And every day a continuous cleaning goes on.
That's what I call meditation.

This professor of philosophy came to Nan-in.
He must have come for wrong reasons.
He must have come to receive some answers.
Those people who are filled with questions
are always in search of answers,
and Nan-in could not give an answer.
It is foolish to be concerned
with questions and answers.

Nan-in could give you a new mind,
Nan-in could give you a new being,
Nan-in could give you a new existence
in which no questions arise,
but Nan-in was not interested
in answering any particular questions.
He was not interested in giving answers.
Neither am I.

You must have come here with many questions.
It is bound to be so,
because the mind gives birth to questions.
Mind is a question-creating mechanism.
Feed anything into it, out comes a question,
and many questions follow;
give an answer to it,
and immediately it converts it into many questions.
You are here filled with many questions.
Your cup is already full.
No need for Nan-in to pour any tea into it,
you are already overflowing.

I can give give you a new existence.
That's why I have invited you here.
I will not give you any answers.
All questions, all answers, are useless,
just a wastage of energy.
But I can transform you, and that is the only answer.
And that one answer solves all questions.

Philosophy has many questions, many answers –
millions.

Religion has only one answer.
Whatsoever the question,
the answer remains the same.
Buddha used to say:
You taste sea water from anywhere,
the taste remains the same, the saltiness of it.

Whatsoever you ask is really irrelevant.
I will answer the same,
because I have got only one answer.
But that one answer is like a master key.
It opens all doors.
It is not concerned with any particular lock –
any lock, and the key opens it.
Religion has only one answer,
and that answer is meditation.
And meditation means how to empty yourself.

The professor must have been tired, walking long,
when he reached Nan-in's cottage.
And Nan-in said:
Wait a little.

He must have been in a hurry.
Mind is always in a hurry,
and mind is always in search
of instantaneous realizations.
To wait, for the mind, is very difficult,
almost impossible.

Nan-in said:
I will prepare tea for you.
You look tired.
Wait a little, rest a little,
and have a cup of tea.
And then we can discuss.

And Nan-in boiled the water,
started preparing the tea.
But he must have been watching the professor.
Not only was the water boiling,
the professor was also boiling within.

Not only was the tea kettle making sounds,
the professor was making more sounds within,
chattering, continuously talking.
The professor must have been getting ready –
what to ask, how to ask, from where to begin.
He must have been in a deep monologue.

Nan-in must have been smiling and watching:
This man is too full,
so much so that nothing can penetrate into him.
The answer cannot be given,
because there is no one to receive it.
The guest cannot enter into the house.
There is no room.

Nan-in must have wanted to become a guest
in this professor.
Out of compassion, a Buddha always wants
to become a guest within you.
He knocks from everywhere, but there is no door.
And even if he breaks a door,
which is very difficult,
there is no room.
You are so full with yourself,
and with rubbish and all types of paraphernalia
which you have gathered in many, many lives,
you cannot even enter into yourself.
There is no room, no space.
You live just outside of your own being,
just on the steps.
You cannot enter within yourself.
Everything is blocked.

And then Nan-in poured tea into the cup.
The professor came to be uneasy,
because he was continuously pouring tea.
It was overflowing.
Soon it would be going out on the floor.
Then the professor said:
Stop!
What are you doing?

Now this cup cannot hold any more tea,
not even a single drop.
Are you mad?
What are you doing?

And Nan-in said:
The same is the case with you.
You are so alert to observe and become aware
that the cup is full and cannot hold any more,
why are you not so aware about your own self?
You are overflowing
with opinions, philosophies, doctrines, scriptures.
You know too much already.
I cannot give you anything.
You have travelled in vain.
Before coming to me
you should have emptied your cup.
Then I could pour something into it.

But I tell you,
you have come to a more dangerous person.
No, an empty cup I won't allow,
because if the cup is there you will fill it.
You are so addicted,
and you have become so habituated
that you cannot allow the cup to be empty
even for a single moment.
The moment you see emptiness anywhere,
you start filling it.
You are so scared of emptiness.
You are so afraid.
Emptiness appears like death.
You will fill it with anything, but you will fill it.
No, I have invited you to be here
to break down this cup completely,
so that even if you want to,
you cannot fill it.

Emptiness means there is no cup left.
All the walls have disappeared;
the bottom has fallen down.

You have become an abyss.
Then I can pour myself into you.

Much is possible, if you allow.
But to allow is arduous,
because to allow, you will have to surrender.
Emptiness means surrender.
Nan-in was saying to that professor:
Bow down, surrender, empty your head.
I am ready to pour.

That professor had not even asked the question,
and Nan-in had given the answer,
because really there is no need to ask the question.
The question remains the same.
You ask me or not, I know what the question is.

So many of you are here, but I know the question,
because deep down the question is one —
the anxiety, the anguish, the meaninglessness,
the futility of this whole life,
not knowing who you are.
But you are filled.
Allow me to break this cup.

This camp is going to be a destruction, a death.
If you are ready to be destroyed,
something new will come out of it.
Every destruction can become a creative birth.
If you are ready to die,
you can have a new life, you can be reborn.

I am here just to be a midwife.
That's what Socrates used to say —
that a master is just a midwife.
I can help, I can protect, I can guide,
that's all.
The actual phenomenon, the transformation,
is going to happen to you.

Suffering will be there,
because no birth is possible without suffering.

Much anguish will come up,
because you have accumulated it
and it has to be thrown.
A deep cleansing and catharsis will be needed.

Birth is just like death,
but the suffering is worth taking.
Out of the darkness of suffering,
a new morning arises, a new sun arises.
And the dawn is not very far
when you feel darkness too much.
When suffering is unbearable, bliss is very near.
So don't try to escape from suffering –
that is the point where you can miss.
Don't try to avoid it, pass through it.
Don't try to find some way which goes round about.
No, that won't do.
Pass through it.

Suffering will burn you, destroy you,
but really you cannot be destroyed.
All that can be destroyed
is just the rubbish that you have gathered.
All that can be destroyed
is something that is not you.
When it's all destroyed, then you will feel
that you are indestructible, you are deathless.
Passing through death,
consciously passing through death,
one becomes aware of life eternal.

These few days you will be here with me,
many things are possible,
but the first step to remember is
to pass through suffering.
Many times I create suffering for you.
Many times I create the situation in which
all that is suppressed within you comes up.
Don't push it down, don't repress it.
Allow it, free it.
If you can free your suffering,

your suppressed suffering,
you will become free of it.
And you can come to the state of bliss
only when all suffering has been passed through,
thrown, completely dropped.

And I can see through you.
The flame of bliss is just near the corner.
Once glimpsed, that flame becomes yours.
I will push you in many ways to have a glimpse of it.

If you miss you will be responsible, no one else.
The river is flowing, but if you cannot bow down,
if you cannot come down
from your egoistic state of mind,
you may go back thirsty.
Don't blame the river.
The river was there,
but you were paralyzed by your ego.

Empty the cup.
That's what Nan-in said.
That means empty the mind.
Ego is there, overflowing.
And when ego is overflowing, nothing can be done.
The whole existence is around you,
but nothing can be done.
From nowhere can the Divine penetrate you,
you have created such a citadel.

Empty the cup.
Rather, throw the cup completely.
When I say throw the cup completely
I mean be so empty
that you don't have even the feeling
that 'I am empty.'

Once it happened,
a disciple came to Bodhidharma and said:
Master, you told me to be empty.
Now I have become empty.
Now what else do you say?

Bodhidharma hit him hard with his staff on the head,
and he said:
Go and throw this emptiness out.

If you say I am empty, the 'I am' is there,
and the 'I' cannot be empty,
so emptiness cannot be claimed.
No one can say: I am empty,
just like no one can say: I am humble.
If you say: I am humble – you are not.
Who claims this humility?
Humbleness cannot be claimed.
If you are humble, you are humble,
but you cannot say it.
Not only can you not say it,
you cannot feel that you are humble,
because the very feeling
will give birth to the ego again.
Be empty, but don't think that you are empty,
otherwise you have deceived yourself.

You have brought many philosophies with you.
Drop them.
They have not helped you at all;
they have not done anything for you.
It is time enough, the right time.
Drop them wholesale,
not in parts, not in fragments.
For these few days you will be here with me,
just be without any thinking.
I know it is difficult,
but still I say it is possible.
And once you know the knack of it,
you will laugh at the whole absurdity of the mind
that you were carrying so long.

I have heard about a man who was travelling
in a train for the first time, a villager.
He was carrying his luggage on his head, thinking:
Putting it down will be too much
for the train to carry,

and I have paid only for my own self.
I have purchased the ticket,
but I have not paid for the luggage.
So he was carrying the luggage on his head.
The train was carrying him and his luggage,
and whether he carried it on his head
or put it down
made no difference to the train.

Your mind is unnecessary luggage.
It makes no difference to this existence
that is carrying you.
You are unnecessarily burdened.
I say drop it.

The trees exist without the mind,
and exist more beautifully than any human being;
the birds exist without the mind,
and exist in a more ecstatic state
than any human being.
Look at children
who are still not civilized, who are still wild.
They exist without the mind.
And even a Jesus or a Buddha
will feel jealous of their innocence.
There is no need for this mind.
The whole world is going on and on without it.
Why are you carrying it?
Are you just thinking that it will be too much
for God, for existence?

Once you can put it down, even for a single minute,
your whole existence will be transformed.
You will enter into a new dimension,
the dimension of weightlessness.
And that's what I'm going to give you:
wings into the sky, into the heaven –
weightlessness gives you these wings;
and roots into the earth –
a groundedness, a centering.

This earth and that heaven.

Both are two parts of the whole.
In this life, your so-called ordinary life,
you must be rooted;
and in your inner space, in the spiritual life,
you must be weightless and flying and flowing,
floating.

Roots and wings I can give to you, if you allow,
because I am only a midwife.
I cannot force the child out of you.
And a forced child will be ugly,
and a forced child may die.
Just allow me.
The child is there; you are already pregnant.

Everybody is pregnant with God.
The child is there,
and you have already carried too long.
Long ago, the period of nine months passed.
That may be the root cause of your anguish –
that you are carrying something in the womb
which needs birth, which needs to come out,
which needs to be born.
Think of a woman, a mother,
carrying a child after the ninth month.
Then it becomes more and more burdensome,
and if the birth is not going to happen,
the mother will die,
because it will be too much to bear.

That may be the reason why you are in
so much anxiety, anguish, tension.
Something needs to be born out of you;
something needs to be created out of your womb.

I can help.
This Samadhi Sadhana Shibir,
this camp for inner ecstasy and enlightenment,
is just going to be a help for you
so that which you have carried like a seed up to now
can come out of your soil and become an alive thing,

an alive plant.
But the basic thing will be
that if you want to be with me
you cannot be with your mind.
Both cannot happen simultaneously.
Whenever you are with your mind you are not with me;
whenever the mind is not there, you are with me.
And I can work only if you are with me.
Empty the cup.
Throw the cup away completely.
Destroy it.

This camp is going to be in many ways different.
This night I start a completely new phase of my work.
You are fortunate to be here,
because you will be witnesses
of a new type of inner work.
I must explain it to you,
because tomorrow morning the journey starts.

The first meditation,
which you will be doing in the morning,
is related to the rising sun.
It is a morning meditation.
When the sleep is broken,
the whole nature becomes alive;
the night has gone, the darkness is no more,
the sun is coming up,
and everything becomes conscious and alert.
So this first meditation is a meditation
in which you have to be continuously alert,
conscious, aware, whatsoever you do.
The first step, breathing;
the second step, catharsis;
the third step, the mantra, the mahamantra, *hoo*.
Remain a witness.
Don't get lost.

It is easy to get lost.
While you are breathing you can forget.
You can become one with the breathing so much

that you can forget the witness.
But then you miss the point.
Breathe as fast, as deep as possible,
bring your total energy to it,
but still remain a witness.
Observe what is happening,
as if you are just a spectator,
as if the whole thing is happening to somebody else,
as if the whole thing is happening in the body
and the consciousness is just centred and looking.
This witnessing has to be carried
in all the three steps.
And when everything stops,
and in the fourth step
you have become completely inactive, frozen,
then this alertness will come to its peak.

In the afternoon meditation –
kirtan, dancing, singing –
another inner work has to be done.
In the morning you have to be fully conscious;
in the afternoon meditation you have to be
half conscious, half unconscious.
It is a noontide meditation –
when you are alert, but you feel sleepy.
It is just like a man who is under
the influence of some intoxicant.
He walks, but cannot walk rightly;
he knows where he is going, but everything is dim;
he is conscious and not conscious.
He knows he has taken alcohol,
he knows his feet are wavering, but he knows this –
half-asleep, half-awake.

So in the afternoon meditation remember this –
act as if you are intoxicated, drunk, ecstatic.
Sometimes you will forget yourself completely
like a drunkard,
sometimes you will remember,
but don't try to be conscious just like the morning, no.
Move with the day –

half-half in the noon.
Then you are in tune with nature.

In the night, just the opposite of the morning –
be completely unconscious;
don't bother at all.
The night has come, the sun has set,
now everything is moving into unconsciousness.
Move into unconsciousness.
This whirling, Sufi whirling,
is one of the most ancient techniques,
one of the most forceful.
It is so deep that even a single experience
can make you totally different.

You have to whirl with open eyes,
just like small children go on twirling,
as if your inner being has become a centre
and your whole body has become like a wheel, moving,
a potter's wheel, moving.
You are in the centre, but the whole body is moving.

Start slowly, clockwise.
If somebody feels it is very difficult
to move clockwise, then anti-clockwise,
but the rule is to move clockwise.
If a few people are left-handed,
then they may feel it difficult.
They can move anti-clockwise.
And almost ten percent of people are left-handed,
so if you feel that clockwise you feel uneasy,
move anti-clockwise;
but start with clockwise, then feel.

Music will be there, slow, just to help you.
In the beginning move very slowly.
Don't go fast,
but very slowly, enjoying.
And then, by and by, go faster.
The first fifteen minutes, go slowly;
the second fifteen minutes, fast;
the third fifteen minutes, faster;

the fourth fifteen minutes, just completely mad.
And then your total energy, you, become a whirlpool,
an energy whirlpool,
lost completely in it,
no witnessing, no effort to observe.
Don't try to see.
Be the whirpool, be the whirling.
One hour.

In the beginning
you may not be able to stand so long,
but remember one thing, don't stop by yourself.
Don't stop the whirling.
If you feel it is impossible,
the body will fall down automatically,
but don't you stop.
If you fall down in the middle of the hour,
there is no problem.
The process is complete.
But don't play tricks with yourself, don't deceive.
Don't think that now you are tired,
so it is better to stop.
No, don't make it a decision on your part.
If you are tired, how can you go on?
You will fall automatically.
So don't stop yourself.
Let the whirling itself come to a point
where you fall down.

When you fall down, fall down on your stomach.
And it will be good
if your stomach is in direct touch with the earth.
Then close the eyes.
Lie down on the earth
as if lying down on the breast of your mother,
a small child lying down
on the breast of the mother.
Become completely unconscious.

And this whirling will help.
Whirling gives intoxication to the body.

It is a chemical thing.
It gives you intoxication, to be exact.
That's why sometimes you may feel giddy
just like a drunkard.
What is happening to the drunkard?
Hidden behind your ears is a sixth sense,
the sense of balance.
When you take any drink,
any alcoholic thing, any intoxicating drug,
it goes directly to the centre of balance in the ear
and disturbs it.
That's why a drunkard cannot walk, feels dizzy.
The same happens in whirling.
If you whirl, really, the same will be the effect.
You will feel intoxicated, drunk.
But enjoy.
This drunkenness is worth something.
This being in a drunken state
is what Sufis have been calling ecstasy, *masti*.

In the beginning you may feel giddy,
in the beginning sometimes you may feel nausea,
but within two, three days,
these feelings will disappear,
and by the fourth day
you will feel a new energy in you
that you have never known before.
Then giddiness will disappear,
and just a smooth feeling of drunkenness
will be there.
So don't try to be alert about what is happening.
Let it happen, and become one with the happening.

In the morning, alert;
in the afternoon, half alert, half unalert;
in the night, completely unalert.
The circle is complete.

And then fall down on the ground on your stomach.
If anybody feels any sort of pain in the navel centre
lying down on the ground,

then he can turn on the back, otherwise not.
If you feel something,
a very deep painful sensation in the stomach,
then turn on your back, otherwise not.

The navel in contact with the earth
will give you such a blissful feeling –
just the same as once you had,
but now you have forgotten,
when you were a child
lying down on your mother's breast,
completely unaware of any worry, any anxiety,
so one with the mother,
your heart beating with her heart,
your breath in tune with her breath.

The same will happen with the earth,
because earth is the mother.
That's why Hindus have been calling
earth the mother and sky the father.
Be rooted in it.
Feel a merger, as if you have dissolved.
The body has become one with the earth;
the form is there no more.
Only earth exists; you are not there.
This is what I mean when I say
break the cup completely.
Forget that you are.
The earth is, and dissolve in it.

During the one hour of whirling,
the music will continue.
Many will fall before the hour,
but everybody has to fall
by the time the music stops.
So if you feel
that you are still not in the state of falling,
then go faster and faster.
After forty-five minutes go completely mad,
so by the time the hour is complete you have fallen.
And the feeling of falling is beautiful,

so don't manipulate it.
Fall, and when you have fallen,
then turn on your stomach,
be merged, close your eyes.
This merger has to be there for one hour.

So the night meditation will be of two hours,
from seven o'clock to nine o'clock.
Don't eat anything before it.
At nine o'clock the suggestion will be given
to come out of this deep drunkenness, this ecstasy.
Even out of it
you may not be able to walk correctly,
but don't be disturbed, enjoy it.
Then take your food and go to sleep.

Another new thing, I will not be there.
Only my empty chair will be there,
but don't miss me,
because in a sense I will be there.
And in a sense
there has always been an empty chair before you.
Right now the chair is empty,
because there is no one sitting in it.
I am talking to you,
but there is no one who is talking to you.
It is difficult to understand,
but when the ego disappears,
processes can continue.
Talking can continue,
sitting and walking and eating can continue,
but the centre has disappeared.
Even now, the chair is empty.

But I was always with you up till now
in all the camps,
because you were not ready.
Now I feel you are ready.
And you must be helped to get more ready
to work in my absence,
because feeling that I am there

you may feel a certain enthusiasm that is false.
Just feeling that I am present,
you may do things which you never wanted to do;
just to impress me you may exert more.
That is not of much help,
because only that can be helpful
which comes out of your being.

My chair will be there.
I will be watching you,
but you feel completely free.
And don't think that I am not there,
because that may depress you,
and then that depression
will disturb your meditation.

I will be there,
and if you meditate rightly,
whenever your meditation is exactly tuned,
you will see me.
So that will be the criterion
of whether you are really meditating or not.
Many of you will be able to see me,
more intensely than you can see me right now,
and whenever you see me, you can be certain
that things are happening in a right direction.
So this will be the criterion.

By the end of this camp
I hope ninety percent of you will have seen me.
Ten percent may miss because of their minds.
So if you see me,
don't start thinking about it, what is happening,
don't start thinking whether it is imagination
or a projection or am I really there.
Don't think,
because if you think,
immediately I will disappear.
Thinking will become a barrier.
The dust will come on the mirror,
and there will be no reflection.

Whenever the dust is not there,
suddenly, you will become aware of me,
more than you can be aware here right now.
To be aware of the physical body
is not much awareness;
to be aware of the non-physical being
is real awareness.

And you must learn to work without me.
You cannot be here always;
you will have to go far away;
you cannot hang around me forever.
You have other works to do.
You have come from different countries
all over the world.
You will have to go.
For a few days you will be here with me,
but if you become addicted to my physical presence,
then rather than being a help,
it may become a disturbance,
because, then, when you go away, you will miss me.
Your meditation should be such here
that it can happen without my presence.
Then wherever you go,
the meditation will not be in any way affected.

And this too has to be remembered,
that I cannot always be
in this physical body with you.
One day or another,
the physical vehicle has to be dropped.
My work is complete as far as I am concerned.
If I am carrying this physical vehicle,
it is just for you.
Someday, it has to be dropped.
Before it happens
you must be ready to work in my absence,
or in my non-physical presence,
which means the same.
And once you can feel me in my absence,

you are free of me.
And then even if I am not here in this body,
the contact will not be lost.

It always happens when a Buddha is there.
His physical presence becomes so meaningful.
And then he dies.
Everything is shattered.
Even a disciple like Ananda,
his most intimate disciple,
started crying and weeping when Buddha said:
Now I have to leave this body.
For forty years Ananda was with Buddha,
twenty-four hours, just like a shadow.
He started crying and weeping like a child.
Suddenly, he had become an orphan.

Buddha asked:
What are you doing?
Ananda said:
It will be impossible now for me to grow.
I couldn't grow when you were there,
so how can I grow now?
It may be now millions of lives
before I come across a Buddha again.
So I am lost.

Buddha said:
My understanding is different, Ananda.
When I am not there,
you may become enlightened immediately,
because this has been my feeling –
that you have become too much attached to me,
and that attachment is working like a block.
You have become too much attached to me.
That very attachment is working like a barrier.

And this happened as Buddha said.
The day Buddha died, Ananda became enlightened.
There was nothing to cling to then.
But why wait?

When I die, then you will become enlightened?
Why wait?

My chair can be empty.
You can feel my absence.
And remember, only when you can feel my absence,
can you feel my presence.
If you cannot see me while my physical vehicle
is not there,
you have not seen me at all.

This is my promise –
I will be there in the empty chair.
The empty chair will not really be empty.
So behave, the chair will not be empty.
But it is better that you learn to be in contact
with my non-physical being.
That's a deeper, more intimate touch and contact.
That's why I say a new phase of my work
starts with this camp.
And I am calling it a Samadhi Sadhana Shibir.
It is not only meditation,
it is absolute ecstasy
that I am going to teach to you.
It is not only the first step, it is the last.

Only no mind on your part is needed,
and everything is ready.
Just be alert not to think much.
The remaining time between these three meditations,
remain more and more silent, don't talk.
If you want to do something, laugh, dance,
do something intense and physical, but not mental.
Go for a long walk,
go jogging on the grounds,
jump under the sun,
lie down on the earth,
look at the sky, enjoy,
but don't allow the mind to function much.
Laugh, cry, weep, but don't think.

If you can be without thinking
for these three meditations
and the time between them,
then after three, four days you will feel
suddenly a burden has disappeared.
The heart has become light, the body weightless
and you are ready
to take a jump into the unknown.

Anything more?

Bhagwan,

The last part of what you said to us
is very beautiful and blissful,
but the first part is very frightening –
breaking the cup, suffering,
falling down on the ground,
you not being there.

And then our minds come in
and we play tricks with our bodies.
We say:
I have this pain.
I have this blister.

Can you give us some clue
as to how we can get over the barriers
we create for ourselves
when we come up against fear?

Any conflict will create more barriers.
If there is fear
and you start doing something about it,

then a new fear has entered,
fear of the fear.
It has become more complex.
So the one thing to be done is, if fear is there,
accept it.
Don't do anything about it,
because doing will not help.
Anything that you do out of fear
will create more fear;
anything that you do out of confusion
will add more to confusion.
Don't do anything.
If fear is there, note down that fear is there,
and accept it.
What can you do?
Nothing can be done.
Fear is there.

See, if you can just note down
the fact that fear is there,
where is the fear then?
You have accepted it; it has dissolved.
Acceptance dissolves.
Only acceptance, nothing else.

If you fight you create another disturbance,
and this can go on ad infinitum.
Then there is no end to it.
People come to me and they say:
We are very afraid.
What should we do?
If I give them something to do,
they will do it
with the being which is full of fear,
so action will come out of their fear.
And the action that comes out of fear
cannot be anything other than fear.

I have heard that Adolf Hitler
was suffering from deep depression, melancholy,
and psychologists were saying that it was due

to some hidden inferiority complex.
So all the Aryan psychologists were called.
They tried, but they couldn't help.
Nothing came out of their analysis.
So they suggested
that a Jewish psychoanalyst should be called.
Hitler was not ready in the beginning to call a Jew,
but seeing no way out of it, he had to yield.

A great Jewish psychoanalyst was called.
He analyzed,
penetrated deep into Hitler's mind, dreams,
and then he suggested:
Nothing much is a problem.
You simply repeat one thing continuously:
I am important, I am significant, I am indispensable.
Let it be a mantra.
Night, day, whenever you remember, repeat:
I am important, I am significant, I am indispensable.

Hitler said:
Stop!
You are giving me bad advice.
The psychoanalyst couldn't understand.
He said:
What do you mean?
Why do you call this bad advice?

Hitler said:
Because whatsoever I say,
I am such a liar, I cannot believe it.
I am such a liar,
whatsoever I say, I cannot believe it.
If you say:
Repeat 'I am indispensable,'
I know that this is a lie.
I am saying it.
I am a liar.

Out of lies, if you repeat something,
it will become a lie;

out of fear, if you do something,
it will become a fear again;
out of hate, it you try to love,
that love will just be a hidden hate.
It cannot be anything else.
You are full of hate.

Go to the preachers and they will say:
Try to love.
They are talking nonsense,
because how can a person who is full of hate
try to love?
If he tries to love,
this love will come out of hatred.
It will be poisoned already,
poisoned from the very source.
And this is what the misery of all preachers is.

Gandhi said to people who were violent:
Try to be non-violent.
Then their non-violence comes out of violence.
So their non-violence is just a facade,
just a face to show.
Deep down, they are boiling with violence.

If your *brahmacharya,* your celibacy,
comes out of too much sexuality,
it will be perverted sex, nothing else.

So please don't create any conflict.
If you have one problem, don't create another,
remain with the one.
Don't fight and create another.
It is easier to solve one problem
than to solve another.
And the first is near the source,
the second will be removed.
The further removed,
the more impossible it becomes to solve it.

If you have fear, so you have fear.
Why make a problem out of it?

Then you know that you have fear,
just as you have two hands.
Why create a problem out of it,
as if you have only one nose, not two?
Why create a problem out of it?

Fear is there.
Accept it, note it.
Accept it, don't bother about it.
What will happen?
Suddenly, you will feel it has disappeared.
And this is the inner alchemy –
a problem disappears if you accept it,
and a problem grows more and more complex
if you create any conflict with it.
Yes, suffering is there,
and suddenly, fear comes.
Accept it.
It is there, and nothing can be done about it.

And when I say nothing can be done about it,
don't think that I am talking pessimism to you.
When I say nothing can be done about it,
I am giving you the key to solve it.

Suffering is there.
It is part of life and part of growth.
Nothing is bad in it.
Suffering becomes evil
only when it is simply destructive,
and not creative at all;
suffering becomes bad only when you suffer
and nothing is gained out of it.

But I am telling you
the Divine can be gained through suffering.
Then it becomes creative.
Darkness is beautiful
if the dawn is coming out of it soon;
darkness is dangerous if it is endless,
leads to no dawn, simply continues and continues,

and you go on moving in a rut, in a vicious circle.

This is what is happening to you.
Just to escape from one suffering,
you create another;
then to escape from another, another.
And this goes on and on,
and all those sufferings which you have not lived,
are waiting for you.
You have escaped,
but you escape from one suffering to another,
because a mind which was creating a suffering
will create another.
So you can escape from this suffering to that,
but suffering will be there,
because your mind is the creative force.

Accept the suffering and pass through it.
Don't escape.
This is a totally different dimension to work in.
Suffering is there.
Encounter it.
Go through it.

Fear will be there.
Accept it.
You will tremble, so tremble.
Why create a facade that you don't tremble,
that you are not afraid?
If you are a coward, accept it.

Everyone is a coward.
People you call brave are just facades.
Deep down they are as cowardly as anyone else,
rather, more cowardly,
because just to hide that cowardliness
they have created a bravery around them,
and sometimes they act in such a way
that everyone knows they are not cowards.
Their bravery is just a screen.

How can man be brave, because death is there?

How can man be brave,
because man is just a leaf in the winds?
How can the leaf help not to tremble?
When the wind blows, the leaf will tremble.
But you never say to the leaf:
You are a coward.
You only say that the leaf is alive.
So when you tremble and fear takes grip of you,
you are a leaf in the wind.
Beautiful.
Why create a problem out of it?

But society has created problems
out of everything.
If a child is afraid in the dark, we say:
Don't be afraid, be brave.
Why?
The child is innocent.
Naturally he feels fear in the dark.
You force:
Be brave.
So he also forces.
Then he becomes tense.
Then he endures the darkness, but now tense.
Now, his whole being is ready to tremble,
and he suppresses it.

This suppressed trembling
will follow now the whole life.
It was good to tremble in the darkness.
Nothing was wrong.
It was good to cry and run.
Nothing was wrong.
The child would have come out of darkness
more experienced, more knowing.
And he would have realized,
if he passed through darkness
trembling and crying and weeping,
that there was nothing to fear.

Suppressed, you never experience

the thing in its totality;
you never gain anything out of it.
Wisdom comes through suffering,
and wisdom comes through acceptance.
Whatsoever the case, be at ease with it.

And don't look to society and its condemnation.
Nobody is to judge you here,
and nobody can pretend to be a judge.
Don't judge others
and don't be perturbed and disturbed
by others' judgment.
You are alone, and you are unique.
You never were before; you never will be again.
You are beautiful.
Accept it.
And whatsoever happens, allow it to happen,
and pass through it.
Soon, suffering will be a learning.
Then it has become creative.

Fear will give you fearlessness.
Out of anger will come compassion.
Out of the understanding of hate,
love will be born to you.
But this happens not in a conflict,
this happens in a passing-through
with alert awareness.
Accept, and pass through it.

And if you make it a point
to pass through every experience,
then there will be death,
the most intense experience.
Life is nothing before it,
because life cannot be so intense as death.
Life is spread out over a long time –
seventy years, one hundred years.
Death is intense because it is not spread out –
it is in a single moment.
Life has to pass one hundred years or seventy years.

It cannot be so intense.
Death comes in a single moment.
It comes whole, not fragmentary.
It will be so intense,
you cannot know anything more intense.

But if you are afraid,
if before death comes you have escaped,
if you have become unconscious because of the fear,
you have missed one of the golden opportunities,
the golden gate.
If your whole life you have been accepting things,
when death comes,
patiently, passively you will accept,
and enter into it without any effort to escape.
If you can enter death passively, silently,
without any effort,
death disappears.
When Krishna, Christ, Buddha, Mahavir
say you are deathless,
they are not talking about a doctrine,
they are talking about their own experience.

And this can happen here in this camp also,
because *samadhi* is death,
dhyan is death, meditation is death.
Many times there will be moments
when you will suddenly feel you are dying.
Don't escape, allow it to happen.
If you allow it to happen, death has gone.
Death is there no more,
and the inner flame, beginningless, endless,
has come into being.
It has always been there.
Now you can feel it.

So this should be the *sutra*.
With fear, hate, jealousy, anything whatsoever,
don't create a problem out of it.
Accept it, allow it, pass through it,

and you will defeat all suffering, all death.
And you will become a Jaina, a victorious one.

Anything more?

Bhagwan,

When you talk about our having to suffer,
you tell us to be joyful at the same time.

Trying to compromise these two things
seems difficult.

When I say suffer joyfully, it looks paradoxical.
And your mind starts thinking
how to compromise both,
because to you they are contradictory.
They are not.
They only appear contradictory.
You can enjoy suffering.

What is the secret?
How to enjoy suffering?
The first thing is, if you don't escape,
if you allow the suffering to be there,
if you are ready to face it,
if you are not trying somehow to forget it,
then, you are different.
Suffering is there, but just around you.
It is not in the centre; it is on the periphery.
It is impossible for suffering to be in the centre.
It is not in the nature of things.
It is always on the periphery,
and you are the centre.

So when you allow it to happen,
when you don't escape, you don't run,
you are not in a panic,
suddenly you become aware that suffering is there
on the periphery,
as if happening to someone else, not to you,
and you are looking at it.
A subtle joy spreads all over your being,
because you have realized
one of the basic truths of life –
that you are bliss, and not suffering.

So when I say enjoy it,
I don't mean become a masochist.
I don't mean create suffering for yourself
and enjoy it.
I don't mean go on, fall down from a cliff,
have fractures and then enjoy it, no.
There are people of that type,
and many of them have become ascetics, *tapasvis,*
and they are creating suffering for themselves.
They are masochists.
They are ill.
They are very dangerous people.
They wanted to make others suffer,
but they are not so courageous.
They wanted to kill others,
be violent with others, cripple others,
but they are not so courageous.
So their whole violence has turned within.
Now they are crippling themselves,
torturing themselves,
and enjoying it.

I am not saying be a masochist.
I am simply saying suffering is there,
you need not seek for it.
Enough suffering is there already;
you need not go in search.
Suffering is already there.

Life by its very nature creates suffering.
Illness is there, death is there, the body is there.
By their very nature suffering is created.
See it.
Look at it with a very dispassionate eye.
Look at it –
what it is, what is happening.
Don't escape.
Immediately, the mind says:
Escape from here.
Don't look at it.
But if you escape, then you cannot be blissful.

Next time you fall ill,
and the doctor suggests to remain in bed,
take it as a blessing.
Close your eyes and rest on the bed
and just look at the illness.
Watch it, what it is.
Don't try to analyze it, don't go into theories,
just watch it, what it is.

The whole body tired, feverish –
watch it.
Suddenly, you will feel surrounded by fever
but there is a very cool point within you.
The fever cannot touch it, cannot influence it.
The whole body may be burning,
but that cool point cannot be touched.

I have heard about one Zen nun.
She died,
but before she died she asked her disciples:
What do you suggest?
How should I die?

It is one old tradition in Zen that masters ask.
They can die consciously, so they can ask.
And they are so playful even about death,
so humorous about it, joking, laughing.
They enjoy devising methods how to die.

So disciples may suggest:
Master, this will be good,
if you die standing on your head.
Or someone suggests:
Walking, because we have never seen
anyone die walking.

So this Zen nun asked:
What do you suggest?
They said:
It will be good if we prepare a fire,
and you sit in it and die meditating.
She said:
This is beautiful, and never heard of before.

So they prepared a funeral pyre.
The nun made herself comfortable in it,
sat in a Buddha posture,
and then they lit the fire.

One man from the crowd asked:
How does it feel there?
It is so hot that I cannot
even come nearer to ask you.
That's why I am shouting.
How does it feel there?

The nun laughed and said:
Only a fool can ask such a question –
How does it feel there?
There it always feels cool, perfectly cool.

She is talking of her inner being, her centre.
There it is always cool,
and only a foolish person can ask.

Why does she say
that only a foolish person can ask it?
It is obvious.
When a person is ready
to sit in a pyre meditating,
and then the pyre is burned
and she is sitting silently,

obviously it shows that this person
must have achieved the innermost cool point
which cannot be disturbed by any fire.
Otherwise, it is not possible.

So when you are lying on your bed,
feverish, on fire,
the whole body burning,
just watch it.
Watching, you will recede back towards the source.
Watching, not doing anything . . .
What can you do?
The fever is there.
You have to pass through it.
It is no use unnecessarily fighting with it.
You are resting,
and if you fight with the fever
you will become more feverish, that's all.

So watch it.
Watching fever, you become cool.
Watching more, you become cooler.
Just watching, you reach to a peak,
such a cool peak,
even the Himalayas will feel jealous.
Even their peaks are not so cool.
This is the Gaurishankar, the Everest within.

And when you feel that the fever has disappeared . . .
It has never really been there;
it has only been in the body,
very, very far away.

Infinite space exists between you and your body –
infinite space, I say.
An unbridgeable gap exists
between you and your body.
And all suffering exists on the periphery.
Hindus say it is a dream,
because the distance is so vast, unbridgeable.
It is just like a dream happening somewhere else –

not happening to you –
in some other world, on some other planet.

When you watch suffering,
suddenly you are not the sufferer,
and you start enjoying.
Through suffering
you become aware of the opposite pole,
the blissful inner being.
So when I say enjoy, I am saying:
Watch.
Return to the source.
Get centred.
Then, suddenly, there is no agony.
Only ecstasy exists.

Those who are on the periphery
exist in agony.
For them, no ecstasy.
For those who have come to their centre,
no agony exists.
For them, only ecstasy.

And when I say break the cup,
it is breaking the periphery.
And when I say be totally empty,
it is coming back to the original source,
because through emptiness we are born,
and into emptiness we return.
'Emptiness' is the word, really,
which is better to use than 'God,'
because with 'God' we start feeling
there is some person.
So Buddha never used 'God,'
he always used *sunyata* – emptiness, nothingness.
In the centre you are a non-being, nothingness,
just a vast space, eternally cool, silent, blissful.

So when I say enjoy,
I mean watch,
and you will enjoy.

When I say enjoy,
I mean don't escape.

Second Talk

11th June 1974

Bhagwan,

The student Doko came to the master and said:
In what state of mind should I seek the truth?

The master replied:
There is no mind,
so you cannot put it in any state,
and there is no truth,
so you cannot seek it.

Doko said:
If there is no mind and no truth,
why do all these students gather before you
every day to study?

The master looked around and said:
I don't see anyone.

The inquirer asked:
Then who are you teaching?

I have no tongue, so how can I teach?
replied the master.

Then Doko said sadly:
I cannot follow you; I cannot understand.

The master said:
I don't understand myself.

Life is such a mystery, no one can understand it,
and one who claims that he understands it
is simply ignorant.
He is not aware of what he is saying,
of what nonsense he is talking.

If you are wise, this will be the first realization –
that life cannot be understood.
Understanding is impossible.
Only this much can be understood –
that understanding is impossible.
That is what this beautiful Zen anecdote says.

The master says:
I don't understand it myself.
And if you go and ask the enlightened ones,
this will be their answer.
But if you go and ask the unenlightened ones,
they will give you many answers,
they will propose many doctrines,
they will try to solve the mystery
which cannot be solved.
It is not a riddle.
A riddle can be solved.
A mystery is unsolvable by its very nature.
There is no way to solve it.

Socrates said:
When I was young, I thought I knew much.

When I became old, ripe in wisdom,
I came to understand that I knew nothing.

It is reported of one of the Sufi masters, Junnaid,
that he was working with a new young man.
The young man was not aware
of Junnaid's inner wisdom,
and Junnaid lived such an ordinary life
that it needed very penetrating eyes to realize
that you were near a Buddha.
He worked like an ordinary labourer,
and only those who had eyes would realize.

To realize Buddha was very easy –
he was sitting under a Bodhi tree;
to realize Junnaid was very difficult –
he was working like a labourer,
not sitting under a Bodhi tree.
He was in every way absolutely ordinary.

One young man working with him,
and that young man
was continually showing his knowledge,
so whatsoever Junnaid would do, he would say:
This is wrong.
This can be done in this way.
It will be better –
about everything he new,
and finally Junnaid laughed and said:
Young man, I am not so young to know so much.

This is really something.
He said:
I am not so young to know so much.
Only a young man can be so foolish,
so inexperienced.
Right was Socrates when he said:
When I was young, I knew too much.
When I became ripened, experienced,
I came to realize only one thing –
that I was absolutely ignorant.

Life is a mystery.
That means it cannot be solved.
And when all efforts to solve it prove futile,
the mystery dawns upon you.
Then the doors are open; then you are invited.
As a knower, nobody enters the Divine;
as a child, ignorant, not knowing at all,
the mystery embraces you.
With a knowing mind you are clever, not innocent.
Innocence is the door.

Right was this Zen master when he said:
I don't understand it myself.
It was very deep, really deep,
the deepest answer possible.
But this is the last part of the anecdote.
Start from the very beginning . . .

The disciple came to the Zen master and said:
In what state of mind should I seek the truth?
The master said:
There is no mind,
so there cannot be any state of mind.

Mind is the illusion,
that which is not but appears,
and appears so much
that you think that you are the mind.
Mind is *maya,*
mind is just a dream,
mind is just a projection,
a soap bubble floating on a river.
The sun is just rising,
the rays penetrate the bubble,
a rainbow is created,
and nothing is there in it.
When you touch the bubble, it is broken,
and everything disappears –
the rainbow, the beauty.
Nothing is left.
Only emptiness becomes one

with the infinite emptiness.
Just a wall was there, a bubble wall.

Your mind is just a bubble wall –
inside, your emptiness; outside, my emptiness.
It is just a bubble.
Prick it, and the mind disappears.

The master said:
There is no mind,
so what type of state are you asking about?
It is difficult to understand.
People come to me and they say:
We would like to attain a silent state of mind.
They think that the mind can be silent.
Mind can never be silent.
Mind means the turmoil, the illness, the disease;
mind means the tense, the anguished state.

The mind cannot be silent.
When there is silence there is no mind.
When silence comes, mind disappears;
when mind is there, silence is no more.
So there cannot be any silent mind,
just as there cannot be any healthy disease.
Is it possible to have a healthy disease?
When health is there, disease disappears.
Silence is the inner health;
mind is the inner disease, inner disturbance.

So there cannot be any silent mind,
and this disciple is asking:
What type, what sort,
what state of mind should I achieve?
Point blank, the master said:
There is no mind, so you cannot achieve any state.

So please drop this illusion.
Don't try to achieve any state in the illusion.
It's as if you are thinking to travel on the rainbow,
and you ask me:
What steps should we take to travel on the rainbow?

I say:
There is no rainbow.
Rainbow is just an appearance,
so no steps can be taken.
A rainbow simply appears.
It is not there;
it is not a reality.
It is a false interpretation of the reality.

The mind is not your reality.
It is a false interpretation.
You are not the mind, you have never been a mind,
you can never be the mind.
That is your problem.
You have become identified
with something which is not.
You are like a beggar
who believes that he has a kingdom.
He is so worried about the kingdom –
how to manage it, how to govern it,
how to prevent anarchy.
There is no kingdom, but he is worried.

Chaung Tzu once dreamt
that he had become a butterfly.
In the morning he was very much depressed.
His friends asked:
What has happened?
We have never seen you so depressed.
Chuang Tzu said:
I am in a puzzle, I am at a loss,
I cannot understand.
In the night, while asleep,
I dreamt that I had become a butterfly.

So the friends laughed:
Nobody is ever disturbed by dreams.
When you awake, the dream has disappeared,
so why are you disturbed?
Chuang Tzu said:
That is not the point.

Now I am puzzled.
If Chuang Tzu can become a butterfly in the dream,
it is possible
that now the butterfly has gone to sleep
and is dreaming that she is Chuang Tzu.

If Chuang Tzu can become a butterfly in the dream,
why not the other?
The butterfly can dream and become Chuang Tzu.
So what is real —
whether Chuang Tzu dreamt
that he has become a butterfly
or the butterfly is dreaming
that she has become Chuang Tzu?

What is real?
Rainbows are there.
You can become a butterfly in the dream.
And you have become a mind
in this bigger dream you call life.
When you awaken,
you don't achieve an awakened state of mind,
you achieve a no-state of mind,
you achieve no-mind.

What does no-mind mean?
It is difficult to follow,
but sometimes, unknowingly, you have achieved it,
but you may not have recognized it.
Sometimes, just sitting ordinarily,
not doing anything,
there is no thought in the mind.
When there is no thought, where is the mind?

When there is no thought, there is no mind,
for mind is just the process of thinking.
It is not a substance, it is just a procession.
You are here, I can say a crowd is here,
but is there really something like a crowd?
is a crowd substantial, or are only individuals there?
By and by, individuals will go away,

then will there be a crowd left behind?
When individuals have gone, there is no crowd.

The mind is just like a crowd;
thoughts are the individuals.
And because thoughts are there continuously,
you think the process is substantial.
Drop each individual thought,
and finally, nothing is left.
There is no mind as such, only thinking.
But thoughts are moving so fast,
that between two thoughts
you cannot see the interval.
But the interval is always there.
That interval is you.

In that interval,
there is neither Chuang Tzu nor the butterfly –
for the butterfly is a sort of mind,
and Chuang Tzu is also a sort of mind.
Butterfly is a different combination of thoughts,
Chuang Tzu again a different combination,
but both are minds.

When the mind is not there, who are you –
Chuang Tzu or a butterfly?
Neither.
And what is the state?
Are you in an enlightened state of mind?
If you think
you are in an enlightened state of mind,
this is, again, a thought,
and when thought is there, you are not.
If you feel that you are a Buddha,
this is a thought.
The mind has entered,
now the process is there,
again the sky is clouded, the blueness lost.
The infinite blueness you can see no more.

Between two thoughts, try to be alert.
Look into the interval, the space in between.

You will see no mind.
That is your nature.
For thoughts come and go –
they are accidental
but that inner space always remains.
Clouds gather and go, disappear –
they are accidental –
but the sky remains.
You are the sky.

Once it happened
that a seeker came to Bayazid, one Sufi mystic,
and asked:
Master, I am a very angry person.
Anger happens to me very easily.
I become really mad and I do things.
I cannot even believe later on
that I can do such things.
I am not in my senses.
So, how to drop this anger,
how to overcome it, how to control it?

Bayazid took the head of the disciple in his hands
and looked into his eyes.
The disciple became a little uneasy,
and Bayazid said:
Where is that anger?
I would like to see into it.

The disciple laughed uneasily and said:
Right now, I am not angry.
Sometimes it happens.
So Bayazid said:
That which happens sometimes
cannot be your nature.
It is an accident.
It comes and goes.
It is like clouds.
So why be worried about the clouds?
Think of the sky which is always there.

This is the definition of the Atma –
the sky which is always there.
All that comes and goes is irrelevant.
Don't be bothered by it,
it is just smoke.
The sky that remains eternally there never changes,
never becomes different.
Between two thoughts, drop into it.
Between two thoughts, it is always there.
Look into it, and suddenly you will realize
that you are in no-mind.

The master was right when he said:
There is no mind,
so there cannot be any state of mind.
What nonsense you are talking.

But the nonsense has its own logic.
If you think that you have a mind,
you will start thinking in terms of states –
ignorant state of mind, enlightened state of mind.
Once you accept mind, the illusory,
you are bound to go on dividing it.
And once you accept that the mind is there,
you will start seeking something or other.

The mind can exist
only if you continuously seek something.
Why?
It is because seeking is desire.
Seeking is moving into the future.
Seeking creates dreams.
So somebody is seeking power, politics,
somebody is seeking riches, kingdoms,
and then somebody is seeking the truth.
But seeking is there,
and seeking is the problem,
not what you are seeking.
The object is never the problem.
Any object will do.
The mind can hang on to any object.

Any excuse is enough for it to exist.

The master said:
There is no state of mind, because there is no mind.
And there is no truth.
So what are you talking about?
There can be no seeking.

This is one of the greatest messages ever delivered.
It is very difficult.
He cannot conceive that there is no truth.
What is the meaning of this master
when he says that there is no truth?
Does he mean that there is no truth?
No, he is saying that for you, who are a seeker,
there can be no truth.

Seeking always leads into the untrue.
Only a non-seeking mind realizes that which is.
For whenever you seek,
you have missed that which is.
Seeking always moves into the future.
Seeking cannot be here and now.
How can you seek here and now?
You can only be.
Seeking is desire –
future enters, time comes in –
and this moment, this here and now is missed.
Truth is here, now.

If you go to a Buddha and ask:
Is there God,
he will deny it immediately:
There is no God.
If he says there is, he creates a seeker.
If he says there is God, you will start seeking.
How can you remain quiet
when there is God to be sought?
Where will you run?
You have created another illusion.

So Buddha said:

There is no God.
Nobody understood him;
people thought he was an atheist.
He was not denying God,
he was simply denying the seeker.
But if he had said that there is God,
the seeker would have been there.
And seeker is the world;
seeking is all that *maya* is.
For millions of lives you have been a seeker,
after this or after that,
this object, that object,
this world or that world,
but a seeker.
Now you are a seeker after truth,
but the master says there is no truth.
He cuts the very ground of seeking,
he pulls away the very ground
where you are standing,
where your mind is standing.
He simply pushes you into the abyss.

The inquirer said:
Then why these many seekers all around you?
If there is nothing to seek and no truth,
then why this crowd?
You must have been there,
sitting around the master.

Somebody comes to me and I say:
There is no seeking.
Nothing is to be sought,
because there is nothing to seek.
He is bound to ask:
Then why these people here?
Why these *sannyasis* here?
What are they doing here?

But the inquirer went on missing the point.
The master looked around and said:
I don't see anyone.

There is no one here.
The inquirer went on missing the point,
for the intellect always goes on missing.
He could have looked.
This was the fact.
There was no one.

You can be in two ways,
but just one if you are seeking.
If you are not seeking, you are not,
for seeking gives you the ego.
Right this moment,
if you are not seeking anyone, anything,
you are not here, there is no crowd.
If I am not teaching anything,
because there is nothing to be taught,
no truth to be taught –
if I am not teaching anything,
and if you are not learning anything –
who is here?

Emptiness exists, and the bliss of pure emptiness.
Individuals disappear,
and it becomes an oceanic consciousness.
Individuals are there because of individual minds.
You have a different desire.
That's why you differ from your neighbour.
Desires create distinctions.
I am seeking something,
you are seeking something else;
my path differs from yours,
my goal differs from yours.
That's why I differ from you.
If I am not seeking and you are not seeking,
goals disappear, paths are no more there.
How, then, can the minds exist?

The cup is broken.
My tea flows into you,
and your tea flows into me.
It becomes an oceanic existence.

The master looked around and said:
I don't see anyone.
There is no one.
The intellect goes on missing,
and the inquirer said:
Then to whom are you teaching?
If there is no one,
then to whom are you teaching?
And the master said:
I have got no tongue, so how can I teach?

He goes on giving hints,
to become alert, to look,
but the inquirer is engulfed in his own mind.
The master goes on hitting, hammering on his head.
He is talking nonsense
just to bring him out of his mind.

If you had been there,
you would have been convinced by the inquirer,
not by the master.
The inquirer would have appeared exactly right.
This master seemed to be mad, absurd.
He was talking and he said:
There is no tongue, so how can I talk?
He was saying:
Look at me, I am without form.
Look at me, I am not embodied.
The body appears to you, but I am not that,
so how can I talk?

The mind goes on missing.
This is the misery of the mind.
You push, it again gathers itself;
you hit, and for a moment
there is a sinking and a trembling,
and again, it is established.

Have you seen a Japanese doll?
They call it a *daruma* doll.
You throw it, in whatsoever way –

topsy-turvy, head upside-down –
but whatsoever you do
the doll sits in a Buddha posture.
The bottom part is so heavy, you cannot do anything.
Throw it in any way and
the doll again sits in a Buddha posture.
The name *daruma* comes from Bodhidharma;
in Japan, Bodhidharma's name is Daruma.
Daruma used to say, this Bodhidharma used to say
that your mind is just like this doll.
He would throw it, kick it,
but whatsoever he did,
he could not disturb the doll,
the bottom part was so heavy.
You throw it upside-down, it will be right-side-up.

So this master went on pushing.
A little shaking and the doll sat again,
missed the point.
Finally, desperate, the inquirer said:
I don't follow, I don't understand.
And with the ultimate hit, the master said:
I don't understand myself.

I go on teaching you,
knowing well there is nothing to be taught.
That's why I can go on infinitely.
If there were something to be taught,
I would have finished already.
Buddhas can go on and on,
because there is nothing to be taught.
It is an endless story.
It never concludes,
so I can go on and on.
I will never be finished.
You may be finished before my story ends,
for there is no end to it.

Somebody was asking me:
You go on talking every day?
I said:

Because there is nothing to be taught.
Someday you will suddenly feel it –
that I am not talking, that I am not teaching.
You have realized
there is nothing to be taught
because there is no truth.

What discipline am I giving to you?
None.
A disciplined mind is again a mind,
even more stubborn, more adamant;
a disciplined mind is more stupid.
Go and see the disciplined monks
all over the world,
Christian, Hindu, Jain.
Whenever you see a man
who is absolutely disciplined,
you will find a stupid mind behind it.
The flowing has stopped.
He is so much concerned with finding something,
that he is ready to do whatsoever you say.
If you say: Stand on your head for an hour,
he is ready to stand on his head.
It is because of desire.
If God can be achieved
only through standing on his head for hours,
he is ready, but he must achieve.

I am not giving you any achieving, any desiring.
There is nowhere to reach and nothing to achieve.
If you realize this,
you have achieved this very moment.
This very moment, you are perfect.
Nothing is to be done, nothing is to be changed.
This very moment, you are absolute Brahma.

That's why the master said:
I don't understand it myself.
It is difficult to find a master who says:
I don't understand it myself.
For a master must claim that he knows,

only then will you follow him.
A master must not only claim that he knows,
he must claim that only he knows, nobody else:
All other masters are wrong, I alone know.
Then you will follow.
You must be absolutely certain,
then you become a follower.
The certainty gives you the feeling
that here is the man,
and if you follow, you will reach.

I will tell you one story.
It happened once, a so-called master was travelling.
In every village he would go, he would declare:
I have achieved; I have known the Divine.
If you want, come and follow me.

People would say:
There are many responsibilities.
Someday, we hope we will be able to follow you.
They would touch his feet, give him respect,
serve him, but nobody would follow,
because there were many other things to be done first
before one went to seek the Divine.
First things first.
The Divine is always the last.
And the last thing never comes
because the first are so infinite
they are never finished.

But in one village, a madman –
mad he was, otherwise who would follow –
said: Right, you have found?

The master hesitated a little, looking at the madman –
because this man seemed dangerous;
he might follow and create trouble –
but before the whole village he couldn't deny it,
so he said: Yes.

The madman said:

Now, initiate me.
I will follow you to the very end.
I want to realize God myself.

The so-called master became perturbed,
but what to do?
The madman started following him.
He became a shadow.
One year passed.
The madman said:
How far, how far is the temple?
And he said:
I am not in a hurry,
but how much time will be needed?

By this time, the master had become very uncomfortable
and uneasy with this man.
This madman would sleep with him,
he would move with him.
He had become his shadow.
And because of him his certainty was dissolving.
Whenever he would say, in a village:
Follow me,
he would become afraid,
because this man would look at him and say:
I am following you, master,
and still I have not reached.

Second year passed,
third year passed,
sixth year passed,
and the madman said:
We have not reached anywhere.
We are simply travelling in villages
and you go on telling people:
Follow me.
And I am following.
Whatsoever you say, I do it,
so you cannot say I am not following the discipline.

The madman was really mad,
so whatever was said, he would do.

So the master couldn't deceive him
that he was not doing well.
So finally, one night, the master said to him:
Because of you, I have lost my own path.
Before I met you I was certain.
Now I am no more.
Now you please leave me.

Whenever there is someone certain
and you are mad enough,
you start following.
Can you follow this type of man who says:
I myself don't know.
I myself don't understand.
If you can follow this man, you will reach.
You have already reached
if you decide to follow this man,
for the mind asks for certainty,
the mind asks for knowledge.
The mind also asks for dogmatic assertions,
so if you can be ready to follow a man who says:
I don't know myself,
seeking has stopped,
for now you are not asking for knowledge.
One who is asking for knowledge cannot ask for being.
Knowledge is rubbish; being is life.

When you stop asking for knowledge,
you have stopped asking about the truth,
for truth is the goal of knowledge.
If you don't inquire what is,
rather you become so silent, so mindless,
that which is
is revealed.

I myself say I don't know.
You cannot come across a more ignorant man than me.
There is no truth and there is no way.
I have not reached anywhere,
I am simply here and now.
If you can follow this ignorant man,

your mind will drop.

For the mind always follows knowledge,
and when the mind drops,
there is no need to go anywhere.
Everything is available, has been available always.
You have never missed it.
But just because of your seeking of the future,
of the goal,
you cannot look.
The truth surrounds you; you exist in it.
Just like the fish exist in the ocean,
you exist in the truth.

God is not a goal.
God is what is here and now.
These trees, these winds blowing,
these clouds moving, the sky, you, I –
this is what God is.
It is not a goal.

Drop the mind and the Divine.
God is not an object, it is a merger.
The mind resists merger;
the mind is against surrender.
The mind is very cunning and calculating.

This story is beautiful.
You are the inquirer.
You have come to me to inquire how to achieve truth,
you have come to me to inquire
how to achieve a state of mind which is blissful.
You have come to acquire knowledge,
to solve the mystery,
and I repeat to you:
There is no state of mind, because there is no mind;
there is no truth, so no seeking is allowed.
All seeking is futile; search as such is foolish.
Seek and you will lose,
don't seek and it is there,
run and you will miss.

Stop. . .
It has always been there.

And don't try to understand.
Be.
Understanding is superficial.
Under the Bodhi tree, Buddha has not known more.
You may know more.

Many scholars came to Buddha.
They knew more than Buddha.
Maha-Kashyap came.
He was a great pundit.
Sariputra came.
He was a great pundit.
Sariputra came
and five hundred disciples came with him,
disciples of Sariputra.

And when Sariputra came to Buddha,
he came for more than knowledge,
for of knowledge he had had enough.
Really, he may have known more than Buddha.
He was a very deep, penetrating scholar.
He knew all the scriptures.
He was a great Brahmin pundit
and all the Vedas were on his tongue.
He could have recited,
but he asked Buddha:
Give me something that is more than knowledge.
Of knowledge I have got enough,
and I am fed up with it.

And what did Buddha say to Sariputra?
He said:
Unlearn.
Drop knowledge,
and that which is more will happen to you.

A real master teaches you unlearning.
It is never learning.
You have come to me to unlearn whatsoever you know,

never learning.
You have come to me learned,
so whatsoever you know, please drop it.
Become ignorant, become like a child.
Only the heart of a child
can knock at the doors of the Divine,
and only the heart of a child is heard.
Your prayers cannot be heard.
They are cunning.
Only a child,
only a heart which doesn't know can be.

This is the meaning of this anecdote,
and it is good for you,
for the same is the case with you.

Anything more?

Bhagwan,

You just told us you have nothing to teach us,
and last night it was a great shock when you said
as far as you are concerned your work is done,
that you're carrying your body for us.

A young Jesus also said:
Wist ye not that I am about my Father's business.

What is or what was your business?

When I say my work is done,
I mean I'm finished with any seeking.
I mean I have come to realize
that there is nothing to be realized,

nothing to be known, nowhere to go.
This moment is enough; this moment is eternity.
When I say my work is done,
I mean now there is no desire.

Desire is business.
You have to do something.
Only then will you be happy.
I am simply happy.
It is not concerned with any doing;
it is now uncaused.

That is the difference between happiness and bliss.
Happiness is caused –
you have a friend and you are happy,
your beloved has returned and you are happy,
you have won a lottery and you are happy.
Causes are there.
They are beyond you; they are outside you.
So your happiness comes from the outside.
It is caused,
and that which is caused cannot be forever.
The beloved may go back,
the friend may turn enemy –
friends turn enemy –
and whatsoever you have achieved may be lost.
That which is caused cannot always be there,
cannot be eternal.

When I say my work is done,
I mean now my happiness is uncaused.
There is nothing that is helping me to be blissful.
I am simply blissful.
It cannot be taken away.
You cannot uncause it if it is not caused.
You cannot do anything to it.
It is simply beyond.
It cannot be destroyed.

My business is finished.
And when I say my business is finished,
I am finished,

because I can exist only with the business.

Then why am I here?
This is one of the oldest questions.
Buddha lived for forty years
after he became enlightened.
After his business was finished,
he lived for forty years more.
Many times it was asked:
Why are you?
When the business is finished,
you should disappear.
It looks illogical.
Why should Buddha exist within the body
even for a moment?
When there is no desire,
how can the body continue?

There is something very deep to be understood.
When desire disappears,
the energy that was moving in desire remains.
It cannot disappear.
Desire is just a form of energy.
That's why you can turn one desire into another.
The anger can become sex;
the sex can become anger.

Sex can become greed,
so whenever you find a very greedy person,
he will be less sexual.
If he is really perfectly greedy,
he will not be sexual at all.
he will be a *brahmachari,* a celibate,
because the whole energy is moving into greed.
And if you find a very sexual person,
you will always find he is not greedy,
because nothing is left.

If you see a person who has suppressed his sex,
he will be angry.
Anger will be always ready.

You can see in his eyes, in his face,
he is just angry.
The whole sex energy has become anger.
That's why your so-called monks and *sadhus*
are always angry.
The way they walk, they show their anger;
the way they look at you, they show their anger.
Their silence is just skin-deep —
touch them and they will become angry.
Sex becomes anger.
These are forms.
Life is the energy.

What happens when all desires disappear?
Energy cannot disappear; energy is indestructible.
Ask the physicists.
Even they say
that energy cannot be destroyed.

A certain energy was existing in Gautam Buddha
when he became enlightened.
That certain energy
was moving in sex, anger, greed, in millions of ways.
All forms disappeared,
so what became of that energy?
Energy cannot go out of existence,
and when desires are not there,
it becomes formless, but it exists.
Now, what is the function of it?
That energy becomes compassion.

You cannot be in compassion,
because you have no energy.
All your energy is divided,
sometimes in sex, sometimes in anger,
sometimes in greed.
Compassion is not a form.
Only when all your desires disappear,
that energy becomes compassion, *karuna*.

You cannot cultivate compassion.

When you are desireless, compassion happens.
Your whole energy moves into compassion
and this movement is very different.
Desire has a motivation in it, a goal;
compassion is non-motivated.
There is no goal to it,
it is simply overflowing energy.

So when I say I exist for you,
I don't mean
that I am doing something to exist for you.
Now I am not doing anything.
Forms of desire have disappeared.
Now the energy is there, without me.
The energy is moving and overflowing,
and you can partake, you can feed on it.
That is what Jesus meant when he said:
Eat me.
Let me become your blood;
let me become your food.
This overflowing energy can become food to you,
food of the eternal.

I am not doing anything.
When I say I exist for you,
it is only language,
for there is no other language.
I am not doing anything.
This is how it is happening.

My forms have disappeared.
Now a formless energy has remained,
and it will go on overflowing.
Those who are wise can partake,
because soon, it will become bodiless also.
First energy becomes formless, desireless,
and then it becomes bodiless.

The body has its own momentum.
When one is born,
when a Buddha is born,

he is born out of a communion of two bodies,
the father and the mother.
Then particular chromosomes, particular cells,
create his body.
Those cells have a built-in momentum.
That built-in momentum means
that this body will exist
for seventy or eighty years.
This is a body blueprint.
For eighty years this body can exist.

The body doesn't know, cannot know,
that the soul that has entered
is going to become enlightened.
This house cannot know
that the person who has entered this house to live
will become enlightened,
and when this man becomes enlightened,
even then this house will not know.
The house will continue.
It has its own life.
The body has its own life,
and the body is completely unaware
that a person has become enlightened.
It continues.
It has its own momentum, its own fuel.

At the age of forty Buddha became enlightened.
The body became irrelevant, but it continued.
It continued; it completed its circle.
It was there for eighty years.

It is good, for these forty years
were the overflowing years,
and we were able to know what enlightenment is.
If Buddha had disappeared that very moment,
there would have been no religion.
If the body had dropped,
if Buddha had become enlightened
and the body had dropped,
he would not have been—

even to tell what had happened.
This was good.
Existence was very compassionate.
Buddha lived for forty years more.
Not with any motivation,
but with the momentum of the body
he just went on overflowing.
This body will also disappear.
The momentum has to be completed.

I am not doing anything for you,
for that too is sort of egoistic,
anybody thinking he is doing something for you.
It is happening.

The form of desires disappears
and energy becomes compassion.
The body has to complete its momentum.
It has to complete its momentum;
it has to complete its blueprint.
This gap will be an overflowing.
It is a feast, not by me given to you.
it is a feast given by the whole.

Language creates problems.
Language is always dualistic;
language is always of this world.
Language belongs to desire
and it carries all the connotations,
so it is very difficult to say anything
about that which is not of this world.
Either you have to be silent —
even then, silence too can be misunderstood —
or you have to use language.
And every word is loaded.

If I say I am here for you,
you can interpret it in such a way
that it looks like a business, looks like a work.
It is not, it is none of it.
It is simply an overflowing of love.

And I am not the doer,
for if I am the doer, there can be no love.

Just a light is burning.
You may find the path, the light is there.
You may use it.
It may become a flame for you,
it may kindle a light within you,
but that depends on you.
I am simply here.

You are initiated, not by me,
by the energy itself.
Eat me as much as you can.
Let me become part of you.
Celebrate this occasion.

Jesus' words again create problems.
Words always create problems.
Had Jesus been here, had he been here
in the country of the Upanishads, Buddha and Mahavir,
the language would have been totally different.

Jesus was born a Jew.
He had to use Jewish language, myth, phraseology.
So he said:
The work, the business,
that was given from my Father to me, is done.
If he had been here,
he would never have talked about the Father.
The Father is a Jewish concept.
It is good, beautiful, but very anthropomorphic.
God is not the Father, God is not a person,
and God is not in any sort of business.

But Jews are businessmen,
and their God is also a businessman,
the super-businessman,
controlling, managing, manipulating.
And just like a businessman,
you can seduce him, you can bribe him.
He is a very real person.

He will be angry.
If you don't surrender to him,
he will throw you in hell;
if you follow him, you will achieve the paradise –
heaven and heavenly pleasures.

This whole language
belongs to the world of profit, business.
But every language has its own problems.
This language is concrete,
and gives a very family-type appearance to existence.
Father, Son and the work . . .
You can reach to the Father through the Son . . .
Jesus was simply using the language available.

In this country
we have tried many linguistic patterns.
Hindus use millions of types,
for Hinduism is not a religion,
it is many religions.
All types of religions exist in Hinduism.
It is a crowd.
It is a phenomenon in itself.
Every type that has ever existed in the world
exists in Hinduism.

This is a miracle.
Even an atheist can be a Hindu –
an atheist cannot be a Christian –
and even an atheist can become enlightened.
Buddha was an atheist.
He didn't believe in God.
He said there is no God, and even more mysterious,
he said there is no soul.
He said nothing exists,
and he became one of the incarnations of a Hindu God.

It is really mysterious.
This atheist, Gautam Buddha, became the Tenth Avatar.
He said there is no God and Hindus said:
This man is God's Incarnation.

He is Bhagwan.

Hindus say even a denial is a way of assertion;
Hindus say even to say no is to say yes.
This is very mysterious.
They say even to say there is no God,
is to say God in a negative way.
If God can be asserted in positive language,
why not in negative?
'It' is a word; 'nothing' is also a word.
And one is just as relevant as the other.

Buddha said no.
Then no became absolute;
nothingness became the nature.
Shankara said yes.
Then yes became absolute;
that 'yesness', Brahma, became the source.
But Hindus say both mean the same.

Each language, each pattern of expressing it,
has its own benefits
and its own dangers and pitfalls.
I myself am inclined towards the negative,
hence so much emphasis on Zen masters.
I have really loved these anecdotes –
no mind, no truth, no understanding.

Your desire is positive.
If God is asserted in a positive way,
your desire will not die,
your desire will turn towards God,
and you will start desiring God.
Negativity is to say no to all your desires,
to all your objects of desire.
Then all desires and all objects disappear,
and only you are left in your purity.
That purity, that innocence,
the benediction of it,
is what I want you to enjoy with me.

It is not a teaching.

I am not a teacher.
It is not a doctrine.
It is just you enjoying with me.
I am available here,
and if you put your mind aside,
we can celebrate.
I am in an inner dance.
You can also become a partner in it.
You may call this my business.

My work is done as far as I am concerned,
because I am done.
Now the energy
has become a compassion and an overflowing,
and all those who really want to taste
are invited to do so without any condition.
You are not to give anything,
you simply are to take.
No discipline, no bargain,
nothing is expected on your part.
It is a gift.
It has always been so;
it will always be so.
The ultimate bliss is always a gift.
That's why we have been calling it grace, *prasad,*
as if the Divine gives to you
out of his overflowing energy.

I will tell you one story Jesus used to say.
He repeated it many times.
He must have loved this story.
He said:
Once it happened, a very rich man
needed some labourers in his garden, to work,
so he sent a man to the market place.
All the labourers who were available were called,
and they started working in the garden.
Then others heard,
and they came in the afternoon.
Then others heard,

and they came just when the sun was setting.
But he employed them.
And when the sun went down,
he gathered all of them and paid them equally.

Obviously those who had come in the morning
became disappointed and said:
What injustice!
What type of injustice is this?
What are you doing?
We came in the morning and we worked the whole day,
and these fellows came in the afternoon.
Just for two hours they worked.
And a few have just come.
They have not worked at all.
This is injustice.

The rich man laughed and said:
Don't think of others.
Whatever I have given to you,
is it not enough?
They said:
It is more than enough, but it is injustice.
Why are these people getting when they have just come?

The rich man said:
I give them because I have got too much.
Out of my abundance I give them.
You need not be worried about this.
You have gotten more than you expected,
so don't compare.
I am not giving them because of their work,
I am giving them because I have got too much,
out of my abundance.

Jesus said some work very hard to achieve the Divine,
some come just in the afternoon,
and some when the sun is setting,
and they all get the same Divine.

Those who had come in the morning must object:
This is too much.

You just see.
You have been meditating so much,
and then suddenly someone comes just by the evening
and becomes enlightened.
And you have been such a great ascetic.
Just look.
If all the ascetics reach,
and see that sinners
are sitting just by the side of the throne of God,
what will happen?
They will become so sad.
What is happening?
These sinners never disciplined their lives,
they never worked,
and they are here.
And we were thinking they would be in hell.

There is no hell.
There cannot be.
How can hell exist?
Out of God's abundance everything is heaven.
It should be so, it must be so, it has to be so.
Out of his abundance is heaven.
There can be no hell.
Hell was created by these ascetics
because they cannot conceive of sinners in heaven.
They have to make compartments.
They cannot think that you will be there.

It is reported that one Hassid, a rabbi, Baal Shem,
was visited by a woman.
She was about seventy.
Her husband was eighty,
and now, by and by, was becoming a virtuous man.
His whole life he had been a sinner,
so she had come to give her thanks
that he had finally converted her husband –
which was impossible,
as he had been a sinner his whole life.
But now he was turning,

so she was very thankful to Baal Shem.

She had always been a pious lady,
never wavered, never went wrong,
always had been on the right track,
and always thinking
that heaven was just waiting to welcome her,
and always knowing well
that this husband of hers was going to hell.
So she said to Baal Shem:
There can be hope now,
and even my husband may reach heaven.
Baal Shem laughed and said:
Greater the sinner, greater the saint.
The woman became sad and said:
Then why didn't you tell me before?
You should have told me forty years before.

Greater the sinner, greater the saint.
This woman will be in such hell
if she finds her husband in heaven.
These so-called virtuous people have created hell,
otherwise, out of Divine abundance,
hell cannot exist.
Saints will receive,
for they come in the morning;
sinners will receive,
and they may have come in the evening.
Everyone is going to receive.
It is a gift.

I am here, not as a business now,
but as a gift.
But you are so afraid and fearful.
You can understand business.
You know the terms.
You cannot understand a gift.
You don't know the terms.
You can understand
if you have to fulfill some condition;
if nothing is required of you,

you are simply at a loss.

All expectations belong to the mind,
all disciplines belong to the mind,
all so-called saintliness and so-called sin
belong to the mind.
When there is no mind,
there is no sinner and no saint,
and the gift simply showers on you.

Third Talk

12th June 1974

Bhagwan,

A warrior came to the Zen master Hakuin
and asked:
Is there such a thing as heaven and hell?

Hakuin said:
Who are you?
The warrior replied:
I am chief samurai to the emperor.
Hakuin said:
You, a samurai?
With a face like that,
you look more like a beggar.

At this the warrior became so angry
he drew his sword.

Standing calmly in front of him,
Hakuin said:
Here open the gates of hell.

Perceiving the master's composure,
the soldier sheathed his sword and bowed.

Hakuin then said:
And here open the gates of heaven.

Heaven and hell are not geographical.
If you go in search of them,
you will never find them anywhere.
They are within you.
They are psychological.

The mind is heaven,
the mind is hell,
and the mind has the capacity to become either.
But people go on thinking
everything is somewhere outside.
We always go on looking for everything outside,
because to be inwards is very difficult.
We are outgoing.
If somebody says there is a God,
we look at the sky.
Somewhere, sitting there, will be the Divine person.

One psychologist in an American school
asked small children what they thought about God.
Children have clearer perception.
They are less cunning, more truthful.
They are more representative of the human mind.
They are unperverted.
So he asked the children
and the answers were collected.

The conclusions were very ridiculous.

Almost all the children
depicted God something like this –
an old man, very tall, bearded, and very dangerous.
He created fear.
If you didn't follow him,
he would throw you into hell;
if you prayed and followed him,
he would give you paradise and all the pleasures.
He was sitting on a throne in the sky,
watching everybody.
You couldn't escape him.
Even in your bathroom, he was looking.

The outgoing mind projects everything outside.
This is your God too.
Don't laugh,
don't think this is a child's conception.
No.
This is you.
This is how you think about God –
as a cosmic spy,
always searching to condemn, to punish,
to throw you into hell;
as very ferocious, revengeful.

That's why all religions are based on fear.
Religions say
if you do this,
you will be appreciated, rewarded;
if you don't do this, you will be punished.
The base seems to be fear.
God just seems to be a very powerful emperor,
sitting on a throne in heaven.

The whole concept is foolish, but human.
The human mind is foolish.
The whole concept is anthropocentric.
In the Bible it is said
God created man in his own image.
In reality, it seems to be quite otherwise –
man created God in his own image.

We have projected God in our own image.
He is just a blow-up of the human mind.
He is a bigger human mind, that's all.

Remember,
if you think God is somewhere outside you,
you have not even taken the first step
towards being religious.

The same happens with all such concepts.
We say heaven is without, hell is without.
It is as if there exists nothing within.

What is within you?
The moment you think of the within,
it seems that everything goes empty.

What is within?
The world is without;
sex is without;
sin is without; virtue is without.
God, heaven, hell –
everything is without.
What is within you?
Who are you?

The moment you think of the within,
your mind goes blank.
There is nothing.
In reality, everything is within.
The outer is just a projection.

Fear is within you.
It is projected as a hell.
Hell is just a projected image on the screen –
of the fear that is within you,
of the anger, of the jealousy,
of all that is poisonous in you,
of all that is evil in you.
Heaven is, again, a projected image on the screen –
of all that is good and beautiful,
of all that is blissful within you.

The devil is the fallen human being,
God is the risen human being.
God is the ultimate possibility of your beatitude;
the devil is your ultimate fall.
There is nobody like the devil existing somewhere.
You will never meet him unless you become him.
And you will never encounter God,
unless you become God.

In the East,
religions transcended this anthropocentric attitude
very long ago, in the past.
Eastern religions are non-anthropocentric.
They say:
You cannot encounter God,
you can become God.
They say:
When you reach to the ultimate point of existence,
there will be no God to receive you and welcome you.
Only you will be there in your godliness.

So this can be said,
and I go on insisting:
There exists no God; existence is Divine.
There exists no one like a person, a super-person,
no one.
God is non-existential; godliness is existential.
The moment I say godliness,
it becomes something inward;
the moment you say God, you have projected it.

This story is beautiful.
The Zen master Hakuin
is one of the rare flowerings.

A warrior came to him, a samurai, a great soldier,
and he asked:
Is there any hell; is there any heaven?
If there is hell and heaven, where are the gates?
Where do I enter from?
How can I avoid hell and choose heaven?

He was a simple warrior.
Warriors are always simple.
It is a difficult to find a businessman who is simple.
A businessman is always cunning, clever,
otherwise he cannot be a businessman;
a warrior is always simple,
otherwise he cannot be a warrior.
A warrior knows only two things, life and death –
nothing much.
His life is always at stake;
he is always gambling.
He is a simple man.

That's why businessmen
could not create a single Mahavir, a single Buddha.
Even Brahmins
could not create a Ram, a Buddha, a Mahavir.
Brahmins are also cunning, cunning in a different way.
They are also businessmen,
of a different world, of the other;
they deal in business,
not of this world, but of the other world.
Their priesthood is a business;
their religion is mathematics, arithmetic.

They are also clever,
more clever than businessmen.
The businessman is limited to this world;
their cunningness goes beyond.
They always think of the other world,
of the rewards they are going to get there.
Their rituals, their whole mind
is concerned with how to achieve more pleasures
in the other world.
They are concerned with pleasure.
They are businessmen.
Even Brahmins could not create a Buddha.

This is strange.
All the twenty-four Jain Teerthankaras were Kshatriyas,
warriors.

Buddha was a warrior; Ram and Krishna were warriors.
They were simple people,
with no cunning in their minds, with no arithmetic.
They knew only two things, life and death.

This simple warrior came to Hakuin
to ask where is heaven and where is hell.
He had not come to learn any doctrine.
He wanted to know where the gate was
so he could avoid hell and enter heaven.
And Hakuin replied in a way
only a warrior could understand.

If a Brahmin had been there,
scriptures would have been needed.
He would have quoted
the Vedas, the Upanishads, the Bible, the Koran.
Then a Brahmin would have understood.
All that exists for a Brahmin is in the scriptures.
Scriptures are the world.
A Brahmin lives in the word, in the verbal.

If a businessman had been there,
he would not have understood the answer,
the response Hakuin gave,
the way he acted with this warrior.
A businessman always asks:
What is the price of your heaven?
What is the cost?
How can I attain it?
What should I do?
How virtuous should I be?
What are the coins?
What should I do so heaven can be attained?
He always asks for the price.

I have heard one beautiful story.
It happened in the beginning
when God created the world.
God came to earth
to ask different races about the Ten Commandments,

the ten rules of life.

The Jews have given so much significance
to those ten rules –
Christians also; Mohammedans also.
All these religions are Jewish.
The source is the Jew.
And the Jew is the perfect businessman.

So God came to ask.
He came to the Hindus and asked:
Would you like to have Ten Commandments?
The Hindus said:
What is the first?
We must have a sample.
We don't know what these Ten Commandments are.

God said:
Thou shalt not kill.
The Hindus said:
It will be difficult.
Life is complex; killing is involved.
It is a great cosmic play.
There is birth, death, fighting, competition.
If all the competition is taken away
the whole thing will become flat, dull.
We don't like these Commandments.
They will destroy the whole game.

Then he went to the Mohammedans and said:
Thou shalt not commit adultery.
He also gave them one example.
They had also asked for a sample.

The Mohammedans said:
This will be difficult.
Life will lose all beauty.
At least four wives are needed.
You call it adultery,
but this is all that life can give,
all that a virtuous man should have.
Who knows of the other world?

This is the world.
You have given it to us to enjoy
and now you have come with these Ten Commandments.
This is contradictory.

God went around and around.
Then he came to Moses, leader of the Jews.
Moses never asked for a sample.
And God was afraid.
If Moses said no, nobody was left.
Moses was the last hope.

When God asked Moses –
the moment God said: I have Ten Commandments –
what did Moses reply?
He said:
How much do they cost?
This is how a businessman thinks.
The first thing he wants to know is the cost.

God said:
They cost nothing.
And Moses said:
Then I will have ten.
If they cost nothing, there is no problem,
That's how the Ten Commandments were born.

But this samurai was not a Jew;
he was not a businessman.
He was a warrior.
He had come with a simple question.
He was not interested in scriptures,
not in cost,
not in any verbal answer.
He was interested in reality.

And what did Hakuin do?
He said:
Who are you?
And the warrior replied:
I am a samurai.

It is a very proud thing to be a samurai in Japan.
It means being a perfect warrior,
a man who will not hesitate a single moment
to give his life.
For him, life and death are just a game.

He said:
I am a samurai; I am a leader of samurais.
Even the emperor pays respect to me.
Hakuin laughed and said:
You, a samurai?
You look like a beggar.

His pride was hurt, his ego hammered.
The samurai forgot what he had come for.
He took out his sword
and was just about to kill Hakuin.
He forgot that he had come to this master
to ask where is the gate of heaven,
to ask where is the gate of hell.

Then Hakuin laughed and said:
This is the gate of hell.
With this sword, this anger, this ego,
here opens the gate.

This is what a warrior can understand.
Immediately he understood:
This is the gate.
He put his sword back in its sheath.
And Hakuin said:
Here opens the gate of heaven.

Hell and heaven are within you.
Both gates are within you.
When you are behaving unconsciously,
there is the gate of hell;
when you become alert and conscious,
there is the gate of heaven.

What happened to this samurai?
When he was just about to kill Hakuin,

was he conscious?
Was he conscious of what he was about to do?
Was he conscious of what he had come for?
All consciousness had disappeared.

When the ego takes over, you cannot be alert.
Ego is the drug, the intoxicant
that makes you completely unconscious.
You act,
but the act comes from the unconscious,
not from your consciousness.
And whenever any act comes from the unconscious,
the door of hell is open.
Whatsoever you do,
if you are not aware of what you are doing,
the gate of hell opens.

Immediately the samurai became alert.
Suddenly, when Hakuin said:
This is the gate,
you have already opened it —
the very situation must have created alertness.

Just imagine what would have happened
if you had been the warrior,
if you had been the samurai,
sword in hand, just about to kill.
A single moment more,
and Hakuin's head would have been severed;
a single moment more,
and it would have been separated from the body.
And Hakuin said:
This is the gate of hell.

This is not a philosophical answer.
No master answers in a philosophical way.
Philosophy exists
only for mediocre, unenlightened minds.
The master responds,
but the response is not verbal.
It is total.

That this man may have killed him is not the point.
If you kill me and it makes you alert,
it is worth it.
Hakuin played the game.
If a single moment had been lost,
this man would have killed him.
But at the right moment Hakuin said:
This is the gate.

You may not have heard about samurais.
Say you are about to kill a samurai.
Your sword is in your hand;
it is just about to touch his neck.
He is standing before you,
unprotected, without any weapon.
Samurais have a particular sound, a *mantra*.

He will just say a single word so loudly
that all your energy will go.
You will become as if dead, a statue.
He may simply say:
Hey!
You will become static; your hand will not move.
That sound will hammer the heart,
which controls everything.
Your hand will become static;
your mind will be shocked.
All activity will disappear.
You cannot kill a samurai,
even if he is without weapons.

A sound becomes a protection.
If you have a gun,
your hands will not move or you will miss the aim.
It is just a sound,
a sound that has to be made in a particular way,
so that it goes deep into your heart
and changes your activity completely,
changes the pattern of your activity.

When Hakuin said:

This is the gate,
the samurai must have remained static.
In that static state,
when all activity ceases,
you become alert.

Some activity is needed,
otherwise your unconscious would break
and you would become conscious.
Zen says if a person can sit for six hours,
without doing anything,
he will become enlightened.
Just for six hours.
But six hours is really too long.
I say six minutes is enough.
Even six seconds will do,
if you can be absolutely without activity.
When you are not occupied, you cannot be unconscious;
when you are unoccupied,
your whole energy becomes consciousness.
A tremendous release occurs.

Your energy is engaged in occupation.
Your mind is thinking, your body is working,
you are occupied.
Your whole energy is moving in activity,
is being dissipated into the world.

When you think, you are dissipating energy.
Each thought takes energy, needs energy.
You are continuously thinking,
and dissipating energy for nothing –
just dissipating energy.
Activity needs energy
and your infinite source of energy
is continuously being dissipated.
You are leaking from everywhere.

That's why you feel so weak, so frustrated,
so impotent.
This impotence feels like helplessness.

You are omnipotent and you feel impotent.
You have all the sources of infinite energy
within you.
You are related to the cosmic source.
But you feel impotent
because you are continuously dissipating energy.

If thought stops even for a single moment
and activity is no more,
if you have become like a statue,
unmoving within or without,
if there is no movement, either of body or of mind,
then tremendous energy is released.
Where will it go now?
There is no activity.
It cannot go without.

You become a pillar of energy,
a flame of energy.
Everything becomes conscious inside.
Everything is lighted.
Your whole being is filled with light.

This must have happened to the warrior –
stopped, sword in hand,
with Hakuin just before him,
with a master, an enlightened master, before him.
The eyes of Hakuin were laughing,
the face was smiling,
and the gate of heaven opened.
He understood.
The sword went back into its sheath.
While putting the sword back into the sheath
he must have been totally silent, peaceful.
The anger had disappeared.
The energy moving in anger had become silence.

If you suddenly awake in the middle of anger,
you will feel a peace you have never felt before.
Energy was moving
and suddenly it stops.
You will have silence, immediate silence.

You will fall into your inner being,
and the fall will be so sudden,
you will become aware.
It is not a slow fall.
It is so sudden that you cannot remain unaware.
You can remain unaware only with routine things,
with gradual things.
You move so slowly you can't feel movement.

This was sudden movement –
from activity to no-activity,
from thought to no-thought,
from mind to no-mind.
As the sword was going back into its sheath,
the warrior realized.
And Hakuin said:
Here open the doors of heaven.

Silence is the door.
Inner peace is the door.
Non-violence is the door.
Love and compassion are the doors.

Heaven and hell are not geographical.
They are psychological.
They are your psychology.
And this is not a question
to be decided on the day of judgment.
The human mind is so clever.
To avoid, to escape,
Christians, Mohammedans and Jews
have created a concept of the last day,
when everybody is to be judged.
You will be taken out of your grave and judged.
Those who have followed Jesus,
who have been good, who have believed,
will go to heaven;
those who have misbehaved,
who have not followed Jesus,
who have not been to church,
will be thrown into hell.

Christian hell is one of the most ridiculous things.
It is eternal; there is no end to it.
This seems injustice, sheer injustice.
Whatsoever sin you have committed,
no punishment which is eternal can be just.

Bertrand Russell somewhere has joked:
If I calculate all my sins,
sins that I have committed,
and sins that I have not committed,
only brooded over –
if even they are included –
the hardest judge can't send me to jail
for more than four years.
And Christianity sends you to hell forever.

Bertrand Russell has written a book,
Why I am not a Christian.
This is one of his arguments.
It is a beautiful argument,
because the whole thing seems to be ridiculous.

If, as Hindus say,
you have committed millions of sins
in millions of lives,
it may look logical
to send a person to hell for eternity.
But Christians believe in only one life,
a life of seventy years.
How can you commit so much sin
that you deserve eternal hell?
If you commit sin continuously for seventy years,
even then, eternal hell doesn't look just.
The whole thing seems to be revengeful.

So God is not throwing you into hell
because of your sins,
because you were disobedient,
because you were rebellious,
because you didn't listen to him.
It seems to be revenge.
But revenge can be unjust.

Is it punishment?
It seems ridiculous.

The human mind has created a last judgment day.
Why?
Why wait for the last day?
The mind always postpones, pushes things ahead:
The problem is not right here and now.
It is a question of the last day, so we will see.
The problem is not urgent.
We will see what happens.

There are ways and means.
In the last moment you can follow Jesus,
in the last moment you can surrender
and say to God:
I was a sinner.
You can confess and be forgiven.
God is infinite compassion.
God is love.
He is going to forgive you.

Christians have evolved a technique of confession.
You commit sin,
and then you go to the priest and confess.
Confessed, you are relieved.
If you confess honestly, you are ready to sin again.
The past sin is forgiven.
Once you know the trick, the key –
that you can commit a sin and be forgiven –
who is going to prevent you from committing more?
So the same people keep on coming to the priest
every Sunday,
and go on confessing.

Sometimes the ego is such
that people confess sins they never committed.
The ego is such that if you start confessing,
you may become so involved in it
that you may start confessing sins
you never committed.
To be a greater sinner is so ego-filling –

the greater the sinner,
the greater will be the forgiveness of the Divine.

It has been said by those
studying Leo Tolstoy's autobiographical notes deeply,
that many sins he says he committed,
he never committed at all.
He is enjoying.
Jean-Jacques Rousseau has written confessions,
his autobiography.
The sins he confesses, he never committed.
The same is possible with Mahatma Gandhi.
In his autobiography
the things he depicts himself as committing
may be exaggerations.

This is how the ego works.
Whatever you say you take to the extreme.
Then there is the beautiful feeling
that you have confessed.

Last judgment, confession
are tricks of the mind.
Heaven and hell are not at the end,
they are here and now.
Every moment the door opens.
Every moment you go on wavering
between heaven and hell.
It is a moment-to-moment question.
It is urgent.
In a single moment you can move from hell to heaven,
from heaven to hell.

This is the meaning of the story.
Not even a single moment had passed and Hakuin said:
This is the gate of hell.
Now the gate of hell opens.
And not a single moment had passed and he said:
Look, this is the gate of heaven.

Heaven and hell are not very distant.
They are neighbours.

Only a small fence divides them.
You can jump that fence, even without a gate.
You go on, jumping from this to that.
In the morning you may be in heaven;
by evening you are in hell.
This moment, heaven; that moment, hell.

It is just an attitude, just a state of your mind,
just how you are feeling.
Many times, in a single life, you may visit hell.
And many times you may visit heaven.
In a single day also . . .

There is a beautiful story of a disciple of Mahavir.
He was a great king.
He renounced and became a disciple of Mahavir.
He was very ascetic, austere,
and did whatever Mahavir said to the very extreme.
His name spread all over the country.
It was Prasannachandra.
Even kings started coming to pay homage to him.

One king, Bimbasar,
who had been a friend of Prasannachandra
when he was also a king,
came to the cave where he was standing
naked under the sun,
with his eyes closed.
Bimbasar bowed down before Prasannachandra and thought:
When will the time come
when I will also become so peaceful,
so silent, blissful?
This man has achieved.

Then he went to Mahavir, Prasannachandra's master.
He was near, somewhere in the same forest.
He said to Mahavir:
Bhagwan, just before coming to you,
I have been to Prasannachandra.
He was standing with his eyes closed,
so blissful, so heavenly.

He has achieved.
When will the moment come for me?
I am not so fortunate; I feel jealous.

I also have a question:
If Prasannachandra had died
that very moment when I was there,
paying my respects to him,
where would he reach?
Which heaven would be attain?

Jains say there are seven heavens and seven hells.
And Mahavir said:
He will fall to the seventh hell.

Bimbasar couldn't understand.
He was puzzled and confused.
He said:
What are you saying, the seventh hell?
Prasannachandra was standing so silently,
so peacefully, so meditatively.
He was in such ecstasy.
If he falls to the seventh hell,
what will happen to me?
Are there more hells beyond the seventh?
No, you must be joking.
Tell me the truth.

Mahavir said:
This is the truth.
Just before you a few people had passed by.
They also went to pay homage to Prasannachandra
They started gossiping around him.
He heard.
And the doors of hell opened.

Those people were coming from his capital
where he had been king.
They said:
This fool has renounced all.
The prime minister,
to whom he has given

the whole responsibility for running the kingdom,
is a thief.
He is looting.
He is destroying.
When Prasannachandra's son comes of age,
when he will come to be king,
there will be nothing left.
And this fool is standing here with his eyes closed.

Prasannachandra heard this.
Suddenly the door of hell opened.
He forgot.
He was also a samurai, a warrior, a Kshatriya.
He completely forgot that he had renounced.
He forgot that there was no sword.
He completely forgot that he was now a monk.

The samurai who had gone to Hakuin had a sword.
Prasannachandra had none; he was standing naked.
He pulled out his sword —
the sword was not there; it was just an illusion —
and completely forgot that he was a *sannyasi*.
The whole thing was so burdensome,
so much anxiety was created out by the news,
that he pulled his sword out of the sheath and said:
I am alive.
What does that prime minister think?
I will go and cut off his head.
I am still here.

Whenever he used to become angry in the old days,
he would always touch his crown.
So he touched his crown.
There was no crown, just a shaven head.
Suddenly he remembered:
What am I doing?
There is no sword.
I am a *sannyasi* and have renounced all.

Mahavir said:
If he had died at the very moment he realized this,
he would have achieved the seventh heaven.

Prasannachandra realized what he had been imagining.
Just through imagination,
the door of hell was opened.
Now it had closed.
If he had died at this moment,
he would have achieved the seventh heaven.

Hell and heaven are within you.
The doors are very close.
By the right hand you can open one;
by the left hand you can open another,
With just a change of your mind,
your being is transformed –
from heaven to hell
and from hell to heaven.
This goes on continuously.

What is the scret?
The secret is
whenever you are unconscious,
whenever you act unconsciously, without awareness,
you are in hell;
whenever you are conscious,
whenever you act with full awareness,
you are in heaven.

If this awareness
becomes so integrated, so consolidated
that you never lose it,
there is no hell for you;
if unconsciousness
becomes so consolidated, so integrated,
that you never lose it,
there is no heaven.

Fortunately,
unconsciousness can never become so consolidated.
A part always remains conscious.
When your whole being seems to be unconscious,
even then,
a witnessing part always remains conscious.

Even while asleep, a part is witnessing.

That's why, in the morning
you sometimes say the sleep was beautiful.
Sometimes you say
the sleep was disturbed, nightmarish;
sometimes you say:
I slept so deeply,
so peacefully –
it was such great happiness.

Who knows this?
You were asleep.
Who knows that you were so happy?
A part has witnessed;
a part was continuously alert, knowing.
Who knows that you were disturbed, uneasy,
uncomfortable?
You were asleep.
Even in sleep a part of you knows.
You cannot become completely unconscious.
Once achieved, consciousness cannot be lost.
You cannot reverse the process.

You cannot be eternally in hell –
this Christian doctrine is absolutely false –
but you can be eternally in heaven.
This is the Hindu doctrine.
Hell can only be temporary;
it can be only for the time being.
It is temporal.
Heaven can be eternal.

To make a distinction
between the momentary heaven and the eternal heaven,
Hindus have a different word – *moksha*.
Hindus have three words;
Christians, Mohammedans, Jews have only two words.
'Heaven' and 'hell' are the two words
for Mohammedans, Christians and Jews.
Hindus say

naraka for hell, *swarga* for heaven,
and *moksha* – beyond both.
A third word.

Hindus say heaven is not worth achieving.
It can be lost.
When the state of heaven becomes permanent,
when it cannot be lost,
it is *moksha.*
It is absolute freedom.
Then bliss has become your nature,
then heaven and hell have disappeared.
Then wherever you are, it will make no difference.
You will be in permanent bliss.
This third state is the aim.

But you cannot reach the third if you are flickering,
if you are wavering between heaven and hell.
Then nothing can be consolidated, integrated.
Then you live in a flux.
There is no crystallization; your being is liquid.
Sometimes it moves to heaven; sometimes, to hell.

Crystallization means
you become more and more conscious,
you become more and more centred,
more and more grounded.
Less asleep, you become more aware.
And a moment comes –
even when you are asleep,
you are conscious.

Ananda used to sleep with Buddha in his room.
A Buddha is worth watching, even in his sleep,
so Ananda used to watch sometimes.
A Buddha asleep is such a beautiful phenomenon.
He looks like a small child, innocent,
with no burden of the day.

You dream only because you carry a burden,
only because the day is incomplete.
You have left many things incompleted.

They have to be completed in the dream.

You looked at a woman.
You desired her, but it was not possible.
Society, the law, the state, morality,
your own conscience, diverted your attention.
You escaped from the woman,
but she will follow you in the dream.
The act has to be completed.
You must make love to this woman,
if not in reality, then in the dream.
Only then will you feel at ease.
The incomplete act becomes a burden.

A Buddha sleeps dreamlessly
because nothing is incomplete.
There is no desire, no passion.
Nothing arises and nothing remains.
Things pass as if in front of a mirror.
A woman passes and Buddha looks,
but no passion arises.
The woman has passed.
The mirror is vacant again.
There is no trace, no mark of it.
He is dreamless.

Even a child is not dreamless.
Even a child has desires.
Maybe the desire is not for a woman,
it may be for a new toy or for something else,
but even a child dreams.

Even a cat, a dog dreams.
Look at a cat
and you will feel it is dreaming of rats.
It is jumping, catching.
It is sometimes frustrated
and sometimes very happy if the rat is caught.
Look at a dog sleeping.
You can feel it is dreaming
about flies, about bones, about fighting.
Sometimes it is tense, sometimes relaxed.

The sleep is disturbed.

To look at a Buddha while he is asleep
is very beautiful,
so Ananda used to watch.
Buddha would go to sleep,
and Ananda would sit and look at him.
He was such a silent pool of being.
Nothing was incomplete.
Everything, every moment was complete and perfect.
There was no dream; there were no traces left.
His mind was a clean mirror.
The stream of consciousness was never muddled.
It was crystal clear.

Ananda became puzzled
because Buddha always slept in the same posture.
He would remain the whole night in the same posture.
He would not change.
He would remain in the same posture.

That posture has become very famous.
It is called the lying posture.
You may have seen Buddha's pictures.
There are many statues
in Ceylon, China, Japan and India.
If you go to Ajanta,
there is a statue of Buddha lying down.
That posture, how Buddha lay,
has been reported by Ananda.
Buddha slept in the same posture the whole night,
not even changing sides.

So one day Ananda asked:
Bhagwan,
everything is okay, but one thing puzzles me —
you remain in the same posture the whole night.
Are you asleep or not?
If someone is asleep he will change his posture.
Are you asleep or not?
Even while you are asleep or appear to be asleep,
it appears you are alert.

It seems you know what the body is doing.
You will not even change your posture unconsciously.

Buddha said:
Yes, when the mind is silent, not dreaming,
only the body sleeps.
Consciousness remains alert.

Krishna has said to Arjuna in the Gita:
While you sleep the yogi remains alert.
Even in the night his sleep is not sleepy.
His sleep is only in the body,
a rest in the body, a relaxation in the body.
His consciousness is alert.

In reality,
a yogi's consciousness needs no relaxation.
It is always relaxed.
There is no tension.
Relaxation is needed because of tension.
You are so tense the whole day,
your consciousness has to be relaxed.

A yogi's body relaxes because the body gets tired.
His body is a mechanism;
his consciousness is always alert,
continually alert.
It is a continuum of alertness.

When your consciousness becomes a continuum
there are no gaps in consciousness;
when there is no darkness within you,
your whole inner temple has become enlightened.
The light has reached to every corner
and no part of your inner house is in darkness.
You are a *mukta,* a free man.

This is the meaning of a Christ.
You are Christ
arisen, resurrected.
Now there is no night for you.
Only the day exists.

Now the sun never sets.

Heaven means consciousness;
hell means unconsciousness.
There is the possibility to move to either.
When the possibility disappears,
there is no hell, no heaven –
there is a third.
The ultimate opens the door.
You become free.
You become freedom.
This is the goal.

Hakuin did well,
but this could only have been done with a warrior.
The warrior responded immediately –
he became angry, totally angry.
If he had been a businessman, he would have smiled.
Anger would have been inside.
He would not have been ready, immediately,
to cut off Hakuin's head.
Hakuin's response would have been useless.

You do this also.
When you are angry, you smile.
You are so inauthentic and false.
Even in anger, you lie.
Your love cannot be believed,
because even your anger is unbelievable.
Your whole life is a continuous lie.
Whatsoever you do, you are not truthful.
Angry, you are not truthful.
You smile, you paint it on, you hide it;
you show something else.
Then you cannot be made alert
that this is the gate of hell.

This warrior was like a child.
He became totally angry.
He became so angry he was going to kill this man
he had come to as a disciple.

He had come in search of a master,
and he was going to kill this man.
He was total.

This totalness helped.
If you are total in your anger,
you will be total when the anger disappears;
if you are false in your anger,
you cannot be real in your silence.

Hakuin said:
Look, you have opened the door of hell.
Immediately he realized.
This can be realized
only if you are total and truthful;
otherwise, it cannot be realized.

You are such a deceiver,
you would have deceived Hakuin.
You would have smiled.
That means the door of hell would have been open,
but painted with the signboard of heaven.
It would have looked from the outside
as if it were heaven,
but inside it would have been hell.
You would have divided and fragmented.
No, it would not have been of much help.

This warrior became so total in his anger,
he lost all his consciousness.
He became angry.
He was not angry —
there was no one who was angry —
he simply became anger.
His whole energy became anger.
He was mad.
At such a peak things can be realized.
Then they become penetrative.
Then somebody can be made alert.

Hakuin said:
Look!

And the warrior could look.
He was a truthful man.
Then Hakuin said:
This is the gate of hell.
And he could realize.
When you are total, you can realize.

Suddenly the anger disappeared.
Because it was total, it disappeared.
Because it was total, it disappeared totally.
If it had been fragmentary
it could not have disappeared totally.
It totally disappeared, totally.
A deep silence was left behind.

This is what I have been telling you continuously:
Be total.
Be authentic; be true.
If you are a sinner, be a true sinner.
Don't try to create a facade of being a saint.
A true sinner is bound to become a true saint,
sooner or later.
Time is irrelevant.
A true sinner is true.
That is the point.
Sin is not the point.

I have heard
a peddlar was caught and brought to court.
He was peddling without a license.
He was a new man in town,
but knew that a license was needed.
There were a few other persons
standing before the magistrate.
Three women had also been caught.
They were prostitutes without licenses.
This is really a wonderful world –
governments even issue licenses for prostitution.

They were caught without licenses,
so the magistrate asked the first woman:

What do you say?
Who are you and what are you doing?
The woman said:
I am a model.
She was lying.
The magistrate sentenced her
to thirty days hard labour.

He asked the second woman.
She said:
Somewhere something is wrong.
I have been caught wrongly.
I am an actress.
The magistrate sent her for sixty days.

He looked at the third woman.
The third woman said:
My lord, I am a prostitute.
The magistrate could not believe
that anybody could be so truthful,
that anybody could confess so truly.
He said:
Authenticity has become so rare
that you have shocked me.
I have never encountered anyone who is truthful.
Go, I forgive you.
I'll not give you any punishment.

Then came the number of the peddlar.
The magistrate asked:
What were you doing?
He said:
To be frank, I am also a prostitute.

This is what is going on.
Faces.
False faces all over.
Deception.
You are not even aware of how you deceive,
and who you are deceiving.
There is no one to be deceived.
You are deceiving yourself trying to escape.

trying to hide.

That warrior was a true man.
This untruthfulness was not there.
He was ready to kill or to die.
He became so inflamed,
he was a fire.
Thc door was open.

Your door is never completely open –
you sneak through the holes.
Your heaven is also never open –
you enter from the back door.

To be total
is a basic thing for any seeker,
for anyone in search of silence and truth.
When you are angry, be angry.
Don't think of the consequences.
Let the consequences be there.
Suffer them.
But don't deceive yourself.

When entering hell, enter totally.
Don't leave half your mind outside.
Go into it.
Pass through it.
Suffer it.
Pain is going to be there,
but pain gives maturity;
suffering is going to be there,
but you can transcend it if you understand.
Only a total mind can understand.
And when anger disappears,
you will become so silent, so meditative.

If you love, love totally;
if you hate, hate totally.
Don't be fragmentary.
Suffer the consequences.
Because of consequences, you try to deceive –
you are a peddlar and you say you are a prostitute;

because of consequences, you are never angry,
never hateful.

Then you will miss heaven also.
One who is incapable
of opening the door of hell completely,
will be incapable
of opening, completely, the door of heaven.

Go through hell.
The path passes through there.
Heaven is achieved through hell.

This is the meaning of the anecdote.
Hakuin first created hell for the warrior.
Hell must be created first.
Hell is easy to create –
you are always ready, always knocking at the door.
You are afraid, but always ready;
you are not courageous, but always ready;
you are not daring, but always ready.
There is continuous turmoil inside.

Hakuin could not have created heaven first.
That is impossible.
No one is ready.
Heaven is very far away.
Hell is nearby, just around the corner.
You move and you are in it.

I, also, cannot create heaven for you.
That is why all my meditation techniques
are designed to create hell first.
People come to me and say:
Make us silent.
Why do you insist on going mad?

I cannot open the doors of heaven first
and you cannot become silent.
Be totally mad first.
I create hell for you
and you will have to pass through it.

It is the nearest thing you can easily do.
Heaven is very far away.
And one who has not travelled through hell
cannot reach heaven.
My insistence is a very considered one.

You can understand the story now.
Hakuin said to the warrior:
You, a samurai?
Your face looks like a beggar's.
The samurai could not tolerate this.
It was too much.
A beggar?
He would never beg, not even for his life.
Immediately he was touched to his very core.
A beggar?
Impossible!
The sword came out.

I am touching you,
hitting you, hammering you
in all my meditation techniques
just to bring your hell out.
But you are such cowards
that even if you bring your hell out,
it will not be total.
You play with it.
You are not involved in it.
You are fragmentary.
You only become lukewarm.

Lukewarm won't do.
You have to be boiling.
Only then can you evaporate.
The ego evaporates only at the boiling point,
not before.
You just become lukewarm.
It is of no use;
it is an unnecessary waste of heat.
Again, you will become cold.
After meditation you will become cold.

cold to the extreme.

In your catharsis, open the door of hell.
I promise you,
if you can open it
I will open the other door immediately.
It is always open.
Once you open the door of hell, it is near.

To say this much is enough:
Look, this is the gate of hell.
Then the gate closes.
And the other gate opens.

Anything more?

Bhagwan,

How does what you said about heaven and hell
tie in with what you've been saying
about roots and wings?

When you say roots into this earth
and wings into that heaven,
I've got a feeling of being infinitely stretched –
that this earth is close
and that heaven is far away.

What is the significance of 'this' and 'that'?

This earth is close,
not because it is close, but because of you.
That heaven is far away,
not because it is far away, but because of you.

'This' means the world.
'This' means the body –
these desires, these passions,
the physical, the visible.
'This' means all that has been condemned by religions.
They are always against 'this' and for 'that'.

'That' means Brahma.
'That' means *moksha.*
'That' means the Divine.
'This' means the material world –
this devilish world, this which is condemned.
All the religions have condemned this world.

I don't condemn it.
I want to give you roots into this world.
All the religions have said
unless you are uprooted from 'this',
you will not get wings into 'that'.
They are against 'this',
against the world, the body,
against the material, the visible.
All you feel as near, they are against.

They are for something very far away,
something abstract –
God, Brahma, *moksha.*
Nobody knows; nobody is in contact with it.
There is no communion, no touch with it.
It looks like a dream, like poetry.
It looks imaginary.

All religions have condemned 'this'.
They say:
Be uprooted.
That's why they call *sannyas* renouncing the world,
renouncing 'this'.
I do not.
They have created a dualism.
Not only dualism,
they have created antagonism between 'this' and 'that',
between the physical and the spiritual.

To me, roots into 'this'
will help to give you wings into 'that'.
I don't create any antagonism where there is none.
Antagonism comes from a mind in conflict,
from a mind in duality.
Out of conflict, dual theories are created,
conflicting theories.

I am not dual.
I create no conflict.
I see 'that',
not against 'this',
but as a flowering of 'this'.
I see wings,
not against roots,
but as a flowering of the roots.

Trees have wings into the sky.
Their branches are their wings.
They have roots into the earth
and branches into the sky.
I would like you to be a strong tree –
with roots into 'this',
and wings into 'that'.

My God is not against the world,
my God is in the world.
My God is the world.
This earth is not against that heaven.
They are two polarities of the same phenomenon.

'This' appears near to you.
because your mind is not yet in a state
to see the invisible.
Your mind is so disturbed, so coarse,
that you can see only the visible, the rough.
The subtle escapes you.
If your mind becomes silent, thoughtless,
the subtle will become visible.
God is not invisible.
He is visible everywhere.

But your mind is not yet tuned to the subtle;
to the invisible.
The invisible can be seen.
The word means that which cannot be seen,
but no, the invisible can be seen;
only you need more subtle, more refined eyes.

A blind man cannot see.
He cannot see that which is visible to you,
but his eyes can be cured,
and then he can see the sunlight, colours, rainbows.
All that was invisible before has now become visible.

God is not invisible.
You don't have the right eyes, that's all.
You are not a tuned being
for which the subtle opens its doors.

'This' and 'that', for me, are not divided.
'This' reaches into 'that';
'that comes into 'this'.
For you, 'that' means the far away.
Not for me.
For me, 'this' is 'that',
and someday it will be the case for you also –
'this' will be 'that'.
This world is God.
The visible hides the invisible.

That's why my *sannyas* is not a renunciation.
My *sannyas* is not against anything.
It is for the totality, for the whole.

Be rooted in the earth
so that you can stretch to the sky;
be rooted in the visible.
so that you can reach into the invisible.
Don't create duality,
and don't create any antagonism.
If I am against anything, I am against antagonism.
I am against being against anything.

I am for the whole, the complete circle.

The world and God are not divided anywhere.
There is no boundary.
The world goes on spreading into God,
and God goes on spreading into the world.

Really, to use two words is not good,
but language creates problems.
We say the creator and the created.
We divide.
Language is dualistic.
In reality, there is no created and no creator,
only creativity,
only a process of infinite creativity.
Nothing is divided.
Everything is one – undivided.

Language is just like a political map.
India, Pakistan, Bangaladesh
are divided on the political map,
and if you ask the earth
where India begins and Pakistan ends,
the earth will laugh and think you mad.
The earth is round,
it is one.
Only on political maps is it not,
and maps are false.
And politicians are madmen,
madmen who have attained power.
They are more dangerous
than madmen who live in madhouses,
because they have power.

Where do you end and I begin?
Where is the point where we can draw a line
between you and me?
Where?

There cannot be any demarcation.
The air goes on flowing in you.
You breathe.

If, even for a moment,
the air is not flowing in you,
if the breath is not coming,
you will be dead.
And the air in me
just a moment before has left me
and entered you.
It was my life just a moment before;
now it is your life.
And your breath has returned to me.
It was your life;
now it is my life.
Where are we divided?

Life goes on flowing.
Life is something in between you and me.
The tree goes on creating oxygen
and you breathe it.
If the trees disappear, you will disappear.
The trees go on changing cosmic rays into food –
that is what fruit and vegetables are –
and if they disappear, you will be no more.
They are constantly creating food for you.
That's how you exist.
Greenery is in a constant process
of creating food for you.
You depend on it.

The clouds go on moving, bringing water for you.
The whole is connected.
The faraway sun sends its rays to you
and those rays are life.
If the sun disappears, all life will disappear.
Even the sun gets its energy from some source,
scientists have not yet
been able to find that source,
but if that source disappears,
everything will disappear.
Everything is related, joined together.
This world does not exist in fragments,
it exists as a whole, one whole.

To me,
'this' plus 'that' is God.
That's why I say very contradictory things.
I would like to give you two things –
roots into this earth, into all that is earthly,
and wings into that heaven,
into all that is abstract for you now,
into all that you cannot even comprehend,
that cannot be conceptualized.
Roots into the finite;
wings into the infinite.

And you need not renounce 'this'.
If you renounce 'this',
you are renouncing your roots.
That has happened.
That is why your monks, your *sadhus,* look so dead.
They have renounced 'this'.
They are uprooted beings.

Uproot a tree and you are exposing the part
that was hidden in the earth.
Soon the flowers will die,
the branches will die,
the leaves will start falling.

That's what's happening to your *sannyasis,*
the so-called old *sannyasis.*
They destroy their roots
because they are against this earth,
and then their flowering stops.
Have you ever seen an old *sannyasi*
in a flowering state –
one who is blossoming every day,
one who is giving anew every day,
one who is flowering into the unknown every day?
No, you will find
a rigid, patterned, disciplined being there,
a dead being.

Mahavir may have been alive,
but look at the followers of Mahavir.

Look at their faces –
you cannot see any flowers there.
Their eyes are dull and dead.
They are uprooted trees.
They have to be pitied;
they need much help, much compassion.
They are ill.
Without roots they are bound to be ill.
They may have destroyed their sex,
but they don't know
that they have destroyed their love also.

Sex is 'this'; love is 'that'.
When you destroy sex, you destroy love.
I say, go so deep into sex that it becomes love –
so deep that your very roots start flowering,
that your very roots become blossoms.
The beginning becomes the end;
the seed becomes the tree.
Go so deep into it
that the other is found hidden there.
It is always there.

You can control your anger
but then there will be no compassion.
Go so deep into anger
that your anger becomes compassion.
Then something, a miracle, has happened to you.
Then you will be blessed.
Then there will be benediction.
Then, only, there will be ecstasy.

This earth symbolizes all that has been condemned,
and that heaven,
all that has been desired.
But I don't divide.
To me, both are one.
And the day will soon come for you, too,
when you will be able to see
that 'this' is pregnant with 'that'.
This world is just a womb for the Divine.

The earthly is just a cover,
a protective cover for the unearthly.
The seed, the cell of the seed,
is not against the tree,
it is a protection.
Matter is just a protection for the Divine.

Look, and always try to find the unity.
In unity is religion;
in disunity, religion is lost.
And avoid being against.
If you are against, you will become rigid, hard,
and the harder you become,
the more dead you will be.

I have heard that it once happened
that a gang of robbers, by fault, entered a monastery.
They thought this house belonged to some rich man –
the monastery had a look of richness –
so they entered.
But the monks gave them such a hard fight,
they were happy when they succeeded in escaping.

When they met again, outside the town,
one of the robbers philosophized:
Not very bad, we have a hundred rupees among us.
The leader said:
You fools!
I have always told you to avoid monks.
We had five hundred rupees
when we entered the monastery!

And I also say to you:
Avoid monks.
If you enter the monastery with five hundred flowers,
you will have only one hundred when you come out.
They are enemies,
enemies of 'this',
and I say those who are enemies of 'this'
are bound to be enemies of 'that' –
whether they know it or not.

Love 'this'
and love it so deeply
that your love transcends 'this'
and reaches 'that'.
That's what I mean –
roots into this earth,
and wings into that heaven.

Fourth Talk

13th June 1974

Bhagwan,

Joshu, the Zen master, asked a new monk
in the monastery:
Have I seen you before?
The new monk replied:
No sir.
Joshu said:
Then have a cup of tea.

Joshu then turned to another monk:
Have I seen you here before?
The second monk said:
Yes sir, of course you have.
Joshu said:
Then have a cup of tea.

Later the managing monk of the monastery
asked Joshu:
How is it you make the same offer of tea
to any reply?
At this Joshu shouted:
Manager, are you still here?
The manager replied:
Of course, Master.
Joshu said:
Then have a cup of tea.

The story is simple, but difficult to understand.
It is always so.
The more simple a thing,
the more difficult it is to understand.
To understand, something complex is needed;
to understand, you have to divide and analyze.
A simple thing cannot be divided and analyzed.
There is nothing to divide and analyze –
the thing is so simple.
The simplest always escapes understanding.
That is why God cannot be understood.
God is the simplest thing,
absolutely the simplest thing possible.

The world can be understood.
It is very complex.
The more complex a thing is,
the more the mind can work on it.
When it is simple, there is nothing to grind.
The mind cannot work.

Logicians say simple qualities are indefinable.
For example, somebody asks you what yellow is.
It is such a simple quality, the colour yellow,
how will you define it?
You will say:
Yellow is yellow.
The man will say:

That I know, but what is the definition of yellow?
If you say yellow is yellow, you are not defining;
you are simply repeating the same thing again.
It is a tautology.

G. E. Moore,
one of the most penetrating minds of this century,
has written a book, *Principia Ethica.*
The whole book consists of a very persistent effort
to define what is good.
Making efforts from all directions,
in two or three hundred pages –
and two, three hundred pages of G. E. Moore
is worth three thousand pages of anybody else –
he came to the conclusion that good is indefinable.

Good cannot be defined.
It is such a simple quality.
When something is complex,
there are many things in it;
you can define one thing
by another that is present there.

If you and I are in a room,
and you ask me: Who are you?
I can at least say I am not you.
This will become the definition, the indication.
But if I am alone in a room
and I ask myself the question:
Who am I?
the question resounds, but there is no answer.
How to define it?

That is why God has been missed.
Intellect denies it;
reason says no.
God is the simplest denominator in existence –
the simplest and the most basic.
When the mind stops, there is nothing other than God.
So how to define God?
He is alone in the room.

That is why religions try to divide.
Then definition is possible.
They say:
This world is not that,
God is not the world; God is not matter;
God is not body; God is not desire.
These are ways to define.

You have to put something against something,
then a boundary can be drawn.
How do you draw a boundary if there is no neighbour?
Where do you place the fence of your house
if there is no neighbourhood?
If there is no one beside you,
how can you fence in your house?
Your house boundary
consists of the presence of your neighbour.
God is alone; he has no neighbour.
Where does he begin?
Where does he end?
Nowhere.

How can you define God?
Just to define God, the Devil was created.
God is not the Devil –
at least this much can be said.
You may not be able to say what God is,
but you can say what he is not:
God is not the world.

I was just reading one Christian theologian's book.
He says God is everything except evil.
This, too, is enough to define.
He says: All except evil.
This much will draw a boundary.

He is not aware.
If God is everything
then from where does this evil come?
It must be coming from everything.
Otherwise, there is some other source of existence
besides God –

and that other source of existence
becomes equivalent to God.
Then evil can never be destroyed.
Then it has its own source of existence.
Then evil is not dependent on God
so how can God destroy it?
God will not destroy it.
Once evil is destroyed, God cannot be defined.
To define him
he needs the Devil to be there always,
just around him.

Saints need sinners;
otherwise, they would not be there.
How will you know who is a saint?
Every saint needs sinners around him.
Those sinners make the boundary.

The first thing to be understood is
that complex things can be understood;
simple things cannot.
A simple thing is alone.

This Joshu story is very simple.
It is so simple it escapes you.
You try to grip it; you try to grab it.
It escapes.
It is so simple that your mind cannot work on it.

Try to feel the story.
I will not say try to understand,
because you cannot understand it.
Try to feel the story.
Many things are hidden if you try to feel it.
If you try to understand it, nothing is there.
The whole anecdote is absurd.

Joshu saw one monk and asked:
Have I seen you before?
The man said:
No sir, there is no possibility.
I have come for the first time.

I am a stranger.
You could not have seen me before.
Joshu said:
Okay, then have a cup of tea.

Then he asked another monk:
Have I seen you before?
The monk said:
Yes sir, you must have seen me.
I have always been here; I am not a stranger.

The monk must have been a disciple of Joshu's,
and Joshu said:
Okay, then have a cup of tea.

The manager of the monastery was puzzled:
With two different persons
responding in different ways,
two different answers were needed.
But Joshu responded in the same way—
to the stranger and to the friend,
to one who has come for the first time
and to one who has been here always.

To the unknown and to the known,
Joshu responded in the same way.
He made no distinction, none at all.
He didn't say:
You are a stranger.
Welcome!
Have a cup of tea.
He didn't say to the other:
You have always been here,
so there is no need for a cup of tea.
Nor did he say:
You have always been here,
so there is no need to respond.

Familiarity creates boredom.
You never receive the familiar.
You never look at your wife.
She has been with you for many, many years,

and you have completely forgotten that she exists.
What is the face of your wife?
Have you looked at her recently?
You may have completely forgotten her face.
If you close your eyes and meditate and remember,
you may remember the face you looked on
for the first time.

But your wife has been a flux, a river,
constantly changing.
The face has changed;
now she has become old.
The river has been flowing and flowing,
new bends have been reached;
the body has changed.
Have you looked at her recently?

Your wife is so familiar there is no need to look.
We look at something which is unfamiliar;
we look at something which strikes us as strange.
They say familiarity breeds contempt.
It breeds boredom.

I have heard one anecdote.
Two businessmen, very rich,
were relaxing on Miami Beach.
They were lying down, taking a sunbath.

One said:
I can never understand what people see in
Elizabeth Taylor, the actress.
I don't understand what people see,
why they become so mad.
What is there?
You take her eyes away, you take her hair away,
you take her lips away, you take her figure away,
and what is left, what have you got?

The other man grunted, became sad, and replied:
My wife, that's what's left.

That is what has become
of your wife, of your husband –

nothing is left.
Because of familiarity, everything has disappeared.
Your husband is a ghost;
your wife is a ghost,
with no figure, with no lips, with no eyes—
just an ugly phenomenon.

This has not always been so.
You fell in love with this woman once.
That moment is there no longer;
now you don't look at her at all.

Husbands and wives avoid looking at each other.
I have stayed with many families
and watched husbands and wives
avoid looking at each other.
They have created many games to avoid looking;
they are always uneasy when they are left alone.
A guest is always welcome.
Both can look at the guest and avoid each other.

Joshu seems to be absolutely different,
behaving in the same way
with a stranger and a friend.

The monk said:
I have always been here, sir;
you know me well.
And Joshu said:
Then have a cup of tea.

The manager couldn't understand.
Managers are always stupid.
To manage, a stupid mind is needed.
And a manager can never be deeply meditative.
It is difficult.
He has to be mathematical, calculating;
he has to see the world and arrange things accordingly.

The manager became disturbed:
What is this?
What is happening?

This looks illogical.
It's okay to offer a cup of tea to a stranger,
but to this disciple who has always been here?
So he asked:
Why do you respond in the same way
to different persons, to different questions?

Joshu called loudly:
Manager, are you here?
The manager said:
Yes sir, of course I am here.
And Joshu said:
Then have a cup of tea.

This asking loudly:
Manager, are you here?
is calling his presence, his awareness.
Awareness is always new;
it is always a stranger, the unknown.
The body becomes familiar, not the soul.
Never.
You may know the body of your wife;
you will never know the unknown hidden person.
Never.
That cannot be known; you cannot know it.
It is a mystery.
You cannot explain it.

When Joshu called:
Manager, are you here?
suddenly the manager became aware.
He forgot that he was a manager;
he forgot that he was a body.
He responded from his heart.
He said:
Yes sir.

This asking loudly was so sudden,
it was just like a shock.
And it was futile.
That's why he said:

Of course I am here.
You need not ask me; the question is irrelevant.

Suddenly the past, the old, the mind, dropped.
The manager was there no more –
simply a consciousness was responding.
Consciousness is always new, constantly new.
It is always being born; it is never old.

And Joshu said:
Then have a cup of tea.

The first thing to be felt
is that for Joshu,
everything is new, strange, mysterious.
Whether it is the known or the unknown,
the familiar or the unfamiliar,
it makes no difference.

If you come to this garden every day,
by and by, you will stop looking at the trees.
You will think you have already looked at them,
that you know them.
By and by, you will stop listening to the birds.
They will be singing, but you will not listen.
You will have become familiar.
Your eyes are closed; your ears are closed.

If Joshu comes to this garden –
and he may have been coming every day
for many, many lives –
he will hear the birds,
he will look at the trees.
Everything, every moment, is new for him.

This is what awareness means.
For awareness, everything is constantly new.
Nothing is old.
Nothing can be old.
Everything is being created every moment –
it is a continuous flow of creativity.
Awareness never carries memory as a burden.

The first thing:
a meditative mind always lives in the new,
in the fresh.
The whole existence is newly born –
as fresh as a dew-drop,
as fresh as a leaf coming out in the spring.
It is just like the eyes of a newborn babe.
Everything is fresh, clear, with no dust on it.

This is the first thing to be felt.
If you look at the world and feel everything is old,
it shows you are not meditative.
When you feel everything is old,
it shows you have an old mind, a rotten mind.

If your mind is fresh, the world is fresh.
The world is not the question –
the mirror is the question.
If there is dust on the mirror, the world is old;
if there is no dust on the mirror,
how can the world be old?

If things get old, you will live in boredom.
Everybody lives in boredom.
Everybody is bored to death.

Look at people's faces.
They carry life as a burden – boring, with no meaning.
It seems that everything is just a nightmare,
a very cruel joke,
that somebody is playing a trick, torturing them.
Life is not a celebration.
It cannot be.
With a mind burdened by memory,
life cannot be a celebration.

Even if you laugh, your laughter carries boredom.
Look at people laughing.
They laugh with an effort.
Their laugh may be just to be mannerly;
their laugh may be just etiquette.

I have heard about one dignitary
who went to Africa to visit a community,
a very old, primitive community of aborigines.
He gave a long lecture.
He told a very long anecdote.
For almost half an hour the anecdote continued.
Then the interpreter stood.
He spoke only four words,
and the primitives laughed heartily.

The dignitary was puzzled.
He had been telling the anecdote for half an hour.
How could it be translated in four words?
It seemed impossible.
And people understood.
They were laughing, a belly laugh.

Puzzled, he said to the interpreter:
You have done a miracle.
You have spoken only four words.
I don't know what you said,
but how can you translate my story, which was so long,
into only four words?

The interpreter said:
Story too long,
so I say:
He says joke —
laugh.

What type of laughter will come out?
Just mannerly etiquette will come out.
And this man has been labouring for half an hour.

Look at people's laughter.
It is a mental thing; they are making an effort.
Their laughter is false.
It is painted; it is just on the lips;
it is an exercise of the face.
It is not coming from their being, from the source,
it is not coming from the belly.
It is a created thing.

It is obvious that we are bored,
and whatsoever we do
will come out of this boredom
and will create more boredom.

You cannot celebrate.
Celebration is possible
only when existence is a continuous newness,
and existence is always young.
When nothing grows old, when nothing really dies –
because everything is constantly reborn –
it becomes a dance.
Then it is an inner music flowing.
Whether you play an instrument or not
is not the point.
The music is flowing.

I have heard a story.
It happened in Ajmer.
You must have heard
about one Sufi mystic, Muinudin Chishti,
whose *dargah,* whose tomb is in Ajmer.
Chishti was a great mystic,
one of the greatest ever born,
and he was a musician.
To be a musician is to be against Islam,
because music is prohibited.
He played on the sitar and on other instruments.
He was a great musician and he enjoyed it.

Five times every day,
when a Mohammedan is required
to pray the five ritual prayers,
he wouldn't pray –
he would simply play on his instrument.
That was his prayer.

This was absolutely anti-religious,
but nobody could say anything to Chishti.
Many times people would come to tell him so,
and he would start singing.

And the song would be so beautiful
they would forget completely why they had come.
He would start playing on his instrument,
and it would be so prayerful
that even scholars and pundits and *maulvis*
who had come to object,
wouldn't object.
They would remember at home.
When they were back at home
they would remember why they had come.

Chishti's fame spread over the world.
From every part of the world, people started coming.
One man, Jilani,
himself a great mystic,
came from Baghdad just to see Chishti.

When Chishti heard that Jilani was coming
he felt:
To pay respect to Jilani
it will not be good to play my instrument now.
Because he is such an orthodox Mohammedan,
it will not be a good welcome.
He may feel hurt.

So only for that day, in his whole life,
he decided he would not play,
he would not sing.
He waited from morning,
and in the afternoon Jilani came.
Chishti had hidden his instruments.

When Jilani came, and they both sat in silence,
the instruments started to make music.
The whole room was filled.
Chishti became very puzzled over what to do.
He had hidden them,
and such music he had never known before.

Jilani laughed and said:
Rules are not for you.
You need not hide them.

Rules are for ordinary people; rules are not for you.
You should not hide them.
How can you hide your soul?
Your hands may not play,
you may not sing from your throat,
but your whole being is musical.
And this whole room is filled
with so much music, with so many vibrations
that now the whole room is playing by itself.

When your mind is fresh,
the whole existence becomes a melody.
When you are fresh, freshness is everywhere,
and the whole existence responds.
When you are young, not burdened by memory,
everything is young and new and strange.

This Joshu is wonderful.
This has to be felt deeply,
then you will be able to understand.
But that understanding
will be more like feeling than understanding –
not mental, but from the heart.

Many more dimensions are hidden in this story.
Another dimension
is that when you come to an enlightened person,
whatsoever you say makes no difference.
His response will be the same.
Your questions, your answers are not meaningful,
not relevant.
His response will be the same.
To all the three Joshu responded in the same way,
because an enlightened person remains the same.
No situation changes him.
The situation is not relevant.

You are changed by the situation.
You are completely changed;
you are manipulated by the situation.
Meeting a person who is a stranger,

you behave differently.
You are more tense, trying to judge the situation:
What type of man is this?
Is he dangerous, not dangerous?
Will he prove friendly, or not?
You look with fear.
That's why with strangers you feel an uneasiness.

If you are travelling in a train,
the first thing you will see
is passengers asking each other what they do,
what their religion is, where they are going.
What is the need of these questions?
These questions are meaningful,
because then they can be at ease.

If you are Hindu and they are also Hindu,
they can relax –
the man is not very strange.
But if you say that you are Mohammedan,
the Hindu becomes tense.
Then some danger is there, some stranger is there.
He will make a little space between you and him.
He cannot be at ease; he cannot relax.
He may even change his seat.

But even a Mohammedan is religious.
If you say:
I am an atheist; I am not religious at all;
I don't belong to any religion –
then you are even more of a stranger.
An atheist?
Then he will feel that
just sitting by your side, he will become impure.
You are like a disease; he will avoid you.

People start asking questions
not because they are very curious about you;
no, they just want to judge the situation –
whether they can relax,
whether they are in a familiar atmosphere,
or if something strange is there.

They are on their safeguard,
and this is their inquiry for safety.

Your face changes continuously.
If you see a stranger, you have a different face;
if you see a friend, immediately the face changes;
if your servant is there, you have a different face;
if your master is there, you have a different face.
You continuously change your masks,
because you depend on the situation.
You don't have a soul; you are not integrated.
Things around you change you.

That is not the case with a Joshu.
With a Joshu, the case is totally different.
He changes his surroundings;
he is not changed by his surroundings.
Whatsoever happens around him is irrelevant.
His face remains the same.
There is no need to change the mask.

It is reported that once a governor came to see Joshu.
Of course, he was a great politician, a powerful man,
a governor.
He wrote on a paper:
I have come to see you,
his name,
and governor of this-and-this state.

He must have knowingly or unknowingly
wanted to influence Joshu.
Joshu looked at the paper, threw it away,
and said to the man who had brought the message:
Say I don't want to see this fellow at all.
Throw him out.

The man went and said:
Joshu has said, 'Throw him out.'
He has thrown your paper away
and said, 'I don't want to see this fellow.'

The governor understood.

He wrote again on a paper –
just his name, and, 'I would like to see you.'
The paper reached Joshu and he said:
So this is the fellow!
Bring him in.

The governor came in and he asked:
But why did you behave in such a strange way?
You said, 'Throw this man out.'

Joshu said:
Faces are not allowed here.
'Governor' is a face, a mask.
I recognize you very well, but I don't recognize masks,
and if you have come with a mask,
you are not allowed.
Now it is okay.
I know you very well, but I don't know any governor.
The next time you come, leave the governor behind.
Leave it at your house; don't bring it with you.

We are almost continuously using faces.
Immediately we change.
If we see changes in the situation,
we change immediately,
as if we have no integrated soul,
no crystallized soul.

For Joshu, everything is the same –
this stranger, this friend,
a disciple, this manager.
With his response:
Have a cup of tea,
he remains the same inside.

And why have a cup of tea?
This is a very symbolic thing for Zen masters.
Tea was discovered by Zen masters,
and tea is not an ordinary thing for them.

In every Zen monastery they have a tea-room.
It is special, just like a temple.

You will not be able to follow this,
because tea is a very religious thing
for a Zen master or a Zen monastery.
Tea is just like prayer.
It was discovered by them.

In India, if you see a *sannyasi* drinking tea,
you will feel he is not a good man.
Gandhi would not allow anybody in his *ashram*
to drink tea.
Tea was prohibited.
It was a sin; nobody was allowed to take tea.
If Gandhi had read this story, he would have been hurt —
an enlightened person, Joshu,
asking people, inviting people to have tea?

But Zen has a different attitude towards tea.
The very name comes from a Chinese monastery, Ta.
There, for the first time, they discovered tea,
and they found that tea helps meditation,
because tea makes you more alert.
It gives you a certain awareness.
That's why if you take tea
you will find it difficult to go to sleep immediately.
They found tea helps awareness, alertness,
so in a Zen monastery tea is part of meditation.

What more can Joshu offer than awareness?
When he says: Have a cup of tea,
he is saying: Have a cup of awareness.
Tea is very symbolic for them.
He says: Have a cup of awareness.

That is all that enlightenment can do.
If you come to me, what can I offer you?
I have nothing other than a cup of tea.

To the familiar or unfamiliar,
to a friend or a stranger,
or even to the manager
who has always been there managing his monastery:
Have a cup of tea.

That's all a Buddha can offer to anybody,
but there is nothing more valuable than that.

In Zen monasteries they have a tea-room.
It is like a temple, the most sacred place.
You cannot enter with your shoes
because it is a tea-room;
you cannot enter without taking a bath.

Tea means awareness,
and the ritual is just like prayer.
When people enter a tea-room, they become silent;
when they enter the room, no talk is allowed.
They become silent.
They sit on the floor in a meditative posture,
and then the hostess or the host prepares tea.

Everybody is silent.
The tea starts boiling
and everybody has to listen to it,
to the sound, to the kettle creating music.
Everybody has to listen to it.
The drinking has started
though the tea is not even ready.

If you ask Zen people they will say:
Tea is not something that you pour with unawareness
and drink like any other drink.
It is not a drink.
It is meditation; it is prayer.
So they listen to the kettle creating a melody,
and in that listening
they become more silent, more alert.

Then cups are put before them and they touch them.
Those cups are not ordinary.
Every monastery has its own unique cups.
They prepare their own cups.
Even if they are purchased from the market,
first they break them, then glue them again,
so the cup becomes special,
so you cannot find any replica of it anywhere else.

Then everybody touches the cup, feels the cup.
Cup means the body.
If tea means awareness, then cup means the body.
And if you have to be alert,
you have to be alert
from the very roots of your body.
Touching,
they are alert, meditating.

Then the tea is poured.
The aroma comes, the smell.
This takes a long time –
one hour, two hours –
so it is not just within a minute
that you have drunk the tea,
thrown the cup down and gone away.
No, it is a long process –
slow, so that you become aware of each step.
And then they drink.
The taste, the heat –
everything has to be done with very alert mindfulness.

That's why the master gives the tea to the disciple.
With a master pouring tea in your cup,
you will be more alert and aware;
with a servant pouring tea in your cup,
you can simply forget him.
When Joshu pours tea in your cup –
if I come and pour tea in your cup –
your mind will stop.
You will be silent.
Something special is happening, something sacred.
Tea becomes a meditation.

Joshu said:
Have a cup of tea,
to all three.
Tea was just an excuse.
Joshu will give them more awareness.
And awareness comes through sensitivity.
You have to be more sensitive

whatsoever you do,
so even a trivial thing like tea . . .

Can you find anything more trivial than tea?
Can you find anything more mean,
more ordinary than tea?
No, you cannot.
And Zen monks and masters
have raised this most ordinary thing
into the most extraordinary.
They have bridged this and that,
as if tea and God have become one.

Unless tea becomes Divine
you will not be Divine,
because the least has to be raised to the most,
the ordinary has to be raised to the extraordinary,
the earth has to be made heaven.
They have to be bridged.
No gap should be left.

If you go to a Zen monastery
and you see a master drinking tea,
with an Indian mind
you will feel very much disturbed.
What type of man is this, drinking tea?
Can you conceive Buddha under a Bodhi tree
drinking tea?
You cannot conceive it.
It is inconceivable.

The Indian mind has been talking about non-duality
but has created much duality.
You have been listening to *advaita,* the unity, the one,
but whatsoever you have done, you have created two.
And you have created such a gap between the two
that they look unbridgeable.
Because of this
Shankara had to talk about *maya* and illusion.
You have created such a gap
between this world and that world,

they cannot be bridged.
So what to do?

Shankara said:
This world is illusory.
You need not bridge; this world is not.
That is the only way to come to one.
You have to deny the other completely.

But denial won't help.
Even if you say this world is illusory,
it is there.
And why do you insist so much that it is illusory
if it is not really there?
What is the problem?
Why is it that Shankara went his whole life
teaching people this world is illusory?
Nobody bothers if it is illusory.
If Shankara knew it is illusory,
then why bother about it?

It seems some problem is there.
It cannot be bridged, so the only way
is to drop it completely from consciousness,
to say it is not there,
so only one remains.
We have only one way to come to the one —
to deny the other.

Zen has another way to bridge,
and I think it is more beautiful —
there is no need to deny the other.

And you cannot deny.
Even in denial, you will assert.
If you say this world doesn't exist,
you have to indicate this world, which is nowhere,
so what are you indicating?
What are you pointing your finger at
if there is nothing?
Then you are foolish.
This world exists,

and if you say it is illusory,
it is only an interpretation.

If this world is illusory,
that cannot be real,
because from this, that has to be achieved.
If this world is illusory,
then your Brahma cannot be real.
If the creation is illusory,
how can the creator be real,
because the creation comes from the creator.
If the Ganges is illusory,
how can the Gangotri be real?
If I am illusory,
then my parents are bound to be illusory,
because only out of dream is a dream born.
If they are real, then the child must be real.

Zen says both are real, but both are not two.
Bridge them –
so tea becomes prayer,
so the most profane thing becomes the most sacred.
It is a symbol.
And Zen says
if your ordinary life becomes extraordinary,
only then are you spiritual.
Otherwise, you are not spiritual.

In the ordinary
the extraordinary has to be found;
in the familiar, the strange;
in the known, the unknown;
in the near, the far;
in 'this', 'that'.
So Joshu said:
Come and have a cup of tea.

One more dimension is there in the story,
and that dimension is of welcome.
Everybody is welcome.
Who you are is not relevant.

You are welcome.
At the gate of an enlightened master,
at the gate of a Joshu or a Buddha,
everybody is welcome.
The door is, in a sense, open:
Come in and have a cup of tea.
What does this mean:
Come in and have a cup of tea?
Joshu was saying:
Come in and relax.

If you go to other so-called masters,
so-called monks and *sannyasis,*
you will become more tense;
you cannot relax.
Go to a *sannyasi.*
You become more tense; you become more afraid.
And he creates guilt.
He will look at you with condemnatory eyes,
and the very way he will look at you,
will say you are a sinner.
And he will start condemning:
This is wrong, that is wrong;
leave this, leave that.
This is not the way
of a really enlightened person.
He will make you feel relaxed.

There is a Chinese saying
that if you reach a really great man,
you will feel relaxed with him;
if you reach a false great man,
he will create tension within you.
He will make, knowingly or unknowingly,
every effort to show that you are low, a sinner;
that he is high, above, transcendental.

A Buddha will help you to relax,
because only in your deep relaxation
will you also become a Buddha.
There is no other way.

Have a cup of tea, Joshu said.
Come relax with me.
The tea is symbolic.
Relax.

If you are drinking tea with a Buddha,
you will immediately feel that
you are not alien, not strangers.
Buddha pouring tea in your cup . . .
Buddha has come down to you.
Buddha has come to this.
He has brought that to this.

Christians, Jews, cannot conceive it;
Mohammedans cannot conceive it.
If you knock at the gate of heaven,
can you conceive of God coming and telling you:
Come, have a cup of tea!
It looks so profane.
God will be sitting on his throne,
looking at you with his thousand eyes,
looking at every nook and corner of your being,
at how many sins you have committed.
Judgment will be there.

This Joshu is non-judgmental.
He does not judge you; he simply accepts.
Whatsoever you say, he accepts and says:
Come and relax with me.
Relaxation is the point.

And if you can relax with an enlightened person,
his enlightenment will start penetrating you,
because when you are relaxed, you become porous.
When you are tense, you are closed;
when you relax, he will enter.
When you are relaxed, comfortable, drinking tea,
Joshu is doing something then.
He cannot enter through your mind,
but he can enter through your heart.
Asking you to have a cup of tea
is making you relaxed, friendly,

bringing you nearer, closer.

Remember, whenever you are taking food
and drinking something with someone,
you become very intimate.
Food and sex are the only two intimacies.
In sex you are intimate; in food you are intimate.
And food is more basic an intimacy than sex,
because when a child is born
the first thing he will receive from the mother
will be food.
Sex will come later on,
when he becomes mature sexually,
fourteen, fifteen years afterwards.
The first thing you received in this world was food
and that food was a drink.

So the first intimacy known in this world
is between a mother and a child.
Joshu was saying:
Come, have a cup of tea.
Let me become your mother.
Let me give you a drink.

And a master is a mother.
I insist that a master is a mother.
A master is not a father,
and Christians are wrong
when they call their priests 'Father'.
because father is a very unnatural thing,
a societal phenomenon.
Father doesn't exist anywhere in nature
except in human society.
It is a created thing, a cultured thing.

Mother is natural.
It exists without any culture, education, society.
It is there in nature.
Even trees have mothers.

You may not have heard
that not only does your mother give you life,

but even a tree has a mother.
They have been experimenting in England.
There is a special lab, Delaware,
where they have been experimenting with plants,
and they have come to discover
a very mysterious phenomenon.
If a seed is thrown in the soil,
and the mother from where the seed has been taken
is near,
it sprouts sooner.
If the mother is not near, it takes a longer time.
If the mother has been destroyed, cut,
then it takes a very long time for the seed to sprout.
The presence of the mother, even for a seed,
is helpful.

A master is a mother; he is not a father.
With a father you are related only intellectually;
with a mother your relation is total.
You have been part of your mother.
You belong to her totally.

The same is the case with a master
in the reverse order.
You have come out of the mother;
you will go into the master.
It is a returning back to the source.

So Zen masters always invite you for a drink.
They are saying in a symbolic way:
Come and become a child to me.
Let me become your mother.
Let me become your second womb.
Enter me.
I will give you a rebirth.

Food is intimacy,
and it is so deep-rooted in you
that your whole life is affected by it.
Men all over the world,
in different societies, different cultures,

go on thinking of women's breasts.
In paintings, sculpture, films, novels, whatsoever,
the breast remains the central point.
Why so much attraction for the breast?
That has been the first intimacy with the world;
you came to know existence through it.
The breast was the first touch of the world.
For the first time you came near to existence,
for the first time you knew the other –
from the breast.
That's why so much attraction for the breast.

You cannot be attracted towards a woman
who has no breasts, flat breasts.
It is difficult,
because you cannot feel the mother there.
So even an ugly woman becomes attractive
if she has beautiful breasts –
as if breasts were the point,
the central thing in the being.
And what is the breast?
The breast is food.
Sex comes later.
Food comes first.

Joshu's calling all the three
to come and have a cup of tea,
was calling them to an intimacy.

Friends eat together,
so if you see a stranger coming near you
when you are eating, you will feel uncomfortable.
Strangers feel uncomfortable if they eat together.
That's why in a hotel, in a restaurant,
things have gone very wrong.
Because you are eating with strangers
the food becomes poisonous.
You are so strained and tense.
It is not a family; you are not relaxed.

Food prepared by someone who loves you

has a different quality altogether.
Even the chemical quality changes.
And psychologists say when your wife is angry,
don't allow her to prepare food.
It becomes poisonous.

It is difficult, because the wife
is almost always angry.
And psychologists say when you are eating,
if your wife starts creating trouble –
talking, arguing –
stop eating.
But then you will die,
because the wife almost always creates trouble
while you are eating.

This is a very non-loving world.
The wife knows, if she has a small understanding,
that the worst time to create any conflict
is while the husband is taking food.
Because when he is strained, tense, not relaxed,
food becomes poisonous,
and it will take a longer time to digest it.
Psychologists say
twice the time will be needed to digest the food.
And the whole body suffers.

Food is intimacy; it is love.
And Zen masters always invite you for tea.
They will take you in the tea-room and give you tea.
They are giving you food, drink.
They are telling you:
Become intimate.
Don't stand so far away.
Come nearer.
Feel homey.

These are the dimensions of the story,
but they are dimensions of feeling.
You cannot understand, but you can feel,
and feeling is a higher understanding.

Love is a higher knowing.
And the heart is the most supreme centre of knowledge,
not the mind.
The mind is just secondary, workable, utilitarian.
You can know the surface through the mind;
you can never know the centre.

But you have forgotten the heart completely,
as if it has become a nothingness.
You don't know anything about it.
And if I talk about the heart, the heart-centre,
you think about the lungs, not about the heart.
Lungs are not heart;
lungs are just the body of the heart-centre.
Heart is hidden in the lungs, somewhere deep down.
Just as in your body the soul is hidden,
in your lungs the heart is hidden.

It is not a physical thing,
so if you go to a physician
he will say there is no heart, no heart-centre,
only lungs.
And he is right as far as he knows,
because if you dissect, no heart is found –
only lungs.

The heart has its own ways of knowing.
Joshu can be understood only through the heart.
If you try to understand through the intellect,
it is possible you may misunderstand.
But understanding is not possible.
That much is certain.

Anything more?

Bhagwan,

I feel I want to be close to you,
but at the same time,
I want to run as far away from you as I can.

I don't understand this fear,
since I am not aware of a feeling like this
about anyone else.

It is natural.
It is not something exceptional.
Whenever you have a feeling
to be closer to a man like me,
the fear will come,
because to be close to me means to be dead.
To be close to me means losing yourself.

It is the same fear that grips a river
when it comes to the ocean –
the banks will be lost, the river will be lost –
and every river tries to go back.
But there is no way.
If you feel a deep urge to come closer to me,
there is no way now to escape.
You may try, but you will be a failure.
Others have tried; others will go on trying.

If you have a deep urge to come closer to me,
you will have to come.
You can only delay it;
by escaping, struggling, you can delay it.
You can postpone it, that's all,
because the deep urge is coming from your very being.

Fear is only in the mind.
The urge is coming
from the deepest core of your being,
to be closer.
But fear comes in the mind,
because the closeness means death.

To be close to a master is death.
Your ego will have to go.
The ego thinks, starts thinking:
I must escape before something happens;
before I am lost, I must escape.
The ego will continuously tell you to escape.
The ego will find rationalizations.
It will find faults in me just to help you escape.
It will convince you in every way
that this is the wrong man.

Love is death-like,
and no love is as death-like as loving a master.
If you love a woman, you can dominate her.
That's why lovers
go on playing politics with each other,
dominating, possessing.
The fear is there
that if you don't dominate, you will be lost,
and the other will dominate.
So they continuously fight.
Husbands and wives, lovers, go on fighting.
The fight is for existence, to survive.
The fear is there:
I may be lost in the other.

But when you come to a master,
you cannot dominate him,
you cannot fight with him.
So fear is deeper because of that,
because you cannot create any politics.
Either you have to escape or merge.
No other alternative is there.

If you escape,
from your very deep source of being
you hear you are doing wrong;
if you escape, you will have to come back.
If you come closer, the mind says:
Where are you going?
If you go closer still you may be burned.

And it is right.
The ego is right.
The flame is there,
and if you come closer, you will be burned.
Conflict will be created.
Inner tension, anguish will be created.

You can delay, that's all.
Sooner or later you will have to merge.
No river can escape the ocean.
Once you have come closer, you have come,
and there is no way to go back.
No way exists for going back.

You are here.
You have travelled long.
Not only in physical space,
but also in the inner space
you have travelled long.
Many, many lives
you have been travelling towards this point.
You have desired it,
and now when the point has come nearer,
you become afraid.

The fear is natural.
Understand it.
Don't let it overpower you.
Take a jump.
And that jump will not only be a death,
it will be a rebirth.
But you cannot know that.
Only death, you see only death.

The beyond that is hidden behind the death
you cannot see.
I can see it.
I know you will be reborn.

But nobody can be reborn unless he dies.
So death is not the goal, and death is not the end,
it is just a beginning.
When you are ready to die,
you are ready to be reborn.
The old will disappear, and the absolutely new
will come in its place.
That new is struggling
from the very core of your being;
the old is struggling from the mind,
because the mind has memory—
the old, the past.
The past and future are struggling within you.
That is the problem.

Now it depends on you.
If you are being overpowered by the past,
then you will delay, postpone,
and you can delay it for many lives.
This is not the first time you have delayed.
Many times you have missed before.
Many times you have come across
a Buddha, a Mahavir, a Jesus,
and you escaped.
You tried to avoid.
You closed your eyes.
Again and again you have been playing that game.

But the game is natural to you I say,
because you can see only death.
The river can only see that she will dissolve,
she cannot see that she will become the ocean.
How can she see?
That oceanic existence will be
only when the river is no more.
So the river cannot see.

When your ego is no more,
only then will you know who you are.

Don't allow the fear to overpower you;
allow love to overpower you.
Love comes from the centre;
fear always comes from the periphery.
Don't allow this periphery to be dominant.

And what have you got to lose?
Even if there is no rebirth —
there is rebirth —
but I say even if there is no rebirth
and you simply die,
what have you got to lose?
What will be lost?
What has the river got that is worth preserving?
The life through the hills
has been just a struggle;
the life through the plains
has been just a dirty passage.
What has the river got to lose in the ocean?
Nothing.

So think about it.
What have you got to lose if you come closer?
Your suffering?
Your madness?
What have you got to lose?

There is nothing to lose,
but we never look within
to see that we have got nothing to lose,
because that, too, gives fear.
You like to think that you have got much to lose,
that a treasure is there,
and you will never look.
There is no treasure.
The house is empty.
There has never been anything.
But you are so afraid, you never look

because you know that there is nothing.

Even a beggar dreams that he is an emperor.
In dreams he becomes an emperor, enjoys.
And then he is afraid:
What if the kingdom is lost?
But there has never been any kingdom.

You have come to me
because there has never been any kingdom.
You have nothing to lose,
and now you become afraid.
Look at the tricks of the mind,
the deceptions of the mind.
Look into them.

A man entered a pet shop.
He looked around, and he asked the shopkeeper:
How much will that big dog cost?
It was a very ferocious looking Alsatian.
The man said:
Five hundred rupees.

That was too much for him,
so, logically, he said:
And how much will this small fellow cost?
It was another dog of a smaller size.
The man said:
One thousand rupees.

He tried still.
Then he said:
How much is this tiny one?
It was a very small dog.
The man said:
Two thousand rupees.

The man became very puzzled and disturbed,
and then he asked:
How much will it cost if I don't purchase anything?
The rates are going higher
and the dog is disappearing.

If I don't purchase anything,
how much will it cost?

That is your fear.
What will happen if you come closer to me?
Nothing will happen,
because you have nothing to lose.
And everything will happen,
because once this nothing is lost,
everything becomes possible.
Once this shelter which has become a bondage to you
is lost,
the sky opens infinitely;
once these banks which have been a prison to you
are lost,
you become boundless,
you become infinite.

Let the river move, unafraid,
into the unknown, the uncharted.
Death will be there,
but death is always followed by rebirth.
Die and be reborn.
Lose yourself and find.
Fear comes from the mind;
love comes from your heart.
Listen to the heart.

It happened once in a great palace of a king
that there was a musical organ.
He loved it very much,
but something had gone wrong,
and the organ was so unique,
that nobody knew how to fix it.
Nobody had ever seen one like it.

This king had heard the organ
when he was a very small child,
when his father was alive,
and since then something had gone wrong.
But he loved the organ so much

that he used to keep it in his room.
It was beautiful;
even from the outside it was beautiful.
Many experts were called in vain.
They made many efforts,
and things went from bad to worse.
The organ was more and more destroyed.
The king lost hope.
The organ could not be fixed.

Then suddenly, one day a beggar appeared.
To the doorkeeper he said:
I have heard
that something has gone wrong with the organ.
I can fix it.

The doorkeeper had the urge to laugh,
because great experts
from many capitals of the world had come,
great musicians.
They couldn't find what was wrong.
They couldn't even recognize
what type of organ this was
and what type of music was created by it,
it was so complex.

He had the urge to laugh,
but he looked at the beggar,
and the voice, the beggar's eyes,
seemed to be authentic.
He was absolutely confident.
He was a beggar, but his face looked majestic.

The doorkeeper's mind was saying:
It will be a wastage again,
but his heart said:
This man seems so confident,
what is wrong if he tries?
So he took him to the king.
Looking at the beggar, the king laughed,
and he said:
Are you mad?

Every type of expert has tried and failed.
You must be mad.
You think you can fix it?

The beggar said:
Nothing more, no more harm can be done.
The organ is already out of order, absolutely.
I cannot harm it any more,
so what is the harm if you give me a chance?

The king thought:
He is right,
because nothing more harmful can be done.
So he said:
Okay, you try.

For many days
the beggar disappeared behind the organ.
He was working and working and working,
and suddenly, one midnight,
he started playing on the organ.
The whole palace was filled with an unknown melody,
something so Divine that everybody ran.
The king came out of his bedroom and said:
You have done it.
It must have been very difficult.
It was almost impossible.
You have done a miracle.

The man said:
No it was not difficult,
because in the first place, I made it.
In your father's time I made this organ,
so it was not difficult.

If you are ready,
for one thing, no more harm can be done to you;
you are already harmed.
I cannot harm you any more.
This much is certain.
And look at my eyes and feel my voice.
Give me a chance.

It is not difficult, I say to you.
Once one is dissolved into the infinite,
he is at the source of the thing
from where he has come.

I am not there.
If I were there, if the ego were there,
then it would be difficult.
There is no expert in me;
the expert died long ago.
The ego is the expert;
I don't know anything.
I am not there; I have disappeared.
The ocean exists,
God exists,
not I.

In the first place,
you are close to that thing
from which you have come,
and for God, nothing is impossible.
In the first place, he created you.

And I am not there,
because otherwise it would be a very difficult thing.
If I am there, I will harm you.
The ego can only harm;
experts can only destroy.
They cannot fix you.
You have been with many experts,
and they have done every type of thing
that was possible.
Now you are beyond repair.

But the river can fall in the ocean,
and suddenly, the melody arises.
A music will come out of you,
a music that you have not heard.
It is just hidden in you –
the ego just has to be put out of the way.

I have heard
one school teacher was asking his first graders:
How do you help your family at home?

One small boy said:
I fix my bed myself.
Another said:
I clean dishes.
And so on and so forth.
But then the teacher saw
that one small boy, Johnny,
had not answered.
So he asked:
Johnny, what do you do?

Johnny hesitated a moment,
and then he said:
Mostly, I keep out of the way.

You just keep yourself out of the way,
that's all.
Don't come in between me and you.
Just keep out of the way.
Even if you keep out of the way for a single moment,
the thing can happen.
The old can die;
the new can be born.

Fifth Talk

14th June 1974

Bhagwan,

Hyakujo called his monks together,
as he wished to send one of them
to open a new monastery.
Placing a filled water jar on the ground,
he said:
Who can say what this is
without using its name?

The chief monk,
who expected to get the position,
said:
No one can call it a wooden shoe.
Another monk said:
It's not a pond because it can be carried.
The cooking monk,
who was standing nearby, walked out,
kicked the jar over,
and then walked away.

Hyakujo smiled and said:
The cooking monk becomes the master
of the new monastery.

Reality cannot be known through thinking.
It can be known through action.
Thinking is just a dreamlike phenomenon,
but the moment you act,
you have become part of the reality.
Reality is activity, action;
thinking is fragmentary.
When you act, you are total.
Whatever the action,
your whole being is involved in it.
Thinking goes on in only a part of the mind,
your whole being is not involved.
Without you,
thinking can continue as an automatic process.

This has to be understood deeply.
This is one of the most basic things
for those who are in search of truth
and not in search of anything else.
Religion and philosophy
are distinct in this sense.
Religion is action; philosophy is thinking.

This story has many implications.
The master wanted one, one disciple,
to become the chief of the new monastery
that was going to be opened.

Who should be sent?
Who should be made the guide there —
a man who has much philosophy in his mind,
a man who can talk, discuss, argue,
a man who is bookish, knowledgeable,
or a man who can act spontaneously?
He may not know much;
he may be simple, not intellectual,
but he will be total.

The chief disciple must have started dreaming,
thinking he was going to be chosen.
The mind is always ambitious.
He must have planned how to behave, what to do,
so that he would be chosen
as the chief of the new monastery.
He must not have slept for many days.
His mind must have been revolving around and around.

The ego plans,
and whatsoever it plans will miss reality.
Reality can only be encountered spontaneously.
If you think about it beforehand,
you may be ready but you will miss.
A ready person will miss.
This is the contradiction.
A person who is not ready,
who has not planned anything,
who acts spontaneously,
reaches the very heart of reality.

The chief disciple must have theorized.
Many alternatives must have come to his mind:
The master is going to choose;
there is going to be some sort of test.
He must have consulted the scriptures.
In the old days too,
masters had been choosing disciples
to be sent to new monasteries.
How have they chosen?
What sort of examination has to be passed?

How could he succeed?

There are many stories from the ancient days,
but this has been, almost always,
one of the basic tests
Zen masters have put before their disciples –
they ask them to express something
without using language.
They say:
Say something about this thing
but don't use any name.
The name is not the thing.

The chair is here and I am sitting on it.
A Zen master will say:
Say something about this chair
but don't use the name.
The word 'chair' is not the chair.
Don't use any verbal expression.
Don't use language and say something.

The mind feels puzzled
because the mind knows only language,
nothing else.
If language is barred, the mind is barred.
What else is the mind except verbal accumulation –
names, words, language?

A master says:
Don't use the name.
He is saying:
Don't use the mind.
Do something,
so that which the chair is, is expressed

The word 'god' is not God.
The word 'man' is not man.
The word 'rose' is not a rose.
The rose exists when language is not there;
when there is no language, the tree exists.
It is not dependent on language.

This chief monk must have brooded over and over again.

He must have chosen, beforehand, an alternative.
He was dead.
That very moment he failed.

Inside, if you decide what you are going to do
and you act out of that decision,
you will miss reality.
Reality is an ever-flowing movement.
Nobody knows what is going to happen.
Nobody can predict it.
It is unpredictable.

There is a Zen story:
Two monasteries existed side by side,
and both the masters had small boys to run errands.
Both the boys used to go to the market
to fetch things for the masters —
sometimes vegetables, sometimes other things.

These monasteries
were antagonistic towards each other,
but boys will be boys.
They would forget the doctrines
and meet on the way and talk, enjoy.
It was really prohibited to talk —
the other monastery was the enemy.

One day,
the boy from the first monastery came and said:
I am puzzled.
As I was going to the market,
I saw the boy from the other monastery and asked him:
Where are you going?
He replied:
Wherever the wind blows.
I was at a loss as to what to say.
He puzzled me.

The master said:
This is not good.
Nobody from our monastery
has ever been defeated by the other monastery,

not even a servant,
so you must fix that boy.
Tomorrow, ask again where he is going.
He will say: Wherever the wind blows.
So you say: If there is no wind, then?

The boy couldn't sleep the whole night.
He tried and tried
to conceive of what would happen the next day.
He rehearsed many times.
He would ask and the other boy would respond,
and then he would give his answer.

The next day he waited on the road.
The other boy came and he asked:
Where are you going?
The boy said:
Wherever my feet lead me.

He was at a loss as to what to do.
His answer was fixed.
Reality is unpredictable.

He came back very sad and said to the master:
That boy is not trustworthy.
He changed,
and I was at a loss as to what to do.

So the master said:
Next day when he answers:
Wherever my feet lead,
you tell him:
If you are crippled and your legs are cut off, then?

Again he couldn't sleep.
He went early to wait on the road.
When the boy came he asked:
Where are you going?
And the boy said:
To fetch vegetables from the market.

He became very disturbed
and said to the master:

This boy is impossible.
He goes on changing.

Life is that boy.
Reality is not a fixed phenomenon.
You have to be present, spontaneously in it —
only then will the response be real.
If your answer is fixed beforehand,
you are already dead,
you have already missed.
Then tomorrow will come but you will not be there.
You will be fixed in the yesterday,
that which has passed.

All the minds which are too verbal
are fixed like this.
Go to a pundit, a scholar, and ask:
What is God?
Before you have asked he will start answering.
Your question is not answered
because even before you had the question,
this man had the answer.
The answer is dead.
It is there already;
it has just to be brought from the memory.

This is the difference
between a man of wisdom and a man of knowledge.
A man of knowledge has ready-made answers —
you ask, and the answer is already there.
You are irrelevant; your question is irrelevant.
Before the question, the answer exists.
Your question simply triggers the memory.

If you go to a man of wisdom,
he has no answers for you.
He has nothing ready-made.
He is open; he is silent.
He'll respond,
but first your question will resound in his being,
not in his memory.

Through his being, the response comes.
Nobody can predict that response.
If you go the next day and ask the same question,
the response will not be the same.

Once it happened
that a man tried to judge the Buddha.
Every year he would go and ask the same question.
He thought:
If he really knows,
then the answer will be always the same.
How can you change the answer?
If I come and ask:
Is there God?
If he knows, he will say yes or he will say no,
and next year, I will come again and ask.

So for many years the man came,
and he became more and more puzzled.
Sometimes Buddha would say yes,
sometimes no,
sometimes he would remain silent,
and sometimes he would simply smile
and not answer anything.

The man became puzzled and said:
What is this?
If you know, then you must be certain,
your answer fixed.
But you go on changing.
Once you said yes,
then you said no.
Have you forgotten
that I asked this question before?
Once you even remained silent,
and now you are smiling.
That is why I have been coming
with the gap of a year—
just to see if you know or not.

Buddha said:

When you came for the first time
and asked:
Is there God,
I answered.
But my answer was not to the question,
it was to you.
You have changed.
Now the same answer cannot be given.
Not only have you changed,
I also have changed.
The Ganges has flowed much;
the same answer cannot be given.
I am not a scripture to be opened
and the same answer found there.

A Buddha is a living river.
And a river is ever-flowing.
In the morning it is different –
it reflects the gold of the rising sun.
The mood is different.
In the evening it is different.
And when the night comes
and the stars are reflected in it,
it is different.
In the summer it shrinks;
it floods during the rains.

A river is not a painting.
It is a live force.
A painting remains the same,
whether it is raining or it is summer.
A painted river will not be flooded in the rains.
It is dead,
otherwise there would be change.

There is only one thing
that goes on continuously,
and that is revolution.
Everything else is impermanent
except revolution.
It goes on and on.

This chief disciple must have decided;
the conclusion was already there.
He was waiting only for the master to ask.

Then the master put a jug before them,
a pot filled with water, and said:
Say something but don't use the name.
Say something but don't use the mind.
Say something but don't use language.

It sounds absurd when you say:
Say something and don't use language.
You are creating an impossible situation.
How can something be said without using language?
But if you cannot say something
about an ordinary jug filled with water,
without using language,
how will you be able to say anything about God,
who is filled with the whole universe?
If you cannot indicate this jug without language,
how will you be able to indicate the great jug,
the universe, God, the truth?

If you cannot indicate this,
how will you be made chief of a monastery?
People will be coming to you,
not to know words, but to know reality.
People won't be coming to you
to be trained in philosophy.
That can be done by the universities.
They teach words.

So what is the purpose of a monastery?
A monastery has to teach reality, not words;
religion, not philosophy; existence, not theories.
And if you can't say anything about an ordinary pot,
what will you do when someone asks:
What is God?
What will you do when someone asks:
Who am I?

The chief disciple answered,

and whenever the mind faces such a situation,
the only way is to define negatively.
If someone says
to say something about God – without naming,
what will you do?
You can only state it negatively.
You can say:
God is not this world; God is not matter.

Look at the dictionaries.
Go to the Encyclopaedia Britannica
and see how it defines things.
You will be surprised.
If you turn to the page where mind is defined,
you will find it defined as
that which is not matter.
Then turn to the page where matter is defined.
You will find it defined as
that which is not mind.

What type of definition is this?
When you ask about mind, they say no-matter;
when you ask about matter, they say no-mind.
Nothing is defined;
it is a vicious circle.
If I ask about A, you say it is not B;
if I ask about B, you say it is not A.
You define one thing by another indefinable thing.
How can this be done?

This is a tricky thing.
Dictionaries are the trickiest things in the world.
They don't say anything
and they appear to be saying so much.
Everything is defined
and everything is indefinable.
Nothing can be defined.

So the chief disciple said something negatively.
When the mind is at a loss as to what to do,
it starts saying things negatively.

So maybe atheism is just an escape.
God is there, but how to define it?
When the mind feels at a loss,
the easiest escape
is to say there is no God.
Then the problem is finished.

Somebody said:
It is not a pond
because it can be carried by hand.

How can you define a water-filled jug
by just saying it is not a pond?
What is a pond?
Say something without naming it.

Then the cook of the monastery came.
He must have been a more real man
than these pundits –
a cook, who has never been much interested
in the scriptures,
a cook, who has been working with reality,
encountering it, not thinking about it.
This cook kicked the pot and went out.

What did he say?
He said something in a more realistic way.
Kicking is not thinking.
It is action.

He kicked the pot and said to the master:
This is nonsense.
You are talking absurdities.
You say to us to say something without words.
Something can be done without words,
but nothing can be said.

He caught the point.
Something can be done without words,
but nothing can be said.
So he did something.
He kicked the pot.

The master said:
This cook has been chosen.
He goes to the new monastery
and there becomes the master.
He knows how to act without the mind;
he knows how to answer without using the mind.
He has said that the problem is absurd.

Remember one thing.
If the problem is absurd,
you cannot answer it in a rational way.
If you try you will be foolish;
it shows foolishness.
If the problem is absurd,
you cannot answer in a rational way.
For an absurd question
there can be no rational answer.
If you try, you simply prove that you are foolish.

That chief disciple must have been a foolish man;
the other scholar,
who said: This is not a pond,
must have been a foolish man.
Scholars are foolish,
otherwise they wouldn't be scholars.
They are wasting their lives in words, scriptures.
Nobody can waste his life in words
unless he is absolutely stupid.

This cook was wiser.
He kicked.
He was not kicking the pot,
he was kicking the whole problem;
he was not kicking the pot,
he was kicking the whole situation.
He saw that it was absurd.
He was not saying anything, not using a word.

Just imagine that cook kicking the pot
with his whole being.
He was involved in it completely,

mind, body, soul.
The kick was alive, spontaneous.
He didn't know it was going to be there.
He may not even have thought that he was answering,
he was just seeing what was going on.
Suddenly, the kick happened.

In this state of being,
when the cook was just action,
there was no mind in him, just an emptiness.
Out of that emptiness, out of that no-mind,
the action arose.

When the action comes from the actor,
it is dead;
when the action comes from the ego,
it is premeditated.
When the action comes without the ego,
without the mind, without you being there,
when it bubbles up out of your nothingness,
it is from the Divine.
It is total.

The cook didn't kick;
rather, it was as if the whole existence kicked.
He kicked all scholarship, all scriptures,
the whole intellect and its vicious circles,
and he walked out.
He didn't wait.
If he had waited to see what the master said,
he would have missed,
because that would have meant
that the mind was looking for the conclusion,
for the result.

The mind is always result-oriented:
What is going to happen?
If I do this, then what will happen?
If the cause is there, what will be the effect?
The mind is always for the result;
the mind is result-oriented.

This cook simply walked out.
He didn't wait for what was going to happen.
He didn't think that he would be chosen.
How can you think, that just by kicking a pot,
you will be chosen the master of a monastery?
No, he didn't bother.

This is what Krishna says to Arjuna in the Gita:
Do!
Act!
But don't ask for the result.
Kick and walk out.

Arjuna said:
If I fight, if I go through with this war,
what will happen?
What will be the result?
Will it be good or bad?
Will I gain or lose?
Will killing so many people be worth the effort?

Krishna says:
Don't think of the result.
Leave the result to me.
You simply act.

The mind cannot do that.
Before the mind acts, it asks for the result.
It acts because of the result.
If there will be a result, only then will it act.

People come to me and ask:
If we meditate, what will happen?
What will be the result?

Remember, meditation can never be result-oriented.
You simply meditate, that's all.
Everything happens, but it will not be a result.
If you are seeking the result,
nothing will happen.
Meditation will be useless.

When you seek a result, it is the mind;
when you don't seek a result, it is meditation.
Kick the pot and walk out;
meditate and walk out.
Don't ask for the result.
Don't say:
What will happen?
If you think about what will happen,
you cannot meditate.

The mind goes on thinking about the result.
It cannot be here and now;
it is always in the future.
You are meditating and thinking:
When will the happiness come?
It has not come yet.

If you forget the result completely,
if there is not even a flicker in the mind
for the result,
not a single vibration moving into the future –
when you have become a silent pool, here and now –
everything happens.

In meditation, cause and effect are not two –
cause is the effect;
the act and the result are not two –
the act is the result.
They are not divided.
In meditation, the seed and the tree are not two –
the seed is the tree.

For the mind, everything is divided.
The seed and the tree are two;
the act and the result are two.
The result is always in the future and the act is here.
You act because of the future.

For the mind,
the present is always sacrificed for the future,
and the future does not exist.
There is always the present, the eternal now,

and you are sacrificing this now
for something which is nowhere
and cannot be anywhere.

In meditation, the whole process is reversed.
The future is sacrificed for the present;
that which is not
is sacrificed for that which is.
There is no result, no conclusion.
Kick the pot and walk out.

That was the beauty of it.
The cook simply walked out, saying:
The whole thing is absurd –
your question and these people's answers.
This is a nonsense game.
I don't belong here.

He must have gone to his kitchen and started working –
that is how a meditative mind will act –
and the master said:
This man is chosen.
He becomes the chief of the new monastery.
He knows how to be total, to act spontaneously;
he knows how to act without motivation;
he knows how to act without the mind.
This man can lead others into meditation;
this man can become a guide.
This man has achieved.

The story is beautiful and very rare.
Penetrate into it.
You can penetrate it,
but only if you start acting the way the cook acted.

There is a pitfall –
you can premeditate it.
If I put a pot before you and you kick,
you will miss.
You know the answer already.
You will think:
Okay now, this is the opportunity.

I'll kick the pot and walk out.

That won't do.
You cannot deceive,
because whenever your mind is there,
your total being gives a different vibration.
You cannot deceive a master.

And remember,
this incident has been repeated many times.
Zen masters are really unique.
They go on repeating the same problem
again and again,
and those who read the scriptures
behave in the old way.
They think they already know the answer –
kick the pot, walk out, and become the chief.

But you cannot deceive a Zen master.
He is not concerned with what you are doing,
he is concerned with what you are
in that moment of doing.
That is a totally different thing.

You have a perfume, a different perfume,
when you act out of emptiness.
And when I say a different perfume,
I mean it literally,
I'm not using a metaphor.
When you act out of emptiness,
there is a freshness all around you,
as if, suddenly,
a morning has come in the middle of the day.

If you kick the pot, ego will be there.
The ego will do the kicking
and you will be aggressive.
When this cook kicked the pot, it was not aggressive.
It was simply a statement of fact.
There was no violence.

I have heard that one man, a poor beggar –

and I say 'poor beggar'
because there are wealthy beggars also –
came to ask for food.
The lady of the house felt much compassion for him,
and said:
I'll give you food,
and if you want some work,
there is wood to chop.
I'll pay you for it.

So the man worked, chopped the wood,
and in the evening when he was about to go,
the lady of the house said:
There is a hole in your robe.
Give it to me,
and within minutes I will repair it.

The man said:
No, a hole in my robe makes all the difference.
When you have a repaired dress,
it is premeditated poverty;
when you have a hole in your robe,
it may have happened just now, through some accident.
But when you have patched it, it looks ancient –
it has not happened accidentally, just now;
it's happened long before
and now it's been patched and repaired.
It becomes premeditated poverty.
Let my poverty be spontaneous.

Your whole mind is premeditated poverty.
You have all the answers and not a single response.
You have already decided what to do,
and in that decision
you have murdered yourself, committed suicide.
The mind is suicide.

Start acting spontaneously.
It will be difficult in the beginning.
You will feel much discomfort.
With a premeditated answer

there is less discomfort,
you are more certain.

Why are we not spontaneous?
It is because of fear,
the fear that the answer may be wrong.
It's better to decide beforehand,
then you can be certain.
But certainty always belongs to death.

Remember, life is always uncertain.
Everything dead is certain;
life is always uncertain.
Everything dead is solid, fixed –
its nature cannot be changed;
everything alive is moving, changing –
a flow, a liquid thing, flexible,
able to move in any direction.

The more you become certain,
the more you will miss life.
And those who know, know life is God.
If you miss life, you miss God.

Act spontaneously.
If there is discomfort in the beginning,
allow it to be there.
Don't hide it and don't suppress it.
And don't imitate.
Be childlike but don't be childish.
If you are childlike,
you will become a great saint;
if you are childish,
you will become a great, knowledgeable person.

A man returned to his house one day.
He saw his children and the neighbour's children
sitting on the steps,
so he asked:
What are you doing?
They said:
We are playing church.

He was puzzled.
They were just sitting there doing nothing.
He inquired:
What type of church is this?
They said:
We have sung, preached, prayed.
Everything has been done.
Now we are sitting on the steps, smoking.

You can imitate.
Knowledgeability is imitation.
A Buddha says something;
you interpret it,
you play church,
you cram it in your mind, you repeat it.
This is childish.

Be childlike, not childish.
Childlikeness is spontaneity.
A child is fresh,
with no answers, no accumulated experience.
He has, really, no memory.
He acts.
Whatever comes through his being, he acts.
He is not motivated, not thinking about results,
about the future.
He is innocent.

This cook was really innocent.
Innocence is meditation.

Start being meditative in your acts,
just with small things.
While eating, be spontaneous.
While talking, be spontaneous.
While walking, be spontaneous.

Allow life a response, not an answer.
If somebody asks you something,
just watch whether you are repeating
something you always do, just a habit,
or whether the answer is a response.

Just watch whether the mind
is repeating an old habit,
whether the answer is coming from memory,
or whether it is coming from you.

Everybody bores everybody else
because everything is dead, borrowed, stale,
and stinks of death.
It is not fresh.

Look at children playing and you feel a freshness.
For a moment, you may even forget
that you have become old.
Listen to the birds,
look at the trees or flowers
and for a moment, forget.
Here, there is no mind.

Flowers are flowering just like the cook kicked,
they are kicking;
birds are singing,
they are kicking;
life itself is kicking –
but there are no theories.

In the beginning, it will be uncomfortable.
Be patient.
Go through that discomfort.
Soon you will have an upsurge of energy.

It is dangerous.
That's why people avoid it.
To be spontaneous is dangerous,
because when anger comes, it comes.
The mind says:
Think.
Don't be angry.
It may be costly.
So you always think
and throw your anger on those weaker than you,
not on those who are stronger than you.

Love can happen,
but love is not allowed.
You can have a loving attitude
only towards your wife,
but life does not know
who is your wife and who is not.
Life is absolutely amoral.
It knows no morality.
You can fall in love with somebody else's wife,
because life knows no relations,
no fixed institutions.

All institutions are man-made.
That is the danger.
So the mind says:
Think before.
She is not your wife.
Don't look in such a loving way.
Don't smile.
Whether you feel it or not is not the point.
This is duty.

That is how we have killed everybody.
Everybody lives in an institution,
not in life.

Because of these dangers
the mind thinks of what to say beforehand.
You are late,
and when you come home you are thinking:
What will my wife say?
How will I answer?
The wife is waiting,
and she knows whatever you will say is wrong.
She has heard your excuses before,
the same old excuses.

I have heard
that one man phoned his wife one day
and said:
One of my friends has come
and I'm bringing him home for dinner.

The wife screamed and said:
You fool, you know very well
the cook has left,
the baby is cutting his teeth,
and I have had a fever for three days.
The man replied, very calmly:
I know it well.
That is why I want to bring him home.
The fool is thinking of getting married.

The whole of life has become an institution,
a madhouse in which duties are to be fulfilled,
not love;
in which you have to behave,
not be spontaneous;
in which a pattern has to be followed,
not the overflow of life and energy.
That's why the mind thinks and decides everything,
because there is danger.

I call a man a *sannyasi*
who breaks out of these institutions
and lives spontaneously.
To be a *sannyasi*
is the most courageous act possible.
To be a *sannyasi* means to live without the mind,
and the moment you live without mind,
you live without society.

The mind has created society,
and society has created the mind.
They are interdependent.
To be a *sannyasi*
means to renounce all that is false
but not to renounce the world,
to renounce all that is inauthentic,
to renounce all the answers,
to be responsive, spontaneously responsive,
and not to think about the reasons,
but to be real.

This is difficult.
There is much investment in falsity,
in the masks, in the faces,
in the games you go on playing.

To be initiated as a *sannyasi*
means now you will try to be authentic.
Whatsoever the consequences,
you will accept them and live in the present.
you will sacrifice the future for the present;
you will never sacrifice the present for the future.
This moment will be the totality of your being.
You will never move beforehand.

This is what *sannyas* is —
to kick the pot and walk out,
and not to wait for the results.
Results will take care of themselves.
They will follow you.

This story doesn't say it,
but I know,
the master must have run out
to catch hold of the cook
and said:
Wait, you have been chosen.
You go to the new monastery
to guide people in life and meditation.

Anything more?

Bhagwan,

Every day when I sit here,
I try sitting without a question in my mind,
staying in the moment with what I am hearing,
not rehearsing, and trying not to rehearse.

Then you say:
Anything more?

And it's as if a shield comes down
and I can't reach you.
I am talking to myself,
and the mind is always making things safe for me.

It happens because we are always afraid,
afraid something may go wrong.
Don't be afraid before me.
Nothing can go wrong.
If something goes wrong spontaneously,
then that is the right thing.
Spontaneity is right.

The mind manipulates because of fear.
You may ask something,
and others may start laughing.
They may think you are foolish.
So something has to be asked
which nobody can laugh about.
Then everyone thinks
you have asked a serious question,
a meaningful question.
That's why the mind is afraid and fear manipulates.

Near me, there is no need for any fear.
You can ask absurdities, foolish questions,
because to me, the mind is absurd.
It cannot ask anything else,
so there is no problem.
For the mind,
it can only appear as if something is serious,
because it cannot ask anything which is not foolish.
All questions are foolish.
The whole mind has to be dropped,
only then will you not be a fool.

The fear is why we rehearse.
The ego wants to feel important.
Near me, there is no need of fear.
I'm not asking you to ask anything wise.
Nothing wise can be asked;
nobody has ever asked a wise question.
That is impossible.
When you become wise, questions drop;
when you are wise, there are no questions.

You can imitate wisdom also by not asking.
That will not help.
Those who are not asking
should not think that they are wise
and that the questioner is a fool.
He is just your representative,
so he is bound to feel more foolish than you.
With so much foolishness represented in him,
all together,
he is bound to feel afraid.
It is natural.

By and by, drop the manipulations,
because when you drop manipulations
you become natural near me,
and this will give you the first glimpse.
To be natural will give you the first glimpse,
and then you can gather courage to be natural in life.
For if you cannot be spontaneous near me,
how will it be possible to be spontaneous in life?

If you go to other so-called masters,
they will create fear.
You cannot laugh before them.
That would be taken as an offence.
You have to have a serious, sad face.
You have to appear very serious.

Look at the churches and mosques,
at the so-called masters with long faces.
Christians say Jesus never laughed.

How can a Jesus laugh?
If he laughs he becomes ordinary,
he becomes profane.
I say to you such seriousness is a shield.
It will protect all that is nonsensical in you.
Allow it to come up.
Don't force it within;
don't repress it in any way.

Near me, be natural.
And in this being natural,
you will learn that which cannot be learned
in any other way.
Just being near me,
being spontaneous,
you will drop the mind and be meditative.

I answer you,
not because I am concerned with your questions.
They are irrelevant.
I'm not satisfying your questions in any way.
They cannot be satisfied.
Then what am I doing?
I am just being here with you.
The answer is just an excuse,
the question is just an excuse
to be near and closer.

Why can't we sit silently?
I can, but it will be difficult for you.
We can sit silently –
I, not talking, you, not asking –
but inside you will go on talking, chattering.
Tremendous chattering will go on,
more than ordinarily,
because when you say to the mind:
Sit silently,
the mind rebels.
It goes mad.
It creates more words, more questions,
a monologue.

You cannot sit silently.
That's why I ask you to ask;
that's why I answer you.
If I am talking, your mind will not talk.
And my talking is not destructive;
your talking is destructive.
When I talk, you get absorbed in it.
You may even have a few glimpses of silence.

This is how life is paradoxical –
you have glimpses of silence while I am talking.
You get so absorbed, engaged, occupied,
your mind gets so tense listening, so alert,
that nothing is missed.
In that alertness the inner talk stops.
You become silent.

That gap is my answer.
My answers are not the real thing,
so they go on changing.

People feel that I am inconsistent.
I go on saying things –
today something, tomorrow something else.
They are irrelevant.
I am not concerned with consistency.
My answering is like music
being played on a guitar.

You never ask inconsistently.
You play the same thing again and again.
The musician goes on changing,
and if you get absorbed into the music
you will have some gaps of silence.
In those gaps, you will become aware
for the first time,
and that awareness, by and by,
will become crystallized.

So don't bother about what you are asking.
Whatever you ask is okay.
Don't rehearse it; let it be more spontaneous.

It will be difficult for you.
Spontaneity is difficult.

I have heard about one preacher.
He was going into the pulpit for the first time,
so for the whole night he rehearsed what to say.
He had chosen a very beautiful passage about Jesus,
and this was to be a great crisis in his life –
whether he would succeed or fail.
The first success or failure means much,
so the whole night, standing in his room,
he rehearsed and rehearsed,
lecturing to the audience.
But by the morning he was so tired, so sleepy,
that when he stood at the pulpit,
his mind went blank.

He had chosen a beautiful passage:
Behold I come!
He said:
Behold I come!
and his mind went blank.
He couldn't find anything,
so he thought:
If I repeat it again, maybe the flow will come.

Again he leaned forward and said:
Behold I come!
but nothing came.

To appear nonchalant, he leaned forward more,
as if it was not by accident that he was repeating,
and again he said:
Behold I come!

Under his pressure the pulpit collapsed,
and he fell into the lap of an old woman.
He said, feeling very embarrassed:
Sorry, I never meant it to happen.
The woman said:
No need to say anything.
You warned me three times

when you said:
Behold I come!
It's not your fault.

There is no need to rehearse, to premeditate.
Let things happen.
But the way things go in the world,
questions and answers have to be thought over.
Both are dead.
And when the dead things meet,
there is no spark.

I know it is difficult for you,
but try.
By and by, it will happen.
And once it happens,
you will have a freedom from the mind.
You will become weightless
and have wings into the sky.

Anything more?

Bhagwan,

My mind is already working on the paradox I find between yesterday's talk and today's.

Today you have been talking
about spontaneity of response to new situations,
seeing them as fresh.
Yesterday, one of the messages
from the story about Joshu
was that situations are all the same,
people the same.
Hence Joshu offered three people a cup of tea.

To me, this is a paradox.

Yesterday is no more.
Joshu has died.
Only today is –
and even that has passed.
Only this moment is.

The mind looks at things and finds paradoxes,
because the mind thinks of the past, the present
and the future.
Only the present is.
The mind finds paradoxes
because the mind is always moving
from the past to the present
and then to the future.

Once you were a tiny cell in the womb of your mother,
so tiny that you could not be seen by naked eyes.
Now, you are totally different.
You are young,
but sooner or later, you will be old, crippled.
Now you are alive,
but the day will come when you are dead.

When the mind thinks all these things together,
a child and an old man become a paradox.
How can a child be old, a young man old?
For the mind,
birth and death become a paradox
because they can both be thought;
for existence,
when there is birth, there is no death,
when there is death, there is no birth.
For existence, there is nothing paradoxical,
but the mind can look at the past,
the present and the future,
and these are paradoxes.

Yesterday, you heard me.
Be finished with it.
There is no more yesterday,
but the mind carries it.

If you really heard me yesterday,
you will not carry it,
for if you carry it,
how can you hear me today?
The smoke of yesterday will be a disturbance.
There will be that smoke
and you will only hear me through yesterday
and you will miss.

Yesterday should be dropped,
so you can be here and now.
There is no paradox,
but if you compare yesterday and today,
then it comes.
If you compare birth and death,
the paradox comes.
Today and yesterday cannot exist together.
They can exist together only in the memory.
Existence is non-paradoxical; the mind is paradoxical.

Why think about yesterday?
If you are thinking about it,
how can you be here?
That will be difficult.
Because of yesterday
you will not be able to hear me today.

Did you hear me yesterday?
For there have been other yesterdays.
And will you be able to hear me tomorrow?
For this today will have become yesterday.
The film of all the yesterdays is there.
Through that film
it is difficult to penetrate into the present.

So all that I can say is be here,
Joshu is dead.
The man who was talking here yesterday is no more.
He is dead.
There is no question of consistency or inconsistency.

Tomorrow, I will not be here,

you will not be here.
It will be absolutely fresh.
And when two freshnesses meet, there is a spark,
a spark that dances,
and a dance that is always consistent.

A carried past creates problems.
The problem is not what I said yesterday
or what I am saying today,
the problem is that you carry yesterdays
and miss today.
And whatever you think you have heard,
I've not said.
You may think you have heard it,
but through so many yesterdays
you will interpret whatever I say.
You will think meanings into it
which are not there;
you will miss things that are there,
and it will become something of your own.
Then you will create many paradoxes
and the mind will become puzzled and confused.
Go on dropping the yesterdays.

I am not a philosopher or a systematizer.
I am absolutely anarchistic,
as anarchistic as life itself.
I don't believe in systems.

If you go to a Hegel or a Kant and say
that this is contradictory,
immediately they will say no.
They will immediately show
that it is not contradictory.
If you can prove that it is contradictory,
they will drop one part
so their system becomes consistent.

One gambler was saying to another gambler:
Yesterday I met this guy,
a wonderful man,

a great mathematician and economist.
He has discovered a system
through which a family can live
without money.

The other gambler became interested,
wanting to know immediately what the system was.
He asked:
Does it work?
The friend replied:
The system is wonderful, but there is one loophole –
it doesn't work.
That's the only loophole,
otherwise the system is wonderful.

All systems are wonderful.
Those of Hegel, Kant, Marx, are all wonderful.
The only loophole is this –
they are dead.

I have no system.
Systems can only be dead,
they cannot be alive.
I am a non-systematic, anarchistic flow –
not even a person –
just a process.
I don't know what I said to you yesterday.
The person who said it is not here to answer.
He is gone; I am here.
And I am answerable only for this moment,
so don't wait for tomorrow,
for I will not be there.
And who is going to make consistency,
who is going to find a thread
that is not contradictory?
There is nobody.
And I would like you to be the same.

Just this moment exists, absolutely consistent,
for there can be no comparison.
There is no past, no future.

Only this moment is.
How can you compare?

If you live in this moment,
there will come a consistency
which is not of a system,
which is of life,
which is of the energy itself.
That will be an inner consistency
of your very being,
not of the mind.

I am interested in the being,
not in the mind,
so don't take my answers very seriously.
They are just play, play with words.
Enjoy them and forget them;
enjoy me,
but don't try to systematize me.
The whole effort is useless,
and in that effort,
you miss much that is beautiful.
You miss much that can become a deep ecstasy in you.

Look at me,
and don't be bothered with what I say.
Be with me,
and don't be bothered about theories and words.
Act with me,
listen to me,
and don't try to think about it.
And this listening should be an act,
not a mental effort.
I am not trying to convince you.
I am not trying to give you a belief.
I am not trying to create any religion or sect.
No doctrine is implied.

When talking to you, I am there.
Talking is just an excuse.
I may be using one sect today, another tomorrow.

If you look at my sect, you will say:
You are inconsistent.
Yesterday you had this sect, and today, this.

I say look at me.
Words are just dressings.
I am consistent; my being is consistent.
It cannot be otherwise.
How can your being be inconsistent?
There is no gap in it.
It is a continuum.
But the mind starts thinking, comparing,
and then problems arise.

Once it happened
that a disciple came to a Zen master and asked:
Why are a few people so intelligent
and a few so stupid?
Why are a few people so beautiful
and a few so ugly?
Why this inconsistency?
If God is everywhere,
if he is the creator,
then why does he create one ugly
and another beautiful?

And don't talk to me about *karmas.*
I have heard all those nonsensical answers –
that because of *karmas,* past lives,
one is beautiful, another is ugly.
I am not concerned with past lives.
In the beginning, when there was no yesterday,
how did the difference come?
Why was one created beautiful and another ugly?
And if everyone was created equal,
equally beautiful and intelligent,
how can they act differently,
how can they have different *karmas?*

The master said:
Wait!

This is such a secret thing
that I will tell you when everybody has left.
So the man sat, eager,
but people kept coming and going
and there was no chance.
But by the evening everybody had left,
so the man said:
Now?
And the master said:
Come out with me.

The moon was coming up,
and the master took him in the garden and said:
Look, that tree there is small;
this tree here is so tall.
I have been living with these trees for many years,
and they have never raised the question
of why that tree is small and this tree is big.

When there was mind in me,
I used to ask the same question
sitting under these trees.
Then my mind dropped,
and the question dropped.
Now I know.
This tree is small and that tree is big.
There is no problem.
So look!
There is no problem.

The mind compares.
How can you compare when the mind is not?
How can you say
this tree is small and that tree big?
When the mind drops, comparison drops,
and when there is no comparison,
the beauty of existence erupts.
It becomes a volcanic eruption; it explodes.
Then you see the small is big and the big is small.
Then all contradictions are lost
and the inner consistency is seen.

Drop the mind and listen to me.
Then you will not ask:
Why yesterday?
Why this today and that yesterday?
Then there is no yesterday and no today;
then I am here and you are here.
There is a meeting.
And this here and now, when the mind is not there,
becomes a communion.

I am not interested
in communicating something to you,
I am interested in communion.
Communication means my mind talking to your mind.
Communion means
I am not a mind, you are not a mind –
just your heart melting into my heart.
No words.

That's what the story is:
Say something about this pot without using words.
The cook kicked and walked out.
Whatsoever I say,
kick and go in.

Sixth Talk

15th June 1974

Bhagwan,

Bankei was preaching quietly
to his followers one day
when his talking was interrupted
by a priest from another sect.
This sect believed in the power of miracles,
and thought that salvation came
from repeating holy words.

Bankei stopped talking,
and asked the priest what he wanted to say.

The priest boasted
that the founder of his religion
could stand on one bank of the river
with a brush in his hand
and write a holy name on a piece of paper
held by an assistant
on the opposite bank of the river.

The priest asked:
What miracles can you do?

Bankei replied:
Only one.
When I am hungry I eat,
and when I am thirsty I drink.

The only miracle,
the impossible miracle,
is to be just ordinary.

The longing of the mind is to be extraordinary.
The ego thirsts and hungers
for the recognition that you are somebody.
Somebody achieves that dream through wealth,
somebody else achieves that dream
through power, politics,
somebody else can achieve that dream
through miracles, jugglery,
but the dream remains the same:
I cannot tolerate being nobody.

And this is a miracle –
when you accept your nobodiness,
when you are just as ordinary as anybody else,
when you don't ask for any recognition,
when you can exist as if you are not existing.
To be absent is the miracle.

This story is beautiful,
one of the most beautiful Zen anecdotes,
and Bankei is one of the superb masters.
But Bankei was really an ordinary man.

Once it happened that Bankei

was working in his garden.
Somebody came,
a seeker, a man in search of a master,
and he asked Bankei:
Gardener, where is the master?

Bankei laughed and said:
Wait.
Come from that door,
inside you will find the master.

So the man went round and came inside.
He saw Bankei sitting on a throne,
the same man who was the gardener outside.
The seeker said:
Are you kidding?
Get down from this throne.
This is sacrilegious.
You don't pay any respect to the master.

Bankei got down, sat on the ground, and said:
Now then, it is difficult.
Now you will not find the master here,
because I am the master.

It was difficult for that man to see
that a great master could work in the garden,
could be just ordinary.
He left.
He couldn't believe that this man was the master.
He missed.

We are all in search of the extraordinary.
But why are you in search of the extraordinary?
It is because you also long to be extraordinary.
With an ordinary master,
how can you become extraordinary, exceptional?

Bankei was talking, lecturing,
and one man stood and asked about miracles.
He belonged to some other sect,
a sect which worked through *mantras,* holy names.

Remember that a *mantra* is a secret technique
to achieve more power.
A *mantra* is not spiritual, it is political,
but the politics are of the inner space,
not of the outer.

The mind can become powerful if you narrow it down.
Narrowing is the method.
The more narrow the mind,
the more powerful it becomes.
It it just like the sun's rays
falling to the ground.
If you focus those waves, those rays,
through a lens,
fire can be created.
Those rays were falling all spread out,
but now they have been narrowed down through the lens.
They have become one-pointed, concentrated.
Now fire is possible.

The mind is energy,
in fact, the same energy
that comes through the sun, the same subtle rays.
Ask the physicists.
They say the mind has a voltage of electricity,
that it is electrical.

If you can focus the mind through a lens,
the *mantra* is a lens,
and you go on repeating Ram, Ram, Ram,
or Om, Om, Om, or anything,
just one word—
if you go repeating and repeating and repeating it,
and the mind's whole energy
is centred in that one word—
it becomes a lens.
Now all the rays are passing through that lens.
Narrowed to one point, it becomes powerful.
You can do miracles.
Just by thinking, you can do miracles.

But remember, those miracles are not spiritual.

Power is never spiritual.
Powerlessness, helplessness, to be nothing, is spiritual.
Power is never spiritual.
This is the difference between magic and religion.
Magic is after power;
religion is after nothingness.

A *mantra* is a part of magic, not of religion at all,
but everything is a big mess, mixed up.
People who are doing miracles are magicians,
not spiritual in any way.
They are even anti-spiritual,
because they are spreading magic
in the name of religion,
which is very dangerous.

Through a *mantra* the mind is narrowed.
It is more narrowed, more powerful,
and then anything can be done.
There is only one thing you will miss –
you will miss yourself.
All miracles will be possible;
the ultimate miracle you will miss.
You will miss yourself,
because through narrowing down
you can achieve an object.
The more the mind is narrowed,
the more it becomes fixed to an object.
It becomes objective.
You are hidden behind and the object is outside.

So if you are a man of *mantras*
you can say to this tree: Die,
and the tree will die;
you can say to a man: Be healthy,
and the disease will disappear,
or: Be unhealthy,
and the disease will enter.
Many things you can do.
You can become somebody,
and people will recognize you as a man of power,

but never a man of God.

A man of God is born
when the mind is not narrowed at all,
when the mind is not flowing in one direction,
but is overflowing in all directions.
There is no lens, no *mantra,*
just the energy flowing in all dimensions,
everywhere.
That flowing energy,
that energy overflowing everywhere,
will make you alert about yourself,
because then there is no object.
Only you, only subjectivity exists,
and through you, you will become aware of God,
not through any power.

This man asked Bankei:
What type of miracles can you do?
My master, through *mantra,* through the holy name,
can do miracles.
He will stand on one bank of the river,
and disciples will stand on the other bank
with a paper in their hands, a half-mile distant,
and he will write from here
and the words will come on the paper
on the other bank.
This our master can do.
What can you do?

And Bankei said:
We know only one miracle here,
and that is
when I feel hungry I eat,
and when I feel sleepy I sleep.
Only this much.

Not much of a miracle.
Your mind will say: What type of a miracle is this?
It is nothing to be proud of.
But I say to you Bankei has said the real thing.

That's what a Buddha can do,
that's what a Mahavir is doing,
that's what a Jesus is to do.
Only then is he a Christ, otherwise not.

What he is saying is such a simple thing.
He says: When I feel hungry I eat.
Is it so difficult that he calls it a miracle?
I say it is difficult for you.
For the mind, it is the most difficult thing –
not to interfere.
When you feel hungry the mind says:
No, this is a religious day and I am on a fast.
When you don't feel hungry the mind says:
Eat, because this is the time every day that you eat.
And when the stomach is overfilled the mind says:
Go on eating, the food is delicious.
Your mind interferes.

What is Bankei saying?
He is saying:
My mind has stopped interfering.
When I feel hungry I eat,
when I don't feel hungry I don't eat.
Eating has become a spontaneous thing;
the mind is not a continuous interference.

When I feel sleepy I go to sleep.
No, you are not doing this.
You go to sleep as a ritual, not when you feel sleepy.
You get up as a ritual because it is *brahmamuhurta,*
and you are a Hindu,
and you must get up before sunrise.
Because you are a Hindu, you get up.

Who is this Hindu?
It is the mind.
You cannot be a Hindu; you cannot be a Mohammedan.
There is no sect for you but the mind.
The mind says:
You are a Hindu, you must get up.
So you get up.

When the mind says:
Now it is time to go to sleep,
you go to sleep.
You follow the mind, not nature.

Bankei is saying:
I flow with nature;
whatsoever my whole being feels, I do it.
There is no fragmentary mind manipulating it.
Manipulation is the problem.
You go on manipulating,
and this disturbance, interference,
this manipulation from the mind is the problem.

Even in dreams you go on manipulating.
Ask the psychologists.
They say while awake, you continue manipulating.
The mind doesn't allow you to see what is there,
it projects;
the mind doesn't allow you to hear
what is being said to you,
it interprets.

Even in dreams you are false,
because the mind goes on playing tricks on you.
Freud discovered that our dreams are also false.
You want to kill your father,
so in the dream you don't kill your father,
you kill somebody who looks like your father.
You want to poison your wife,
but you don't poison your wife even in a dream,
you poison some woman
who somehow resembles your wife.
The mind is interfering continuously.

I have heard that one man was saying to another,
to his friend:
Did I dream last night!
What a dream!
I went to Coney Island.
What delicious ice cream,

such a tasteful dinner.
I have never eaten such a thing in my whole life.

The other man said:
You are kidding.
You call that a wonderful dream?
Last night I dreamt
that on one side was Elizabeth Taylor,
on the other side was Marilyn Monroe,
both in the nude.

The other became excited and said:
Then why didn't you call me?
The man said:
I called you, but your wife said
you had already left for Coney Island.

Even in dreams the mind goes on creating the world –
Coney Islands, Elizabeth Taylors –
and you become jealous even about another's dream:
Why didn't you call me?

Bankei is saying:
We know only one miracle.
We allow nature to have its own course;
we don't interfere.
Through interference comes the ego.
The more you interfere, the more you manipulate,
the more you feel you are somebody.

Look at the ascetics.
Their egos are so refined and subtle, so shiny.
Why?
It is because they have interfered the most.
You have not interfered so much.
They have killed their sex,
they have destroyed their love,
they have suppressed their anger,
they have completely destroyed their hunger
and the feeling of the body.
They have reason to be egoists; they are somebodies.
Look in their eyes.

There is nothing except ego.
Their bodies may be almost dead,
but their egos are at the supreme-most peak.
They have become Everests.

These monks and saints
will not be able to understand what Bankei means.
He says:
We know only one miracle –
to allow nature to have its own course.
We don't interfere.
If you don't interfere, you will disappear.
Fighting is the way to be there.

People come to me
and ask how to drop the ego.
I tell them: Who will drop it?
If you try to drop it you will be the ego.
And someday you will claim
that you have dropped the ego.
And who is this claimer, who is claiming it?
This is the ego.
And the most subtle ego
always tries to pretend egolessness.

I also know only one miracle,
to let nature have its course, to allow it.
Whatsoever is happening, don't interfere,
don't come in the way,
and suddenly, you will disappear.
You cannot be there without resistance, fight,
aggression, violence.
The ego exists through resistance.
This has to be understood very deeply –
the more you fight, the more you will be there.

Why do soldiers feel so happy fighting?
Fighting is not such a beautiful thing.
War is just ugly,
but why do soldiers feel so happy fighting?
If you have once been to a war
you will never be happy again in peace,

because the ego comes to such a peak fighting.
Why, in competition, do you feel so happy?
It is because competing, your ego arises;
fighting, you become stronger.

But fighting with another is never so ego-fulfilling
because you may be defeated –
the possibility is there –
but fighting with yourself you cannot be defeated.
You are always going to be the winner.
There is nobody else except you.
Fighting with another there is fear,
the fear of being a failure;
fighting with yourself there is no fear,
you are alone.
You are going to win today or tomorrow,
but finally you will win
because there is nobody else.

The ascetic is fighting with himself;
the soldier is fighting with others;
the businessman, fighting with others;
the monk, fighting with himself.
The monk and the ascetic are more cunning.
They have chosen a path where victory is inevitable.
You are not so calculating.
Your path is hazardous.
You may be a success, you may be a failure,
and your success can turn into a failure any moment
because there are so many fighters around you,
and you are such a small, tiny existence –
you can be destroyed.

But fighting with yourself, you are alone.
There is no competition.
So those who are very cunning escape from the world
and start fighting with themselves.
Those who are not so cunning, are more simple,
are in the world, and go on fighting with others.
But the basic essential thing remains the same –
fighting.

Bankei is saying:
I am not a fighter; I don't fight at all.
When I feel hungry I eat,
when I feel sleepy I go to sleep;
when I am alive I am alive,
and when I die I will die.
I don't come in the way.
And he says:
This is the only miracle we know.

But why call it a miracle?
Animals are doing it already,
trees are doing it already,
birds are doing it already.
The whole existence is doing it already.
Why call it a miracle?
Man cannot do it.

The whole existence is a miracle except man.
The Christian story seems to be very meaningful.
That man has been turned out of the Garden of Eden
seeems to be very relevant, most significant.
The whole existence is a continuous miracle,
it is a continuum;
miracles are happening every moment.
Existence is miraculous,
but man has been turned out.

Why has man been turned out?
The story says because he ate
the fruit of the tree of knowledge,
and God had forbidden it.
God said:
Don't eat the fruit of this tree,
the tree of knowledge.
All the trees are open to you except this one.

But the Devil persuaded.
Of course, he persuaded Eve first.
The Devil always enters through the woman.
Why?

It is because woman is the weakest point of man,
the weakest link from where the Devil can enter.
To enter man directly is difficult
because he will give a good fight.
It will be difficult.
But through woman the Devil can persuade man.

So the Devil said to woman, to Eve:
This is the only fruit worth eating,
and that's why God has prohibited it.
If you eat this fruit you will be like gods.
You will be a god yourself.

Eve couldn't resist; the temptation was too much.
She persuaded Adam.
Adam tried to say it was not good,
because God had prohibited it,
but when it is a problem of choosing
between your wife and God,
you will choose your wife.

Really, there is no real alternative,
because she will create such trouble,
in twenty-four hours, such trouble . . .
God cannot create so much trouble.

So, finally, Adam had to eat.
And the moment he ate the fruit,
be became conscious of the ego;
he became aware that 'I am'.
Immediately, he was thrown out of the Garden of Eden.

It is a beautiful story.
The story is really a key to all the secrets.

This knowledge has turned you out
of the miraculous world that you are in.
Before this, Adam was like a child —
naked, but not aware that he was naked;
naked, but not aware that there was some guilt in it.
He loved Eve, but the love was natural.
He was never aware that something wrong was going on,
or that there was some sin.

There was no sin.
Before knowledge, there is no sin.
A child cannot commit sin;
only an old man can be a sinner.
So all sinners are old.
A child cannot be a sinner.
How can it be a sinner?
A child is innocent
because a child is not aware of himself, that he is.

Adam was like a child; Eve was like a child.
They enjoyed, but there was no one who was enjoying.
They were part of this mystery, of the miracle.
When they felt hungry, they ate,
when they felt sleepy, they slept,
when they felt like loving, they loved.
But everything was a natural phenomenon,
the mind was not there as the manipulator.
They were part of this universe –
flowing like rivers,
flowering like trees,
singing like birds.
They were not separate.
Separation came with the knowledge that 'I am'.

The first thing Adam and Eve did
was to try to hide their nakedness.
The childhood was lost.
Whenever a child begins to feel that he is naked,
that is the point where Adam and Eve
were turned out of the Garden of Eden.

It has always been my feeling
that the answer to the Christian story
exists in Mahavir –
not in Jesus, but in Mahavir –
because if by eating the fruit of knowledge
Adam became aware and felt guilty that he was naked,
then the answer exists in Mahavir.
The moment Mahavir became silent,
the first thing he did was to become naked.

And I say Mahavir entered the Garden of Eden again.
He became a child again.
The Christian story is half;
the Jain story is the other half.
They make the whole.
The whole existence is a miracle;
you have fallen out of it.

Bankei said:
We know only one miracle.
We have entered in this great miracle again.
We are no more separate as egos;
we are not individuals.
Hunger is there, but there is no one who is hungry.
Sleep comes, but there is no one who is sleepy.
The ego is not there to resist or to decide.
We flow, we drift.
Nothing is wrong and nothing is good.
This is the beyondness, the transcendental attitude
where no evil exists and no good.
You have become innocent.

Your saints cannot be innocents,
because their goodness is forced too much.
Their goodness is already ugly.
Their goodness is managed, controlled, cultivated.
It is not innocent.

I have heard about one old woman.
She served a Buddhist monk for thirty years,
did everything for that monk.
She was just like a mother and a disciple both.
And the Buddhist monk
meditated and meditated and meditated.
The day the old woman was going to die,
she called a prostitute from the town and said:
Go to that monk's hut.
Enter the hut, go near him, caress the monk,
and just come and tell me how he reacts.
This night I am going to die,

and I want to be certain
whether I was serving a man who is innocent.
I am not certain.

The prostitute became afraid.
She said:
He is such a good man, so saintly.
We have never seen such a saintly man.

Even the prostitute felt guilty
to go there and touch this man,
but the old woman bribed her.
She went, she opened the door.
The monk was meditating.
It was midnight.
In that isolated part, nobody was near.
The monk opened his eyes, looked at the prostitute,
jumped to his feet and said:
Why are you coming in?
Get out!

His whole body trembled.
The prostitute went nearer.
The monk jumped out of the hut and cried:
This woman is trying to seduce me.

The prostitute returned.
She told the whole thing
and the old woman sent her servants
to burn the hut of the monk.
She said:
This man is of no use.
He has not become innocent yet.
He may be a saint, but his saintliness is ugly.
It is manipulated.
Why should he see a prostitute so suddenly?
A woman was entering, not a prostitute.
Why should he think that she had come to seduce him?
He should have been, at least, gentlemanly.
He should have said:
Come, sit, why have you come?
He should have at least shown a little compassion.

And even if she had embraced him,
why should he be afraid?
He has been telling me for thirty years:
I am not the body.
If he is not the body, then why should he be
so much afraid of the body?
No, his saintliness is cultivated.
It is a pose.
It is not from the inner, it is from the outer.
He has managed it all right,
but, inside, he is not innocent,
he is not childlike.

And unless saintliness becomes childlike,
it is not saintliness at all,
it is just a sinner hiding,
hiding through a facade.

Bankei has said:
We know only one miracle.
What is that miracle?
It is to be childlike.
Whenever a child feels hungry, he starts crying.
He is hungry.
Whenever he feels sleepy, he goes to sleep.

We try to manage even a child.
We destroy him.
In the West now there are books, guides for mothers.
And what type of world is there going to be
when a guide is needed even for a mother –
guidelines that say: After three hours give milk,
never before, but each three hours, give.
The child is crying, but that's not the point;
the child is hungry, but that is not the point,
because the guidebook says after three hours.
The mother is waiting,
and when the three hours are completed,
she will feed the child.

Even motherhood is not enough,

a guide is needed.
And a child's authentic cry is not to be trusted,
as if the child may be trying to deceive.
Why should the child deceive?
If he is hungry, he is crying.

But we are trying to destroy childhood.
Sooner or later, he will follow us.
He will also look at the clock,
and when the three hours are complete
he will give a cry that he is hungry.
This hunger will be false.
And when hunger goes false,
everything goes false.

We go on forcing children to go to sleep
when we think it is time.
But sleep is not to be manipulated by time.
Sleep is something inner.
When the child feels sleepy,
he will go to sleep.
But mother and father go on forcing the child
to go to sleep,
as if sleep can be ordered.

Children must think that you are foolish.
They think that something has gone wrong
in your mind.
How can a child force sleep?
He can pretend.
So when you are there he can close the eyes,
and when you have gone he can open the eyes,
because sleep cannot be forced.
Nobody, not even you, can force sleep.
If you don't feel sleepy, how can you go to sleep?

But this is how society destroys.
That's how the Devil persuades.
That's how we bring every child
out of the Garden of Eden.
Remember, not only were Adam and Eve
born in the Garden,

every child is born there,
because that is the birthplace.
And then society brings the child out.
So society is the Devil.
Society persuades:
Do this, do that, and bring the child out.
Make him an ego, make him a manipulator.

And the only miracle that is possible
is to enter this Garden of Eden again,
to become childlike,
to allow nature its flow.
Don't block it, don't stand in the way,
don't push it.
Just flow with it.
You are nature; you are Tao.
You are part of the continuous mystery
that is happening.

Bankei was right.
It is difficult for us,
because we have become so much addicted to the mind
and its manipulation.
And even if I say to you, be natural,
you will try to be natural
and then you will miss.
How can one try to be natural?
If I say don't do anything,
you try not to do anything;
if I say be inactive,
then you make every effort to be inactive –
but the effort is the activity.

So this has to be understood.
No effort is needed.
Any effort on your part
and you will miss the miracle.

Then what is to be done?
Nothing is to be done,
just a simple feeling –

allow nature.
In the beginning it will be difficult,
because you have always been jumping in the way,
always interfering.
In the beginning it will be difficult,
but for just three weeks allow nature.
When you feel hungry, eat,
when you feel sleepy, go to sleep.

When you don't feel hungry, don't eat.
It is not a fast, remember,
because a fast is from the mind –
and you are feeling hungry, but you are on a fast.
There is no harm if you don't feel sleepy.
There is no harm, because the body doesn't need it,
so don't force it.
Stay awake, enjoy, go for a walk,
have a little dance in the room,
or sing or meditate,
but don't force sleep.
When you feel sleepy,
when the eyes say: Now go to sleep . . .

And don't force yourself in the morning
to come out of bed.
Allow your inner being,
give it a chance.
It will give you the indication,
the eyes will open by themselves.

For a few days there will be difficulty,
but within three weeks . . .
And I say within three weeks if you don't interfere.
If you interfere, then three lives are not enough.
Don't interfere and just wait for things to happen.
And allow them.
Within three weeks, you will fall into nature again,
and suddenly you will see
that you have been existing in the Garden of Eden,
and Adam has never been expelled.
He only thinks he has.

That's what the knowledge of the fruit means.

You simply think that you have been expelled.
Where can you be expelled to?
The whole nature is the Garden of Eden.
Where can you be expelled to?
The whole house is God,
so where can you be expelled to?
Bankei said:
I have entered the Garden again.

Bankei was going to die.
The disciples were very worried and they asked:
What should we do?
What should we do with your body?
Should we preserve it?
Should we burn it, as Hindus do, as Buddhists do?
Should we bury it in the ground,
as Mohammedans and Christians do?
We don't know who you are,
a Hindu, a Buddhist, a Mohammedan?
You have confused us too much,
we don't know who you are.
So what should we do?

Bankei said:
Wait, let me die first.
Why are you in such a hurry?
The mind always jumps ahead.
Why are you in such a hurry?
And you call yourselves my disciples?
Let me die, and do whatsoever you like,
because Bankei will not be there.
Whether you bury, whether you burn,
or whether you preserve,
it makes no difference to Bankei.
Bankei will not be there.
But let me die first,
then do whatsoever you like.
It makes no difference,
but don't jump ahead.

The mind has a tendency to jump ahead,
always to jump ahead.

One minister invited his congregation
for a garden party.
He forgot a little old lady.
Just at the eleventh hour he remembered.
So he phoned, because that lady was dangerous,
very religious,
and very religious people are always dangerous.
He was afraid
that she might create trouble or mischief.
She was one of the oldest members
of his congregation
and contributed to the church and everything.
She could create trouble.
So he phoned and told the old lady:
Come.
Just by mistake I forgot,
but forgive me, and you must come.

The old lady said:
It is too late now.
I have already prayed for rain.

There was going to be a garden party
and she had not been invited,
and she had already prayed for rain.
So it was too late.
See, it was no use.
Now, nothing could be done.

The mind goes on jumping ahead.
That is the way of the mind.
Make jumps less and less,
or, if it is very difficult for you,
then allow the mind to jog, but don't jump ahead
Jogging is meditation;
it is a jogging.
You are jumping on the same ground,
and the mind is accustomed to jump ahead.

It may be difficult to stop it completely,
so do half-half –
don't jump ahead, jump on the ground, jog.
Half is cut.
Then, by any by, slow down;
then stand, then sit down.
When you are here and now,
sitting totally, not jumping ahead,
the miracle has happened.
To be in the moment is the miracle.

But I know Bankei will not appeal to you.
Sai Baba can appeal to you
because with Sai Baba
your mind has a logic, a tuning.
With Bankei your mind cannot be tuned.
It has to be dropped –
only then can that tuning happen.
With Sai Baba you can understand things.
With logic it is the same.
What your mind says is that a miracle is happening.

This is not religion at all.
This is simply magic.
And there is no difference between a Houdini
and a Sai Baba.
The only difference, if there is any,
is that Houdini was more honest than Sai Baba,
because he simply said that he was a magician,
that these were tricks,
and all that Sai Baba can do, any magician can do.
But you will not pay much respect to a magician,
because he is so sincere and honest that he says:
These are tricks.
So you say:
Okay, so these are tricks; no miracle.

When somebody says:
These are not tricks.
This is a miracle,
Divine power manifesting through me,

then your mind starts jumping.
Then you think:
If I can become a close disciple of this man,
then I also can become somebody,
I can also do something.

If you have come in search of such a miracle from me,
you have come to the wrong person.
I am Bankei reborn.
I know only one miracle –
to be here and now:
when feeling hungry, to eat;
when feeling sleepy, to sleep;
just to be ordinary,
and just to be part of the cosmos.

If you are in search of such a miracle,
much can happen near me;
but if you are not in such a search,
nothing will happen near me.
And remember, you will be responsible for it,
because your whole search is wrong,
and then there can be no tuning with me.
So decide clearly in your mind,
come to an understanding of what type of miracle
you are searching for.

I can make you most ordinary.
I can make you simple human beings.
I can make you like trees and birds.
There is no magic around here, only religion.
But if you can see, this is the greatest miracle.

Anything more?

Bhagwan,

You were just talking about food,
and now in the West, food is a big cult.
It's one of the things
coming in as a basis of spirituality.

You said if we're natural,
we'll know what to eat and when to eat,
but now we are out of touch
with our childlike nature.

Also, many religions say
that the food you eat does make a difference
to one's spiritual path.

Is there anything you can tell us about food
as a guide for the West?

It is the other way round.
Food cannot make you spiritual,
but if you are spiritual
your food habits will change.

Eating anything will not make much difference.
You can be a vegetarian,
and cruel to the extreme, and violent;
you can be a non-vegetarian,
and kind and loving.
Food will not make much difference.

In India there are communities
who have lived totally with vegetarian food.
Many Brahmins have lived totally with vegetarian food.
They are non-violent but they are not spiritual.
And Jains are the most materialistic community in India,

the most attracted by possessions, accumulation.
That's why they have become the wealthiest.
They are the Jews in India.
But a non-vegetarian world in the West
is not in any way different
from these vegetarian communities in India.

Rather, on the contrary,
a very important thing has to be remembered –
if you are violent and your food is vegetarian,
then your violence
will have to find some other way of expression.
It is natural, because eating non-vegetarian food
gives release to your violence.

So if you know some hunters
you may have come to realize
that hunters are the most loving people.
Their whole violence is released in hunting.
They are most friendly, loving.
But a businessman vegetarian
has no way for his violence to be released,
so his whole violence
becomes a search for wealth and power.
It becomes narrowed down.

But it happens the other way round.
It happened to Mahavir.
Mahavir came from a warrior family;
he was a Kshatriya.
Violence must have been easy for him.
And then a deep meditative effort,
a twelve year-long silence
changed his inner essence.
When the essence changed,
the expression changed;
when the innermost being changed,
his character changed.
But that character change was not basic,
it was a consequence.
So I say to you,

if you become more meditative
you will become more and more vegetarian automatically.
You need not bother about it.

And only if this happens,
that through meditation
vegetarian food comes into you,
not through mind manipulation,
it is good.
But manipulating by the mind, argument,
reasoning that vegetarian food is good,
that it will help you to gain spirituality,
is not going to help anything.

Your clothes, your food,
your habits of life, your style,
everything will change.
But this change is not basic.
The basic change is going to be in you,
and then everything else follows.

If you meditate long enough, deep enough,
it is impossible for you to hurt anybody for food.
It is impossible.
It is not a question of argument,
it is not a question of scriptures,
it is not who says what,
it is a question of calculating
that if you take vegetarian food
you will become spiritual,
it is automatic.
It is not a question of cunningness,
you simply become spiritual.
The whole thing seems so absurd.
Just for food,
killing animals, birds, seems so absurd,
it falls down.

Your clothes change automatically.
By and by, you like looser and looser clothes.
The more relaxed you are inside—loose clothes.
Automatically, I say;

there will be no decision on your part.
By and by, if you use tight clothes,
you will feel uneasy.
Tight clothes belong to a tense mind;
loose clothes belong to a relaxed mind.

But the inner change is the first thing;
and everything else is just a consequence.
If you reverse the order, you will miss.
Then you will become a food addict.

One man came to me.
He was just lean and thin and pale,
and any moment he could die,
and he said:
I want to live only on water,
because everything else
is a hindrance to spirituality.
Now I want to live on pure water.

This man is going to die.
There have been a few people
who have lived on pure water,
but that happened to them naturally.
It cannot be practised.
They were freaks, accidents;
their body mechanism and chemistry worked differently.
It has happened.
Somebody can survive on water,
but nobody can practise it.

Someday science may be able to find
the basic chemical change,
and then everybody will be able to survive on water.
Then science will change your body chemistry,
and you will survive just on air.
It is possible, but you cannot practise it.
And the whole effort is meaningless,
and the whole suffering is unnecessary,
but there are mad people who try things like that.
It has never happened by effort.

There was one woman in Bengal.
She lived forty years without food –
but it simply happened.
Her husband died, and she couldn't eat
for a few days.
Just out of misery, out of sorrow,
she couldn't eat.
But suddenly she realized that without eating,
she was feeling better than ever.
Then she realized that in the past
whenever she was eating, she was always ill,
and suddenly she become healthy, as she never was.
Then she lived for forty years
without eating anything.
Just the air was the food.
And this has happened in many cases.

There was one woman in Europe.
For thirty years she lived without eating.
She became a saint,
because Christians thought it a miracle.
They examined her with every scientific instrument
to see what was happening,
and they couldn't find out anything.
Then it seemed a miracle.
It was not a miracle.

Yoga says there is a possibility
of a body change, of a body chemistry change.
Right now you are doing the same,
just by an intermediary.
You cannot eat sun-rays directly,
because your body chemistry is not in such a state.
The mechanism is not such
that it can absorb sun-rays directly.
So first the fruit of the tree absorbs the sun-rays,
it becomes vitamin B in the fruit,
then you eat the fruit,
then the vitamin B goes into your body.
The fruit is just an intermediary.

The fruit is working just as your agent
to absorb the sun-rays and then give them to you.
You can absorb them through the fruit, not directly.

But if the fruit can absorb directly,
why not you?
So someday there is going to be a scientific discovery
that some body changes will help you
to absorb directly,
and then fruit will not be needed.
In the future –
and I think not very long, fifty years –
science is bound to discover it.
It has to be discovered,
otherwise humanity is going to die
because food will not be possible.
And birth control is not helping.
Nothing is helping.
The population goes on growing.
Some way has to be found so food can be dropped
and direct absorption of cosmic rays becomes possible.
It has happened in individual cases,
but it was by accident.
If it can happen to one individual,
it can happen to every individual,
but not as an accident.
It will happen as a scientific change.

But don't try such things.
They are not spiritual.
Even if you eat sun-rays directly,
there is nothing spiritual.
What is spiritual?
Just by dropping the intermediary of fruit
you become spiritual?
If you live only on water, nothing is spiritual.

What you eat makes no difference.
What you are is a totally different phenomenon.
And when that changes, everything will change.
But that change will not be from the mind,

it will be from the innermost being.
Then things will change automatically.

Sex will disappear by and by.
So I don't say be a *brahmachari,* be a celibate.
That is foolish,
because if you force celibacy
you will become more and more sexual in the mind,
and your whole mind will become ugly and dirty.
You will think only of sex and nothing else.
That is not the way.
You will go crazy and insane.
Freud says that ninety percent of madmen
are mad because of repressed sexuality.

I don't say change sex.
I don't say change food.
I say change your being,
and then things will start changing.

Why is so much sex needed?
Because you are tense, sex becomes a release.
Your tensions are released through it –
you feel relaxed, you can go to sleep.
If you repress it, you remain tense.
And if you repress sex,
the only release, the only possibility of release –
what will happen?
You will go mad.
Where will you release your tensions then?

You eat food.
It is needed by the body,
and the body rejects only things
which are not needed.
Whatsoever you are eating,
is somehow needed by the body.
If you are taking animal food,
if you are taking non-vegetarian food,
your mind, your body, your whole being is violent.
And it is needed.

Don't change it,
otherwise your violence
will have to find another channel.

Change yourself
and food will change, clothes will change,
sex will change.
But change should come from the innermost core,
it should not come from the periphery.
And all turmoil is on the periphery.
Deep down there is no turmoil.
You are just like the sea.
Go and watch the sea.
All the turmoil, all the waves clashing,
is just on the surface.
Deep, the deeper you go, there is more and more calm.
At the deepest part in the sea
there is no turmoil, not a single wave.

First go deeper into your sea,
so you achieve a calm crystallization,
so you achieve the point
where no disturbance ever reaches.
Stand there.
From there every change comes,
every transformation comes.
Once you are there you have become a master.
Now whatsoever is unnecessary can be dropped,
and can be dropped without any struggle and fight.

Whenever you drop something by fight,
it is never dropped.
You can drop smoking by fighting,
and then you will start doing something else
which will become a substitute.
You may start chewing gum; it is the same.
You may start chewing *pan;* it is the same.
There is no difference.
You need something to do with your mouth —
smoking, chewing, anything.
When your month goes on working, you feel at ease

because through the mouth tensions are released.
So whenever a man feels tense he starts smoking.
Why is it
that through smoking or chewing gum or tobacco
tensions are released?

Just look at a small child.
Whenever he feels tense,
he will take his hand in his mouth,
he will start chewing his own hand.
This is his substitute for smoking.
And why does he feel good
when his thumb is in his mouth?
Why does the child feel good and go to sleep?
This is the way of almost all children.
Whenever they feel sleep is not coming,
they will take the thumb inside the mouth,
feel at ease, and fall asleep.
Why?
The thumb becomes a substitute
for the mother's breast.
And food is relaxing.
You cannot go to sleep on a hungry stomach;
it is difficult to get sleep.
When the stomach is full, you feel sleepy,
the body needs rest.
So whenever the child takes the breast in his mouth,
food is flowing, warmth, love.
He is relaxed; he need not worry.
Tensions are relaxed.
The thumb is just a substitute for the breast.
It is not giving milk, it is a false thing,
but still it gives the feeling.

When this child grows,
if he takes his thumb in public
you will think he is foolish,
so he takes a cigarette.
A cigarette is not foolish; it is accepted.
It is just the thumb,
and more harmful than the thumb.

It is better if you smoke your thumb,
go on smoking to your grave.
It is not harmful.
It is better.
No harm is done,
but then people think you are childish, juvenile,
then people think what you are doing is stupid.
But there is a need,
so it has to be substituted.

And in countries where breast-feeding has stopped,
more smoking will automatically be there.
That's why the West smokes more than the East –
because no mother is ready
to give her breast to the child,
because the shape is lost.
So in the West smoking is increasing more and more.
Even small children are smoking.

I have heard that one mother said to her child:
I don't want neighbours to tell me
that you have started smoking.
Be truthful, and whenever you start smoking,
tell me.
The child said:
Don't bother Mom.
I have already stopped.
It is one year now
that I have stopped smoking.
It is one year now, so don't you bother.
Don't you get worried about it.

Small children smoking,
and the mother is not aware
that it is because the breast has been taken away.

In all primitive communities,
a seven-year-old child,
or even an eight – or nine-year-old child,
will continue breast-feeding.
Then there is a satisfaction
and smoking will not be so necessary.

And that's why in primitive communities
men are not so much interested in women's breasts.
There is no problem that somebody will attack them.
Nobody looks at the breasts.

If you had been given the breast
for ten years continuously,
you would get fed up and bored,
you would say:
Stop now!
But every child
has been taken away from the breast prematurely,
and that remains a wound.
So all civilized countries are obsessed with breasts.
Even an old man, dying, is obsessed with breasts,
goes on searching for breasts.

This seems mad, and it is,
but the basic cause is there –
children should be given the breast,
otherwise they will become addicted to it.
The whole life they will be in search of it.

You cannot stop smoking directly
because it has many related things, implications.
You are tense,
and if you stop smoking
you will start something else,
and the other may be more harmful.
Don't go on escaping problems,
face them.
The problem is that you are tense,
so the goal should be how to be non-tense,
not, smoking or not smoking.

Meditate.
Relax your tensions without any object
into the sky.
Allow catharsis to happen.
When you're non-tense,
these things will become absurd, foolish,

and they will drop.
Food will change, styles of your living will change.

But my insistence is on you.
Character is secondary,
behaviour is secondary,
the essential you is the primary thing.
Don't pay too much attention to what you do,
pay much attention to what you are.
Being should become the focus,
and doing should be left to itself.
When being changes, doing follows.

Anything more?

Bhagwan,

Whenever you speak of our failings,
you usually mention anger, sex and jealousy.

Anger and sex seem fairly straightforward,
but there's some confusion
about exactly what jealousy is,
and it's harder to get to the core.

Would you tell us about jealousy?

Yes, I make more mention of anger, sex,
and less of jealousy,
because jealousy is not a primary thing.
It is secondary.
It is a secondary part of sex.

Whenever you have a sexual urge in your mind,

a sexual happening in your being,
whenever you feel sexually attracted
and related to somebody,
jealousy enters because you are not in love.
If you are in love, jealousy never enters.

Try to understand the whole thing.
Whenever you are sexually related,
you are afraid,
because sex is really not a relationship,
it is an exploitation.
If you are attached to a woman or man sexually,
you are always afraid
that this woman may go to somebody else,
this man may move to somebody else.
There is no relationship, really.
It is just mutual exploitation.
You are exploiting each other,
but you don't love and you know it,
so you are afraid.

This fear becomes jealousy,
so you may not allow things.
You will guard.
You will make every security arrangement
so this man cannot look at another woman.
Even looking will be a danger signal.
This man should not talk to another woman,
because talking . . .
And you feel afraid he may leave.
So you will close all the paths,
all the ways of this man going to another woman,
of this woman going to another man.
You will close all the ways, all the doors.

But then a problem arises.
When all the doors are closed, the man becomes dead,
the woman becomes dead, a prisoner, a slave,
and you cannot love a dead thing.
You cannot love one who is not free,
because love is beautiful

only when it is given freely,
when it is not taken and demanded and forced.

First you make security arrangements.
Then the person becomes dead, becomes like an object.
A beloved may be a person,
a wife becomes an object;
a beloved may be a person,
a husband becomes an object
to be guarded, possessed, controlled.
But the more you control, the more you are killing,
because freedom is lost.
And the other person may be there for other reasons,
but not for love,
because how can you love a person who possesses you?
He looks like an enemy.

Sex creates jealousy,
but it is a secondary thing.
So it is not a question of how to drop jealousy.
You cannot drop it, because you cannot drop sex.
The question is how to transform sex into love.
Then jealousy disappears.

If you love a person,
the very love is enough guarantee,
the very love is enough security.
If you love a person,
you know he cannot go to anybody else.
And if he goes, he goes.
Nothing can be done.
What can you do?
You can kill the person,
but a dead person will not be of much use.

When you love a person
you trust that he cannot go to anybody.
If he goes, there is no love,
and nothing can be done.
Love brings this understanding.
There is no jealousy.

So if jealousy is there, know well there is no love.
You are playing a game;
you are hiding sex behind love.
Love is just a painted word;
the reality is sex.

In India, because love is not allowed much,
not allowed at all,
marriage is arranged and tremendous jealousy exists.
A husband is always afraid.
He has never loved, so he knows,
and the wife is always afraid
because she has never loved, so she knows,
that this has been an arrangement.
The parents arranged, astrologers arranged,
society arranged;
the wife and husband were never asked.
In many cases they never knew each other,
they had never seen each other.
So fear exists.
The wife is afraid, the husband is afraid,
and both are spying on each other.
The very possibility is lost.

How can love grow in fear?
They can live together,
but that living together is also
not living together.
They only tolerate together,
they somehow carry on together.
It is just utilitarian.
And out of utility you may manage,
but ecstasy is not possible.
You cannot celebrate it;
it cannot become festive.
It will be a burdensome affair.

So a husband is dead before death,
and a wife is dead before death.
It is two dead persons
taking revenge on each other,

because each thinks that one has killed the other.
Taking revenge, angry, jealous —
the whole thing becomes so ugly.

But in the West,
a different type of phenomenon is happening
which is the same on the other extreme.
They dropped arranged marriage,
and it is good.
That institution is not worth keeping.
But by dropping it, love has not arisen,
only sex has become free.
And when sex is free you are always afraid,
because it is always a temporary arrangement.
You are with this girl tonight.
Tomorrow she will be with somebody else,
and yesterday she was with somebody else.
Yesterday the girl was with somebody else,
tomorrow she will again be with somebody else.
Only tonight she is with you.

How can this be very intimate and deep?
It can only be a meeting of the surfaces.
You cannot penetrate each other,
because penetration needs seasoning.
It needs time.
It needs depth, intimacy,
living together, being together.
A long time is needed.
Then depth opens.
Depths talking to each other . . .

This is just acquaintance.
It may not even be acquaintance.
In the West you can meet a woman on the train
and make love,
and at midnight you drop her at some station.
She never bothers,
she may never know you again.
She may not even have asked your name.

If sex becomes such a trivial thing –
just a bodily affair
where surfaces meet and separate –
your depth remains untouched.
You are again missing something –
something great, something very mysterious –
because you become aware of your own depth
only when somebody else touches it.
Only through the other
do you become aware of your inner being.
Only in deep relationship
does somebody's love resound in you
and bring your depth into being.
Only through somebody else do you discover yourself.

There are two ways of discovery.
One is meditation –
without the other you search for the depth;
another is love –
with the other you search for the depth.
He becomes a root to reach to yourself.
The other creates a circle.
And both lovers help each other.
The deeper love goes, the deeper they feel they are.
Their under-beings are revealed.
But then there is no jealousy.
Love cannot be jealous.
It is impossible.
Love is always trusting.
And if something happens that breaks your trust,
you have to accept it.
Nothing can be done about it,
because whatsoever you do will destroy the other.

Trust cannot be forced.
Jealousy tries to force it.
Jealousy tries, makes you make every effort
so that trust can be maintained.
But trust is not something to be maintained.
It is there, or it is not there.
And I say that nothing can be done about it.

If it is there, you go through it;
if it is not there, better separate.

But don't fight for it,
because you are wasting time, life.
If you love someone,
and the depth speaks to the other's depth –
you have a meeting in being –
it is okay, beautiful.
If it is not happening, separate.
But don't create any conflict, struggle
or fight for it,
because it cannot be achieved through fight,
and the time is lost –
and not only time,
your capacity will be damaged.
You may start again with another person,
repeating the whole pattern.

If there is no trust, separate –
the sooner, the better –
so you are not destroyed,
so you are not damaged,
so your capacity to love remains fresh
and you can love somebody else.
This is not the place,
this is not the man, this is not the woman for you.
Move, but don't destroy each other.

Life is very short,
and capacities are very delicate.
They can be destroyed.
And once damaged,
there is no possibility of repairing them.

I have heard that once it happened
that Winston Churchill was invited to speak
in a small club of friends.
Everybody knew that Churchill was a drunkard,
and loved alcohol very much,
and the man who introduced him,

the president of the club, said:
Sir Winston has drunk so much wine up to now,
that if we pour all the wine into this hall,
the level will come up to my head.
It was a big hall, and he was just joking.

Winston Churchill stood,
looked at the imaginary line,
looked at the ceiling –
the ceiling was high –
became very sad, and he said:
So much still to be done,
and so little time left to do it.

As far as love is concerned,
so much is to be done for everyone,
and so little time is left to do it.
Don't waste your energy in fighting,
jealousy, conflict.
Move, and move in a friendly way.

Search somewhere else
for the person who exists who will love you.
Don't get fixed with someone who is wrong,
not for you.
Don't be angry.
There is no point in it.
And don't try to force trust.
Nobody can force it,
it never happens.
You will miss the time, you will miss the energy,
and you may become aware when nothing can be done.
Move.
Either trust or move.

Love always trusts.
Or if it finds that the trust is not possible,
it simply moves in a friendly way.
There is no conflict and fight.
Sex creates jealousy.
Find, discover love.

Don't make sex the basic thing.
It is not.

India missed with arranged marriage.
The West is missing with free love.

India missed love
because parents were too calculating and cunning.
They would not allow falling in love:
That is dangerous;
nobody knows where it will lead.
They were too clever,
and through cleverness,
India missed all possibility of love.

In the West they are too rebellious, too young;
not clever — too young, too childish.
They have made sex a free thing,
available everywhere:
No need to go so deep to discover love;
enjoy sex and be finished.

Through sex, the West is missing.
Through marriage, the East has missed.
But if you are alert,
you need not be Eastern, you need not be Western.
Love is neither Eastern nor Western.

Go on discovering love within you.
And if you love, sooner or later
the person will happen to you,
because a loving heart, sooner or later,
comes to a loving heart.
It always happens.
You will find the right person.
But if you are jealous you will not find,
if you are simply for sex you will not find,
if you live only for security you will not find.

Love is a dangerous path,
and only those who have courage can travel it.
And I say to you it is the same,

just like meditation –
only for those who are courageous.
And there are only two ways to reach the Divine –
either meditation or love.
Find out which is your way,
which can be be your destiny.

Seventh Talk

16th June 1974

Bhagwan,

The Japanese master Ekido was a severe teacher,
and his pupils feared him.

One day, as one of his pupils
was striking the time of day on the temple gong,
he missed a beat
because he was watching a beautiful girl
who was passing the gates.

Unknown to the pupil,
Ekido was standing behind him.
Ekido struck the pupil with his staff,
and the shock stopped the heart of the pupil,
and he died.

Because the old custom
of the pupil signing his life over to the master
had sunk to a mere formality,
Ekido was discredited by the general public.

But after this incident,
Ekido produced ten enlightened successors,
an unusually high number.

This type of phenomenon is special to Zen
and to Zen masters.
Only a Zen master beats his disciples,
and sometimes it happens
that the disciple dies through beating.
Ordinarily, this looks very cruel, violent, mad.
Religious people cannot conceive
how a master can be so cruel as to kill a disciple,
but those who know feel differently.

A man who is enlightened knows well
that nobody is ever killed.
The inner is eternal.
It goes on and on.
It may change bodies,
but the change is only of houses.
The change is only of dresses.
The change is only of vehicles.
The traveller goes on and on.
Nothing dies.

The moment of death
can become the moment of enlightenment also
Both are so similar.
When someone becomes enlightened,
it is a death deeper than ordinary death;
when someone becomes enlightened,

he comes to know that he is not the body.
The attachment, the identification disappears.

For the first time,
he can see an unbridgeable gap.
He is here; the body is there.
There is an abyss between.
He has never been the body
and the body has never been him.
This death is deeper than ordinary death.
When you die ordinarily,
you are still identified with the body.

This death is still deeper.
Not only are you unidentified with the body,
your identification with the mind, with the ego,
also disappears.
You are left simply as an emptiness,
as an inner space,
boundless.
You are neither the body nor the mind.

In ordinary death only the body dies.
The mind goes on following you like a shadow.
The mind is the problem, not the body.
Through the mind
you have become one with the body.
And unless the mind disappears
you will go on getting into newer bodies,
into newer vehicles,
and the wheel of life will go on and on.

When you become enlightened,
suddenly you are not the body, you are not the mind.
Only then do you come to know who you are.
The body is a seed.
The mind is also a seed.
Hidden beyond them is you.

Sometimes it happens that a Zen master
can coincide the moment of your death
with your enlightenment.

In the right moment he can hit you.
The body falls down –
everybody can see that –
but deep within the ego falls down also.
Only you and the master know.

It is not cruelty.
It is the highest form of compassion,
and only a very great master can do it.
It is very subtle
to feel the moment of your death,
and to make it a point of inner transformation
and transfiguration.

Look at this story and you may think –
it is how the story appears –
that the master killed his disciple.
That is not the thing.
The disciple was going to die anyhow;
it was the moment for his death.
The master knew it.
He simply used the moment of death
for the disciple's enlightenment.

But this is an inner secret, something esoteric,
and I could not defend Ekido in a court with this.
The court would say he is a murderer.
Anyhow, there would be no way to prove
he knew the disciple was going to die in that moment.

Why not use death?
An ignorant person cannot use life;
an enlightened person can even use death.
That's how a master should be,
using everything for enlightenment.

Ekido was just standing behind the disciple.
He was beating the gong of the temple
and the master was watching.
If this disciple can die in awareness,
death will become the turning-point of the wheel.
If he can die in awareness,

if he can fall but remain conscious,
if the body can fall,
but deep down he can remain centred, alert, aware,
this will be the last death.
He will not need to be reborn again.

Remember,
if you can die with full awareness
the wheel of life stops.
You can enter a new body
only if you are unaware, unconscious.
When someone dies fully conscious,
this world disappears.
There is no birth again.

That's why we say
an enlightened person never comes again.
A Buddha simply disappears.
You will not be able to meet him again in the body.
You can meet him in bodilessness –
he is everywhere then –
but not in the body.

You cannot meet Buddha somewhere,
because only a body exists somewhere.
When the body disappears,
Buddha exists everywhere,
or nowhere.
You can meet him here,
you can meet him there,
you can meet him anywhere,
but don't look for him in the body.

The body exists somewhere.
When the body disappears,
the soul, the consciousness exists everywhere.
You can meet Buddha anywhere.
Wherever you go you can meet him.

The body is there
because the mind seeks desires through the body.
Desires cannot be fulfilled without the body.

You can be completely fulfilled without the body,
but desires cannot be fulfilled without the body.
Desire needs the body.
The body is the vehicle of desire.

That's why possession happens.
You have heard,
you must have heard many stories,
about a ghost possessing somebody else.
Why is a ghost so interested
in possessing somebody else?
It is because of desires.
Desires cannot be fulfilled without a body,
so he enters somebody's body to fulfill his desires.

The same is the case when you enter a womb,
enter into a fresh body,
and start the journey of desires.
But if you die alert,
in that alertness not only the body dies,
all desires evaporate.
Then there is no entering into a womb.
Then entering a womb is such a painful process,
it is so painful
that consciously you cannot do it.
Only unconsciously you can do it.

The English word 'anxiety' comes from a Latin root
which means narrowing down,
and in the beginning the word was used
for the entry of a soul into a womb.
So the first anxiety is felt
when a soul enters a womb,
because everything is narrowed down.
An infinite soul becomes a small body.

This is the most painful process possible,
as if the whole sky
has been forced to enter into a seed.
You don't know it
because it is so painful
that you become totally unconscious.

There are two painful processes.
You may have heard Buddha's saying:
Birth is pain, death is pain.

These are the greatest pains,
the greatest anguishes possible.
When the infinite becomes finite in the womb,
it is painful, it is anxiety.
And when the infinite is taken out of the body
again there is anguish and pain.

So whenever someone dies consciously, he disappears.
Then there is no more entry into the body.
Then there is no more anxiety,
because anxiety is the consequence of desire;
then you need not be narrowed down,
because there is no desire to be fulfilled.
You can remain infinite.
There is no need to enter a vehicle,
because now you are going nowhere.

This disciple who was beating the gong of the temple
must have been near his death, close,
and the master was standing behind him
because of this fact.

The disciple was going to die any moment.
This is not said in the story.
This cannot be said,
but this is how the thing happened.
Otherwise there was no need
for the master to stand behind the disciple
when he was beating the gong.
There are many more important things
for the master to do.
Beating the gong is just an ordinary thing,
an everyday ritual.
Why was the master standing behind him?
This Ekido seems to be a strange fellow.
Had he not anything more significant to do?

At that moment

there was nothing more significant,
because this disciple was going to die anyhow,
and his death had to be used.
And only a master can use death –
out of compassion.
He was waiting to see whether he remained alert
at the moment of death or not.
He missed.

The story is beautiful and very significant.
He saw a beautiful girl passing
and his whole consciousness was lost.
He became a desire;
his whole being became a desire.
He wanted to follow this girl, to possess this girl.

Whenever there is desire, consciousness is lost,
because both cannot exist together.
Desire exists with unconsciousness;
it cannot exist with consciousness.
When you move in desire, consciousness disappears.

Hence so much insistence
by all the Buddhas and Jainas for desirelessness.
When you are desireless, you will be aware;
when you are aware, you will be desireless.
These are two aspects of the same coin –
on one aspect, desirelessness;
on another aspect, alertness, consciousness.

The story is significant.
Seeing a beautiful girl pass,
the disciple missed himself.
He was no more there; he became a desire.
He started following the girl.
He entered a dream.
He became sleepy.
He became unconscious.

Sex is the mid-point between death and birth.
Between birth and death is sex.
Really, between birth and death

there is nothing but sex, an extension of sex.
You are conceived out of sex,
and from the moment you are conceived
you start on a journey of sexual pleasure.
The moment you die, this continues.

And sex is so powerful,
that even if death is standing there,
you will forget it.
If sex takes the grip,
then everything can be forgotten.
You become completely mad.

The form of the girl caught his mind.
He was no more there.
He was alert just a moment before.
Now he was not alert.

You may have heard stories, Indian stories,
of *rishis,* seekers, doing austerities,
meditating in their forest abodes, in the hills.
Always it happens
that wherever they reach a point of awareness
suddenly sex arises.
Apsaras, nymphs from heaven, descend,
as if they are just waiting
for someone to come to a point of awareness,
as if there is a subtle conspiracy
against achieving awareness.

Hidden deep in a forest,
someone achieves a little alertness,
and suddenly nymphs are there —
beautiful girls from heaven,
not of this earth, perfect.
You cannot conceive anything more perfect.
The bodies are as if of gold, transparent.
Suddenly awareness is lost
and the *rishi* has become a man of desire.
He falls.

From where do these *apsaras* come?

Do they really come from heaven?
Is there some conspiracy against awareness?
No.
They come out of the mind of the seeker.

The mind, when it sees
that everything is going to be lost,
uses sex as the last weapon.
When the mind sees
that now awareness is reaching a crystallization,
and that crystallized,
the mind will not have any say,
the mind will be dropped,
this is its last struggle –
suddenly the mind creates sex and the desire for sex,
the mind projects.

I say to you,
there may have been no girl passing.
It was just the moment of death
and this man was aware,
so the mind played the last trick.
That is the last.
If you win that,
you have won the mind.
The mind will play other tricks
and always preserve sex as the last resort.
If sex cannot work, then nothing can work.

The mind depends basically on sex.
Look into your mind.
You will find it is ninety percent sex,
thinking about sex, dreaming about sex.
Projecting in the future,
remembering the past,
it is always about sex.
And sometimes,
even if you feel it is not thinking about sex,
ponder over it, meditate –
it desires other things also because of sex.

You may think about becoming wealthy.
What will you do with your wealth?
Just ask the mind,
and the mind says:
Then you can enjoy the body,
then you can get the most beautiful woman possible.

The mind may think:
Become a Napoleon, a Hitler.
But ask the mind
what you will do with power.
Suddenly you will find, hidden somewhere,
sex and desire.

This girl may not have been passing there.
Or, even if the girl was passing there,
the girl may not have been as beautiful as she looked,
as she appeared.

In the first place,
I think there was no girl –
just the moment of death
and this man's awareness.

He was beating the gong fully alert.
This is part of meditation in a Zen monastery –
whatsoever you do, do it with awareness.
When you walk, walk fully alert;
when you move your head, be fully alert.
Whatsoever you do, follow it with alertness.
Don't miss it;
don't think of anything else.
Be there in it as a light
and everything is revealed.
Every act, every nook and corner of it is lighted.
Nothing is in darkness.
When you eat, eat with awareness.
This is all one has to do in a Zen monastery –
twenty-four hours of alertness.

This disciple must have been beating the gong
with full alertness.

The gong is beaten to make everybody alert,
and he must have been alert
with the sound resounding in the monastery.
Suddenly the girl appeared.
From where?

In the first place
I think there was no girl.
The mind projected.
In the second place,
even if there was a girl,
the girl was not so beautiful as the mind thought.
It projected.
The girl was just a screen.
The dream came from the mind and was projected.

That's how it is happening to everybody.
When for the first time you fall in love,
the girl is not of this world.
She comes from somewhere else.
She is an *apsara,* a nymph from heaven.
But by and by, the more you become acquainted,
the girl becomes more and more earthly,
ordinary, homely.
Suddenly you find there is nothing –
this is just an ordinary girl –
and then you think you have been deceived,
that this girl has deceived you.

Nobody has deceived you.
Your mind projected.
Your mind projected so that desire could move.

Beauty doesn't exist in things.
Beauty is a projection.
Beauty is not objective.
It is subjective.
So one day somebody looks beautiful;
another day the same person becomes ugly.
It is you who projects; it is you who withdraws.
The other works just as a screen.

Once you come to know
that the mind projects beauty and ugliness,
that the mind projects good and bad,
you stop projecting.
Then for the first time,
you come to know what objective reality is.
It is neither good nor bad;
it is neither beautiful nor ugly.
It simply is.
All your interpretations drop
with the projections.

So this disciple, at the moment of death,
was going to be alert and aware,
and the mind did the last thing, its final resort —
a beautiful girl appeared.
The mind created beauty around her
and awareness was lost.
The mind became dim and desire arose.
The soul was there no more.
The disciple became the body.

That's why all religions insist so much
on transcending sex.
Unless you transcend sex,
the mind will play the last trick,
and it will be the winner, not you.
But repression is not transcendence.
It is escape.

Move into desire with full awareness.
Try to be in the sex act, but alert.
By and by, you will see the emphasis changing —
the energy will be moving more into alertness
and less into the sex act.
Now the thing has happened;
the basic thing has happened.
Sooner or later the whole sex energy
becomes meditative energy.
Then you have transcended.

Then, whether you stand in the market
or sit in a forest,
apsaras cannot come to you.
They may be passing on the street,
but they will be there no more for you.
If your mind is there
absent *apsaras* become present;
if your mind is not there,
present *apsaras* disappear.

At this moment, when the disciple missed awareness,
the master hit him hard on the head.
I would like to do the same for you
in your moment of death,
but it cannot be tolerated here.
In Japan it was one of the oldest traditions.
Whenever a disciple came to a master, he said:
My life, my death – both are yours.
If you want to kill me, you can.
This is what surrender is.

And he signed, he wrote it down.
He gave it in writing
because the law, the state, won't listen.
The law will not listen if you say
that because he was going to die,
that's why you hit him.
The law will say:
You hit him, that's why he has died.

The law moves from the visible,
and a master moves from the invisible.
The master is seeing the invisible death reaching,
and he hits just to make the disciple alert.

And a very hard hit is needed.
When the mind is moving in sex,
an ordinary hit won't do.
A real hit is needed,
a real electric shock-like thing.

It is an old story.

If in the future there are monasteries
like old Zen monasteries,
there will be no need to hit with a staff.
An electric shock can be given –
but something so shocking
that the whole being trembles,
something so shocking
that there is a break in the desire
that is leading you out.

The master hit the disciple so hard that he died.
This is the visible part of it –
he fell down and died.
What happened inside?
What is the inside story?

When the master hit the disciple,
it was the moment of his death,
but desire was arising.
And in the moment of death
if sex is there,
only then can you enter into another womb.
Otherwise, you cannot enter.

Men dying on a bed, if they are conscious,
always think of sex.
It may be strange
but an old man, even a man of a hundred years,
dying on a bed,
almost always thinks of sex,
because sex is the first and the last
in the body's life.
He may have been thinking of God before,
he may have been chanting: Ram, Ram, Ram,
but suddenly at the moment of death
everything drops
and sex appears again.

It is natural.
The first must be the last.
You were conceived out of sex

and you must die with sex in your mind.

So, old, dirty men are not just a myth.
The body is almost dead,
but the mind continues to think.
And old men think more about sex than young men,
because young men can do something about it.
Old men cannot do; they can only think.
The whole phenomenon becomes cerebral, mental.

In the moment of death
you are preparing for a re-entry,
for entering the womb.
Try to understand deeply
why there is so much attraction
in entering the feminine body, the female body.
What do you gain out of it?
While making love, when your whole being
wants to penetrate the feminine body,
what do you gain out of it?

Psychologists say –
and spiritualists have always been alert about it –
that it is again the same symbolic act of entry.
It is not only when you are born
that your being enters into the womb of a woman,
this persists your whole life.
Again and again
you want to penetrate the female body.
You want to reach the womb again and again.

Sex means
the urge to penetrate the feminine body,
to enter again into the womb.
They are both the same;
whether you enter as a seed,
or whether you enter just in a sex act,
the urge is to enter.

At the moment of death,
sex must come into the mind,
and if it comes, you have missed.

You have created a desire,
and now this desire
will lead you again into another womb.
You will enter.

The master was waiting behind.
Masters are always waiting behind disciples,
whether physically or non-physically,
and this is one of the greatest moments –
when a person is going to die.
The master hit him hard.

His body fell down,
but inside he became alert.
The desire disappeared,
the girl passing was no more;
the street was there no more.
Everything dropped with the body, shattered.
He became alert.
In that alertness, he died.
And if you can join alertness and death,
you have become enlightened.

That's why a miracle happened.
Ekido's tradition
became one of the most significant traditions in Japan.
Ten persons attained enlightenment.
People started to wonder:
This cruel man who has killed,
this aggressive and violent man who has killed,
why are his disciples becoming enlightened?

It is a rare number.
Ten is rare.
With one master,
ten disciples becoming enlightened
is very rare.
Even to help one to become enlightened is too much.

But there is nothing strange,
it is plain arithmetic –
only this type of master can help.

And whenever I have read this story
I have always wondered why others missed.
This man could have enlightened many.

But those who were afraid, scared, filled with fear,
simply must have escaped from this man.
People would have stopped coming to his monastery
because he was dangerous.

One thing is said about Ekido –
that when this disciple died,
he never said anything about it,
he never said: The disciple is dead.
He continued as if nothing had happened,
and whenever somebody would ask:
What about the disciple?
he would laugh.
He never said anything about it.
He never said the disciple was dead,
he never said something had gone wrong,
he never said it was just an accident.
Whenever someone would ask,
he would laugh.
Why was he laughing?
Because of the inside story.

People can know only from the outside.
If I hit you hard and you die,
people can only know that you are dead.
No one will be able to know
what has happened inwardly.

This disciple achieved something,
something which Buddhas make efforts
for many lives to attain.
And Ekido did it in a single moment.
He was a great artist, a great master.

He used the moment of death so beautifully,
and the disciple attained.
The disciple disappeared not only from the body,
the disciple also disappeared from the mind.

The disciple was never born again.
This was total death, with no rebirth.

But in Japan
people had become accustomed to such things.
You would go to a master –
he would hit you;
he might throw you out of the window;
he would jump on you and start beating you.
You were asking a philosophical question –
whether God exists or not –
and he would start beating you.

Ekido helped many persons to become enlightened.
Only such a man, with such deep compassion,
can help.
But a very great surrender is needed.

It is said that the disciple's parents came
when the disciple was dead.
They came to see Ekido,
and they were very angry, obviously.
They had only one child, and he was dead.
They were old
and they were depending on him.
And they were waiting –
sooner or later
he was to come back from the monastery
and help in their old age.

In Japan,
monastery life is a periodical thing.
You can go to a monastery, become a *sannyasi,*
remain there for a time,
study, meditate,
attain a certain quantity of alertness,
a certain quality of being,
and then come back to live the life
of an ordinary householder.
Sometimes,
if you feel that you are missing

and the mind has become dim and confused,
you go again.

It is not a permanent style of life
to become a *sannyasi* in Japan.
Few people follow it their whole life;
that is their decision.
You can come back,
and this is not thought of with guilt.

In India there is guilt.
If once you become a *sannyasi*
and then come back,
get married and become a householder,
then everyone looks at you as if you have fallen.

This is nonsense.
This is foolish
because the whole country cannot become *sannyasis.*
Only a few people can be *sannyasis,*
not doing anything,
and they will have to depend on others
who are doing, who are active in life.

Sannyas should be available to everybody.
The whole country must be able to become *sannyasis.*
But that is possible
only if you can be a *sannyasi* in ordinary life —
if you can go to the office,
if you can work in a shop,
if you can be a labourer, or a teacher,
or a doctor, or an engineer
and still be a *sannyasi.*

So people move to the monastery.
That is just a training period
so the whole time is devoted to meditation.
Then they come back.
They carry the quality with them
and come back to ordinary life,
become ordinary citizens again,
and work in life —

as far as the outward life is concerned.
Inside they go on trying deeply
for the inner flame.
Whenever they feel something is becoming dim,
whenever they feel they are missing consciousness,
they go again to the monastery,
stay there for a period
and come back again.

This old couple
was waiting for the boy to come back –
and he was dead.
They must have been angry;
they must have thought many things
against this master Ekido.

So they came.
They looked at Ekido
and they were waiting
for him to say something kind to them.
What did Ekido say?
He said:
Why are you waiting?
Follow the boy.
You have wasted enough life.
Don't waste any more.

And when they looked at Ekido's eyes,
they forgot their anger.
This man could not be cruel.
The compassion was flowing.
They had come to complain,
but they simply thanked Ekido
and went back.

When you come to a master, be ready to die.
Beating any gong,
falling in desire, following a girl –
the master can hit you any moment.
If you have not surrendered,
the hit will be useless.

The master will not hit you because you will miss.
It will not be of much use.

This disciple must have been
one of the closest, most intimate,
and so surrendered
that he would die but would not complain.
He fell down without a complaint,
as if the body dropped like an old dress.
And inside there was light, more light.
He entered that light.

Be ready to die.
Only then can you be reborn
into an altogether different dimension.
That dimension is the dimension of the Divine.

Don't protect yourself.
Your protection is your undoing.
Don't try to safeguard.
Near a master be insecure,
because he is your security.
Be unsafe.
Leave everything to him and wait for his hit.
Any moment it can descend on you.

But if you have not surrendered
it will not descend,
because no master is interested in hitting you,
no master is interested in killing you.
Masters are interested
only in making you fully enlightened,
and that can happen
only when your death and your awareness meet –
a very difficult, very rare combination.

A master can see
when you are going to die.
It is written, because your body has a fixed span;
it can be read.
An astrologer may miss it;
a palmist may not be able to read it,

because you are such a liar that even your palm lies.
You are so deceptive
that even your forehead will not say the truth.
And you are so afraid of death
that unknowingly, unconsciously,
you hide the knowledge of it
in the innermost chamber.
If you are a true person, authentic,
you yourself will become aware
of when you are going to die.

Zen masters have been forecasting their deaths.
They can always tell when they are going to die,
but even then people don't believe them:
How can we believe that you can know death?
We have hidden it so deep,
and we never look at it.

Astrology may fail
because it is an outer science,
reading something from the outer towards the inner.
Palmistry may fail
because it cannot be very certain.
Your hands cannot be believed,
you cannot be believed.
Your whole body lies.

And the lines on your palm
can be changed very easily.
For fifteen days think of suicide,
and your life-line will be broken.
Continuously, for fifteen days,
don't think of anything else,
just think of suicide, of committing suicide,
picturing, dreaming.
Within fifteen days
your life-line will be broken.

The mind can create or change.
If you go to a palmist and he says
within three months you are going to die,
he may have misinterpreted,

but if this idea settles deep in you,
you will die in three months.
And within three months
your life-line will be finished.
Your hand is not influencing your mind,
your mind is continuously influencing your hand.

I have heard about one Egyptian king.
He was very much afraid of death.
He was very weak and ill
and always on his death-bed.

He came to know about one astrologer
who predicted the death of one of his ministers,
and exactly on time, the minister died.
The king thought:
This man is dangerous.
The king thought:
This man has done something like black magic.
He has killed,
and to allow this man to be alive is dangerous –
he can do the same to me.

He called the astrologer and asked him:
Tell me something about my death.
When am I going to die?

The astrologer looked at the king's face
and felt something dangerous.
The king was very ferocious.
He suspected something,
so he made the chart, studied it,
and then said:
You will die after I have died,
within one week.

So the king called all his doctors
to look after this man.
A palace was created for him
with the best of food and of everything.
The greatest doctors were called,
just in his service, and told:

Preserve him,
because he says if he dies, within seven days . . .

It is said that the king lived very long,
because that man was alive.
He was a very healthy man,
and the king died only when that man died.
Within a week, the king was dead.

Your mind goes on changing.
And if your mind is a liar,
don't go to any palmist.
The palmist will be deceived.

But you cannot deceive a master
because he never reads your palm,
he never looks at your forehead,
he is not worried about your stars.
He looks deep in you.
He knows the exact moment of your death
and if you surrender, the death can be used.

This story is beautiful.
Meditate on it.
The same can happen to you
but much readiness is needed.
Ripeness is needed.
And surrender.

Anything more?

Bhagwan,

The last line of this Zen story
says ten were enlightened
and that this was a great number.

Ten doesn't seem a great number to me.
Can we buy your stick and use it on ourselves
to help surrender happen?

Ten is really a big number,
because enlightenment is so arduous,
so difficult to achieve,
almost impossible.
Ten is a big number,
but even bigger numbers have happened.
With Buddha, hundreds became enlightened;
with Mahavir, hundreds became enlightened.

The basic thing
is not how to buy my stick –
you cannot buy it –
it is how to allow it.

It is not a question of the master hitting you,
it is a question of receiving the hit,
welcoming it.
If you resist, nothing can be done.
And resistance is there.
In ordinary things resistance is there,
and death is very big, the ultimate.

In ordinary things, resistance is there.
One man was here and he said:
I want to surrender.
I told him:
Think about it.
What do you mean?
It is difficult.
It is not so easy
that you can come and say: I surrender.

I told the man:

Go and first shave your head.
The man said:
That's very difficult; that I cannot do.
I love long hair.

The man had completely forgotten
he was going to surrender to me,
but he could not cut his hair.
And hair is dead already.
Hair is not a live part of you.
That is why you can cut it and you are not harmed.
Hair is dead, already dead,
something which has gone dead
and been thrown out of the body as dead cells.

This man says he cannot cut his hair
because he loves long hair —
and he is ready to surrender.
He doesn't know what surrender means.

Someone comes to me and says:
I am ready to surrender.
And I say to him:
Change to ochre.
Then he says:
That will be awkward; it will be difficult.
He cannot change his dress to ochre,
yet he is ready to surrender.

The word 'surrender' has become meaningless.
It carries no meaning for him.
He is not aware of what he is saying,
otherwise, to utter the word 'surrender'
would make his whole being tremble and shake,
because it means death.

My stick is there.
I can hit you,
but your readiness is not there.
If I hit you before you are ready,
you will simply escape from me.
Many escape, many have escaped

because I have hit them somehow or other.

And don't think that the stick
is really a visible thing.
I use subtle sticks.
Just a word can hit you to death.
You are shattered.
Your logic, your religion, your concepts are hit
and you are shattered,
and you never come back again to me.

I hit your emotions.
Then you become antagonistic to me.
Your ripeness is needed.
You have to welcome the hit,
wait and pray for it.

In Zen it has been one of the oldest traditions
that whenever a disciple is hit,
the whole monastery becomes happy,
and the disciple is received as something special.
The master has hit him;
the disciple has been chosen.
People wait for years to be hit by the master.
They pray, they ask the master:
When will we be capable,
or when will we be fortunate enough to be hit?
When will your stick, your staff,
descend upon us?

A deep receptivity is needed.
There is no need to buy my staff;
it is always yours.
Only have a welcoming heart,
a deep receptivity, patience.
It can descend on you at any moment.

Sometimes it comes near to you
and you become scared.
Sometimes, on many centres of your body I hit,
but then you are scared,
then you want to escape from it.

Be alert to the mind.
The mind will always tell you to escape.
Wherever there is danger,
the mind will tell you:
Run away from here.

The mind has two ways
of encouraging a situation –
one is fight,
another is flight.

Your mind starts fighting with me,
I can see.
When I am talking,
I can see in your eyes
whether you are fighting or fleeing.
Your very look,
the way you sit, the way you hear,
shows that you are fighting, resisting, withdrawn –
creating a space
so I cannot enter in you.

Or you are on a flight,
and then you are sleepy
and you are not listening at all.
Or you are somewhere else, thinking something else,
You are engaged within so you can escape.

When you are ready
neither flight nor fight exists,
just a prayerful patience and waiting.
There is not even an impatience about it,
because impatience creates tension.
You are not even impatient,
just patiently waiting,
passively waiting with a prayerful mood.

The hit is yours.
I am waiting for it,
and many more than Ekido's disciples
can become enlightened.

The possibility is there; the opportunity is there.

The river is flowing,
but whether you will bow down and take a drink,
or whether you will remain egoistic
and turn away from the river,
thinking either of flight or of fight,
and creating all your own ideas around you —
whether you will allow your mind
to take you away from me,
or whether you will put it aside
and allow me to hit you —
everything depends on you.
The hit is always near,
but you go on wavering.

This disciple was hit by Ekido.
He was really surrendered.
And after his death,
many more were ready.

From somewhere the chain is to be broken.
When one light is kindled, many more follow.
Who will be the first to die?
That's the question.
Once this disciple was dead and inside, enlightened,
many followed.
Ten became enlightened.

This word 'ten' is also worth thinking about.
This ten is symbolic,
because ten is the greatest number.
It is not exactly ten;
it is not arithmetical.
Ten is just the greatest number.
Man started counting on his fingers,
and ten are the fingers.
Even now in the villages
people count on their fingers.

Ten is the highest number
and all other numbers are repetitive.
Eleven means one upon one,

twelve means two upon one.
There is repetition.
Ten is the basic number
in all the languages of the world,
because everywhere man has ten fingers.
These are the ten digits,
so ten is the highest number.
It is symbolic.

One dropped into infinity,
then many followed.
Once the abyss is open
and you see someone entering it,
and you see the bliss, the benediction,
you can also enter it very easily.
You can take the jump as well.

Many are getting ready.
But even if you are ninety-nine percent ready,
the hit cannot descend on you.
The hit can descend on you
only when you are one hundred percent ready,
because then it is a revolution.
You can turn back even from ninety-nine percent.
That's the problem.
It is very unfortunate, but it happens.

I have been working with many, many people,
and sometimes they turn
when the right moment was going to be.
Exactly before that moment they turn away.
And the mind is cunning enough.
It can philosophize.
It can say why you have turned away.

Exactly at the moment
when something was going to happen,
you can turn away.
There is more possibility for you
to turn away from that moment
than from any other moment.
It is unfortunate, but it happens.

You wait and wait and wait,
and then the moment is nearing
where the evaporating point can be reached,
and suddenly you turn away.

To resist that turning is very difficult.
It is just like death,
reaching nearer, nearer, nearer,
and seeing the abyss,
you turn away and run as fast as you can.

Remain alert.
This misfortune happens to seekers.
It can happen to you.

Buddha passed through a village many times
in his forty years of travelling.
One man used to come.
He would listen for a few minutes
then get up and go away.
And this had become a habit.
He never listened to Buddha
for the whole time Buddha was speaking.

He would come; that was certain.
And whenever Buddha would come to the town
he would wait for that man.
He would come; that was certain.
He would sit,
and for a few minutes he would listen.
Then, respectfully bowing down to Buddha,
he would go away.

Ananda once asked that man:
Why do you do this?
The man said:
Sometimes this is the peak hour for my business,
but I must come just to pay my respects.
That's why I come.
But my shop is open and customers are there,
and they will not wait.
Enlightenment can wait.

Next time I will hear.
It happened again and again.

The day Buddha died he was near the village,
and before his death he said to Ananda:
That man has not come.
This is exceptional –
he never missed.
He always missed in a sense,
but he never missed.
He has always come.
Now he has not come.

Then Buddha asked his disciples:
Do you have anything to ask,
because soon I will enter into the final *samadhi,*
the final ecstasy,
and then I will not be able to come back
and answer you.

They started weeping and crying,
but there was no question.
And Ananda said:
We have asked everything,
you have answered everything,
and there is nothing.
Our minds are blank
just thinking that you are going to disappear.

Buddha asked thrice, again and again.
There was no question,
so he went behind the tree and closed his eyes,
just to dissolve into the infinite,
to leave the body,
and then suddenly the man came.
He started fighting with the monks and said:
I must see him.
This is the last time;
I will not be able to see him again.
For forty years I have been missing,
and I have a question to ask.

I have never been able to ask it before,
because sometimes there was a marriage in my family,
sometimes business was at a peak,
sometimes I was ill or my wife was ill,
and sometimes there were relatives staying.
I always missed,
but now don't prevent me.

The disciples said:
It is not possible.
Now he is dissolving.

Buddha came out from his ecstasy,
from his final *samadhi*.
He came in front of the tree and he said:
Don't prevent that man.
He may have been foolish,
he may have missed because of his ignorance,
but I cannot be hard on him.
I am still alive,
so let him come.
No one should say that Buddha was alive
and a man who had come begging
was sent back.

Buddha said:
What have you come to ask?
The man had forgotten the question.
He said:
When I came, I knew,
but now I can't remember.
Next time I see you
I will bring the question.

And there was going to be no next time.
Buddha died that day,
and that man must be wandering somewhere
on this or some other earth,
seeking a man who can answer his question.

That man missed Buddha continuously for forty years.
You can miss me.

Always remember that possibility.
But it will be because of you,
not because of me.
I am always ready.
Whenever you are ready I will hit you.

But a deep surrender is needed.
Before that nothing can be done.
You have to die, die as you are,
so that which you really are
can be born out of you.
You have to die as an appearance,
so that the real can be born.
You have to die on the periphery,
so that the centre evolves and comes out
in its luminousness, in its full perfection.

All hits are to destroy the seed
so that the tree is born.

Anything more?

Bhagwan,

There have been several questions
concerning what you were saying
about warriors and businessmen.

Since most of us
were businessmen and professionals,
and not warriors,
are we going to miss enlightenment?

To be a warrior doesn't mean to be a soldier.
It is a quality of the mind.

You can be a businessman,
and be a warrior.
You can be a warrior and be a businessman.

'Businessman' means a quality of the mind
which is always bargaining,
trying to give less and get more.
That's what I mean when I say businessman –
trying to give less and get more,
always bargaining,
always thinking about profit.

A warrior is again a quality of the mind,
the quality of the gambler, not of the bargainer,
the quality which can stake everything
this way or that –
a non-compromising mind.

If a businessman thinks of enlightenment,
he thinks of it as a commodity
like many other commodities.
He has a list –
he has to make a big palace,
he has to purchase this and that,
and in the end,
he has to purchase enlightenment also;
but enlightenment is always the last –
when everything is done, then;
when nothing remains to be done, then.
And that enlightenment is also to be purchased,
because he understands only money.

It happened that a great and rich man came to Mahavir.
He was really very rich.
He could purchase anything,
even kingdoms.
Even kings borrowed money from him.

He came to Mahavir and he said:
I have been hearing so much about meditation, *dhyan,*
and during the time you have been here
you have created a craze in people.

Everybody is talking about *dhyan*.
What is this *dhyan*?
How much does it cost,
and can I purchase it?

Mahavir hesitated,
so the man said:
Don't you think about the cost at all.
You simply say, and I will pay.
There is no problem about it.

How to talk to this man?
Mahavir was at a loss as to what to say to him.
Finally Mahavir said:
You go.
In your town there is a man,
a very poor man.
He may be willing to sell his *dhyan*.
He has achieved,
and he is so poor
that he may be ready to sell it.

The man thanked Mahavir,
rushed to the poor man, knocked on his door
and said:
How much do you want for your *dhyan*?
I want to purchase your meditation.

The man started laughing.
He said:
You can purchase me, that's okay.
But how can I give you my *dhyan*?
It is a quality of my being.
It is not a commodity.

But businessmen have always been thinking
in this way.
They donate to purchase;
they create temples to purchase.
They give, but their giving is never a giving.
It is always to get something.
It is an investment.

When I say to you to be a warrior,
I mean to be a gambler,
to put everything at stake.
Then enlightenment
becomes a question of life and death –
not a commodity –
and you are ready to throw away everything for it.
And you are not thinking about the profit.

People come to me and they ask:
What will we gain out of meditation?
What is the purpose of it?
What will be the profit out of it?
If one hour is devoted to meditation
what will be the gain?

Their whole life is economy.
A warrior is not after gain.
A warrior is after a peak,
after a peak of experiencing.

What does a warrior gain when he fights in a war?
Your soldiers are not warriors any longer,
they are just servants.
Warriors are no more on this earth,
because the whole thing is being done by technology.
You drop a bomb on Hiroshima.
The dropper is not a warrior.
Any child can do that;
any madman can do that.
Really, only a madman can do it.
Dropping a bomb on Hiroshima
is not being a fighter or a warrior.

War is no more the same as it was in the past.
Now anybody can do it,
and sooner or later
only mechanical devices will do it.
A plane without a pilot can do it –
and the plane is not a warrior.
The quality is lost.

The warrior was facing,
encountering the enemy, face to face.

Just imagine two persons with drawn swords
encountering each other.
Can they think?
If they think they will miss.
Thinking stops.
When swords are drawn, thinking stops.
They cannot plan,
because if they plan,
in that moment the other will hit.
They move spontaneously; they become no-minds.
The danger is so much,
the possibility of death is so near,
that the mind cannot be allowed to function.
The minds needs time.
In emergencies, the mind cannot be allowed.

When you are sitting in your chair you can think,
but when you are facing an enemy
you cannot think.
If you pass through a street,
a dark street,
and suddenly you see a snake,
a dangerous snake sitting there,
what will you do?
Will you start thinking?
No, you will jump.
And this jump will not be out of your mind,
because the mind needs time,
and snakes don't have any time.
They don't have any mind.
The snake will strike you –
so the mind cannot be allowed.

While facing a snake you jump,
and that jump comes out of your being.
It comes before thought.
You jump first and then you think.
This is what I mean by

the quality of a warrior.
Action comes without thinking.
Action is without mind; action is total.

You can become a warrior
without going to war.
There is no need to go to war.
The whole of life is an emergency,
and everywhere there are enemies and snakes,
and ferocious wild animals ready to attack you.
The whole of life is a war.
If you are alert you will see
that the whole of life is a war,
and any moment you can die.
So the emergency is permanent.

Be alert!
Be like a warrior,
as if moving amidst the enemy.
Any moment, from anywhere,
death can jump on you.
Don't allow the mind.
And be a gambler –
only gamblers can take this jump.

The jump is so much
that those who think of profit cannot take it.
It is a risk, the greatest risk.
You may be lost, and nothing may be gained.
When you come to me you may lose everything
and you may not gain anything.

I will repeat one of Jesus' sayings:
Whosoever clings to life,
whosoever tries to preserve it,
will lose it;
and whosoever is ready to lose it
will preserve it.

This is talking in the language of a gambler:
Lose it –
this is the way to preserve it.

Die –
that is the way to reach the eternal life,
the immortal life.

When I say 'a businessman',
I say 'a calculating, cunning mind'.
Don't be cunning minds.
No child is ever a businessman,
and it is difficult to find an old man
who is not a businessman.
Every child is a warrior,
and every old man is a businessman.
How every warrior becomes a businessman
is a long story.
The whole society, education, culture, conditioning,
makes you more and more fearful, afraid.
You cannot take a risk,
and everything that is beautiful is risky.
Love is a risk.
Life is a risk.
God is a risk.

God is the greatest risk,
and through mathematics you will not reach –
only through taking the ultimate risk,
putting everything that you have at stake.
And you don't know the unknown.
The known you risk,
and the unknown you don't know.

The business mind will say:
What are you doing –
losing that which you have
for that which no one knows exists or not?
Preserve that which is in hand,
and don't long for the unknown.

The warrior mind says:
The known has been known already.
Now there is nothing in it.
It has become a burden
and to carry it is useless.

The unknown must be known now,
and I must risk the known
for the unknown.

And if you can risk, totally risk,
not preserving anything,
not playing tricks with yourself,
not withholding anything,
suddenly the unknown envelops you.
And when it comes,
you become aware that it is not only the unknown,
it is the unknowable.
It is not against the known,
it is beyond the known.

To move in that darkness,
to move in that uncharted place
without any maps and without any pathways,
to move alone into that absolute,
the quality of the warrior is needed.

Many of you still have a little of it left,
because you were once children.
You were all warriors.
You were all dreamers of the unknown.
That childhood is hidden,
but it cannot be destroyed.
It is there.
It still has its own corner in your being.
Allow it to function.
Be childlike
and you will be warriors again.

That's what I mean.
And don't feel depressed because you run a shop
and you are a businessman.
Don't feel depressed.
You can be a warrior anywhere.
To take risks is a quality of the mind,
a childlike quality –
to trust
and to move beyond that which is secure.

Eighth Talk

17th June 1974

Bhagwan,

The Zen master Mu-nan had only one successor.
His name was Shoju.

After Shoju had completed his study of Zen,
Mu-nan called him into his room and said:
I am getting old, and as far as I know
you are the only one who will carry on this teaching.
Here is a book.
It has been passed down from master to master
for seven generations,
and I have also added many points
according to my understanding.
This book is very precious,
and I am giving it to you
to represent your successorship.

Shoju replied:
Please keep the book.
I received your Zen without writing,
and I was very happy with it, thank you.

Mu-nan replied:
I know that,
but this great work
has been carried from master to master
for seven generations,
and it will be a symbol of your learning.
Here, take the book.

The two were talking in front of a fire,
and the instant Shoju felt the book in his hands,
he thrust it into the flames.

Mu-nan, who had never in his life been angry before,
shouted:
What are you doing?

And Shoju shouted back:
And what are you saying?

All books are dead,
and that is how it should be.
They cannot be alive.
All scriptures are graveyards.
They cannot be anything else.

A word, the moment it is uttered, goes wrong.
Unuttered, it is okay;
uttered, it is falsified by the very utterance.
Truth cannot be said, cannot be written,
cannot be indicated in any way.
If it can be said, you will attain to truth
just by hearing it;
if it can be written, you will attain to truth
just by reading it;
if it can be indicated, you will attain to truth
by mere indication.
This is not possible.
There is no way to transfer truth to you.
There exists no bridge.
It cannot be given, it cannot be communicated.

But people become addicted
to scriptures, books, words, theories,
because for the mind
it is easy to understand a theory,
it is easy to read a book,

it is easy to carry a tradition.
With anything dead,
the mind is always the master;
with anything alive,
the mind becomes the slave.

So the mind is always afraid of life.
It is the dead part in you.
Just as I said that hairs and nails
are dead parts of your body,
the parts that have died already
and that the body is throwing out,
so the mind is the dead part of your consciousness.
It is the part that has already become dead,
and the consciousness wants to get rid of it.

What is the mind?
It is the past, the memory,
the accumulated experience.
But the moment you have experienced the thing,
it is dead.
Experiencing is in the present;
experience is in the past.

Why are you listening to me?
Just in the moment, just here and now,
it is an experiencing,
it is an alive process,
but the moment you say: I have heard,
it has become dead,
it has become an experience.
While listening to me, the mind is not there,
you are there.
The moment the mind comes in, it says:
I have understood, I have heard, I know.

What do you mean?
You mean the mind has taken possession.
The word can be possessed by the mind –
anything dead can be possessed by the mind –
and only dead things can be possessed.

If you try to possess a live thing
there are only two ways —
either you will not be able to possess it,
or you will have to kill it first
and then you can possess it.
So wherever there is possession,
there is murdering, killing.

If you love a person,
love in itself is an experiencing,
a moment-to-moment flow, with no past being carried.
The river remains fresh.
But the mind says:
Possess this woman, possess this man,
because who knows about the future?
Possess!
She may escape, she may go to somebody else,
she may fall in love with someone else.
Possess her and block all the ways of escape,
close all the doors so she remains always yours.

The mind has entered,
and now this woman will be killed,
now this man will be murdered.
There will be a husband, there will be a wife,
but there will not be two live persons.

And this is the mischief
the mind goes on doing everywhere.
The moment you say: I love,
it has become an experience,
it is already dead.
Loving is something else.
It is a process.

Why when in love can you not say: I love?
That would be profane.
How can you say: I love?
In love, you are not,
the possessor is not,

so how can you say: I love?
In love there is no 'I'.
Love is there of course, but you are not.

While an experience is alive, experiencing,
there is no ego.
The process is there,
and you can say love is there,
but you cannot say: I love.
In that love, you have dissolved.
You have merged and melted.

Anything live, alive, is greater than you;
anything dead, and the mind can jump,
just like a cat jumps on a mouse
and catches hold of it.

Truth cannot be delivered;
there is no way to deliver it.
Once delivered it is dead,
it has already become untrue.

Lao-Tse insisted
no not saying anything about the truth
his whole life.
Whenever someone asked about truth
he would say many things,
but he would not say anything about the truth.
He would avoid it.
In the end he was forced to say something.
Disciples, lovers, said he should write
because he had known something
which was rarely known,
he had become something which was unique –
there would be no Lao-Tse again.

So he wrote a small book, *Tao Te Ching,*
but the first thing he said in it was:
Tao cannot be said.
Truth cannot be uttered.
And the moment you utter it,

it is already false.
And then he said:
Now I can write at ease.
I have declared the basic fact –
uttered, truth becomes false;
written, it has already gone wrong.

Why is the word false?
One thing –
it always belongs to the past;
another thing –
the word in itself
cannot carry the experience to you.

I say I am silent.
You hear the words.
The word 'silent' is heard,
but what do you understand?
If you have never been silent,
if you have never tasted it,
if it has never stirred your heart,
if it has never overwhelmed you, overpowered you,
how can you understand?

And if it has overpowered you,
if there has been a gap when you disappeared
and silence was there,
there will be no need for me to talk about silence.
The moment you see me, you will know;
the moment you come near me, you will feel.
The word will not be needed.
The word is needed because you don't know.
This is the problem.
Because you don't know, the word is needed.
So how can the word express?

That which you don't know,
the word cannot say to you.
The word may be heard,
you may memorize it,

you may understand the meaning
written in the dictionary –
what silence means is written in the dictionary,
and you know it already –
but that is not the meaning.

When I say I am silent,
the silence that I am here
is not written in the dictionary,
cannot be written in the dictionary,
cannot be written there.
If you are silent, you will understand,
but then there is no need to say.
If you are not silent,
whatsoever you understand will be wrong –
but then there is need to say.

I have heard a story.
Once a villager entered a big bank.
Many people were coming and going
and much business was going on.
Suddenly the villager cried,
shouted at the top of his voice:
Did somebody drop a wad of notes
with a rubber band around it?
Many people cried:
Yes, I did.
And they ran towards him.
A crowd gathered,
and everybody was claiming the money.
The villager said:
I have found the rubber band.

Whenever I say 'truth',
whenever I say 'silence',
you will only find the rubber band.
The notes will be missing.
The word will reach you,
but not with the weight of the notes.
Those notes will be left behind –

they are in my heart.
The word will reach,
but it is just a rubber band.
It may have been around the notes,
but still it is just a rubber band.

Truth is incommunicable.
But then what have masters been doing?
They seem to be involved
in an absurd activity.
Yes, that is right.
They are trying to say something
which cannot be said,
and they are indicating something
which cannot be indicated.
They are trying to communicate something
which has never been communicated
and never will be communicated.

Then what are they doing?
Their whole effort is absurd,
but still there is something in their effort –
their compassion.

Knowing well that I cannot say
that which I want to say,
the easiest course is that I should remain silent,
because if I know it cannot be said
then why bother?
You cannot understand my words,
but will you be able
to understand my silence?
So it is a trial between two evils.

It is better I remain silent.
That would be more consistent.
It cannot be said,
therefore I should remain silent.
But will you be able to understand my silence?

The word you may not be able to understand,
but you can hear it,

and some possibility is open.
Hearing it continuously,
you may become aware of something
which has not been said in the word.
Listening to me, by and by,
you may become aware of me,
not of what I am saying.
The word will help, just as a bait –
you may be caught in the net.
But if I am silent,
you will pass by my side.
You will not even become aware
that I am there,
and even that possibility will be lost.

So when masters speak,
they don't speak
to tell the truth that cannot be told.
They have a choice.
Either they can remain silent or they can talk.
With silence you will miss them completely.
With words a possibility opens,
not a certainty because everything depends on you,
but a possibility opens.

Listening continuously to a Buddha
you will someday become silent,
because just being near a Buddha
is being near a pool of silence, an energy,
a tremendous energy which has become silent.

This is what Indians call *satsang* –
to be near the truth.
It is not a question of communication.
Just to be near the truth can be infectious –
just as you come near a river
and the breeze becomes cooler.
You may not see the river;
it may still be far away,
but the breeze carries the message

and you feel a coolness coming.
When you come near a Buddha
the words are carrying just such a coolness –
Buddha is somewhere near.

You may start groping for him;
you may be lost in his words.
Then you are lost in the forest
and the river is missed.
But if you are alert, intelligent,
then, by and by,
you will feel from where this wind is blowing,
from where these words are coming.
And these words carry a silence around them.
It may be just a rubber band,
but that rubber band
has been in deep contact with the notes.
It carries something, something of the sound
from where this breeze is coming.
If you can follow intelligently
sooner or later you will reach the source.

The words of a Buddha
may not be able to communicate the truth,
but they can communicate the music,
the music that exists in one who is enlightened.
They carry the melody, something of the source,
a tiny part, a very tiny part,
but something of the source.

It should be so,
because when a word comes out of a Buddha
it carries something of the Buddha.
It has to be so.
The word has been vibrating in his being,
it has been in touch with Buddha's heartbeat,
it has passed through the Buddha's silence,
it has been in the womb, the womb of the Buddha.
It carries the scent, the fragrance.
It is a very far off cry, but still . . .

You may be lost in the words –
then you miss the Buddha –
but if you are aware
that the word cannot carry the truth,
then you will always
put aside the word and follow the perfume,
put aside the word and follow the music,
put aside the word and follow the presence.

If I suddenly say:
Hey,
you look at me.
The word is meaningless, but the look . . .
Suddenly you become aware of me.
That awareness has to be followed,
so then, words can become a help.
They may not tell the truth
but they can become a help,
a step towards the truth.

This story is beautiful.
A master is on his dying bed,
and soon he has to leave this earth
and its vehicle,
the body,
and he would like to have a successor
who can carry the flame that he has kindled,
one who will be able to continue the work
that he has started.

He chooses a disciple, calls him near,
and says to him:
You are the most capable of those around me
and you are going to be my successor.
You will have to continue this work.
For seven generations a book has been passed
from the master to the disciple
who is going to be the successor.
I received this book from my master
and I give it to you.

It is very precious, a unique treasury.
Seven enlightened persons
have noted down their experiences of truth in it,
and I have also added
a few of my own understandings.
Preserve it.
Don't lose it; don't let it be lost.

The disciple said:
But I have achieved the experience
without any book,
and I am happy and blissful.
I am not even a little bit dissatisfied,
so why add this burden to me,
why give an unnecessary responsibility to me?
I have already experienced the truth
and the book was not needed.
It is unnecessary.

The master still insisted:
Much that is valuable is written in it.
It is no ordinary book,
it is the book, the Bible,
so don't be sacrilegious.
Pay respect to this book,
keep it and hand it over to your successor.
By giving this book to you,
I certify this book is a representation
that you are my successor.

The master gave the book to the disciple.
It must have been a cold night
because the fire was burning.
In one hand the disciple received the book,
and in the same instant
he thrust it into the fire.

The master, who had never been angry in his life,
shouted:
What are you doing?
And the disciple shouted,

even louder than the master:
What are you saying?

This is beautiful.
The master must have died peacefully.
This was the right man.
The book had to be thrust into the fire
or the disciple would have missed.
If he had kept the book, he would have missed,
and then he would not have been the successor.

You keep the book
only when the thing has not happened to you.
Who is bothered about words
when the truth is with you?
Who is bothered about a book
when the real thing has happened within?
Who is bothered about explanations
when the experience is there?
Explanations are precious
because the experience is lacking;
theories are significant
because there is no knowledge.
When you know, you can throw theories.
They are rubber bands.
And when the notes are with you,
you can throw the rubber band.
Preserving a rubber band shows foolishness.

This book was not precious –
no book is precious –
and the master was playing a game,
the same that his master must have played with him.
Nobody knows what was written in the book,
but I tell you nothing was written in it.
It was empty.
Had the disciple preserved it,
when the master died he would have opened it,
and then he would have cried.
Nothing was written in the book.

It was just a game, an old game.
Every master
tries to test the experience of a disciple,
whether he knows.
And if he knows,
he will not be addicted to the book.
Why?
There is no point in it.
That is why the disciple said:
What are you saying?
To preserve the book
when I have achieved without it,
when I have already achieved?
What are you saying?

The master provoked a situation,
and in that situation
the disciple proved his mettle.
He proved that he knew.
Even a slight inclination to preserve
and he would have missed,
he would not have been the successor.
He didn't even look in the book
to see what was there.
He was not even curious,
because only ignorance is curious.
If you know, you know.

What is curiosity?
What would have happened to you?
The first thing the mind would have said was:
At least look in it; see what is there.
But that gesture would have been enough
to prove that you had not achieved.

Curiosity means ignorance.
Wisdom is not curious.
Curiosity asks questions;
wisdom has no questions to ask.

What would you have done?
The first thing that comes to the mind:
At least see what is there.
If my master insists
that this precious book has to be preserved,
handed down from one generation to another
with seven enlightened persons having written in it,
and with my own master
having added his own understanding to it,
at least have a look
before you throw it in the fire.

But I tell you – if he had looked,
he would have been thrown out of the house
with the book:
Get out, and never come back again!

He acted out of a deep understanding.
How can the master who knows
insist that the book is precious?
There must be some game.
The master had never been angry,
never in his life,
and suddenly he was angry and said:
What are you doing?
He created the whole situation.

In the anger the disciple may have yielded,
may have said:
I have done something wrong, forgive me.
This is how the mind functions.
The mind might have come in and thought:
I have done something wrong.
The master may not appoint me as successor now.
If my master is so angry,
it means I have done something wrong,
and I may miss being the successor.
I was going to be the chief,
I was going to be the master of the monastery
and millions would have followed me.

Thousands would have been my disciples,
and now I have done something wrong.
A man who has never been angry
is angry, shouting.

If you had been there,
you would have touched the feet of the master
and said:
Forgive me, but appoint me.
But the disciple said:
And what are you saying?
If the master can play at anger
the disciple can also play.
But this can happen only when both know,

He answered in the right coin.
He answered correctly
and the master was satisfied:
This is the man.
He became the successor.
He was the successor.

But this has been done by every religion.
They preserve books and do nothing else.
Christians preserve their Bible,
Mohammedans preserve their Koran,
Hindus preserve their Gita,
and they have missed.
They are not the successors.

Mohammedans do not belong to Mohammed.
They cannot belong.
The Koran must be in the fire
before they can belong.
Christians don't know anything about Christ
because they preserve the Bible,
and Hindus have no understanding of Krishna
because of the Gita.
They go on carrying the burden.
All the Vedas, and all the Bibles,

and all the Korans
are for those who don't understand.
They carry the burden
and the burden becomes so much
that they are crushed under it.
They are not freed through it.
They become slaves to it.

A religious person is always beyond the book;
a religious consciousness
is never addicted to words and the verbal.
The whole thing is childish.

A religious man
is in search of authentic experience,
not borrowed words, not experiences of others.
Unless he knows,
Buddhas may have existed, but they are useless;
unless he knows, there is no truth
because truth can only be his experience.
Only then is it there.

The whole world may say there is light
and there is a rainbow in the sky,
and the sun is rising,
but if my eyes are closed,
what does it mean to me?
The rainbow, the colours, the sunrise,
the whole thing is non-existential to me.
My eyes are closed; I am blind.
And if I listen to them too much,
and if I start believing in them too much,
and if I borrow their words
and I also start talking
about the rainbow that I have not seen,
about colours which I cannot see,
about the sunrise which is not my experience,
I may be lost in the forest of words.

It is better to say:
I am blind.

I don't know any colour and I don't know any light,
and unless my eyes open, there is no sun
and there can be no sunrise.

Insist, so that you can work upon your eyes.
Don't carry the books.
They talk about rainbows seen by others;
they talk about sunrises experienced by others.
Don't carry the borrowed God
when you can encounter him directly, immediately.
Why create barriers of books between you and him?
Burn the books!
That is the message.
Throw them in the fire.

That doesn't mean
go and throw your Gita in the fire.
That will not be of much help,
because if a Gita cannot help towards truth,
how can burning a Gita be helpful?
That is not the point.
You can throw away all the books
and you can remain addicted to theories, doctrines.
When I say burn the books,
I say:
Burn the mind,
drop the mind,
don't be verbal.
Seek authentic experience.

But your inquiry may have arisen out of the books.
That is the problem –
your questions may have arisen out of books.
If your questioning is itself bookish,
your whole inquiry has started in a wrong direction.
People come to me and ask:
What is God?
And I ask them:
Did this question come out of your own life
or have you read some book which talks about God

and so you have become curious?

If your curiosity has arisen out of learning,
it is useless.
It is not your question.
And if the question is not yours,
no answer can be of any help.
When the basic thing is borrowed,
when even the question is borrowed,
you will go on borrowing the answers.
Seek your authentic question.
What is your question?

I have heard about a philosopher
who entered a London car-showroom.
He looked around
and became fascinated with a beautiful car,
a streamlined sports car.
The salesman became alert
because he was looking so interested.
He came nearer and asked:
Are you interested in this car?
The man said:
Yes, I am interested.
Is it fast?
The salesman said:
Fast?
You cannot find a faster car than this.
If you get in it right now,
by tomorrow morning at three o'clock,
you will be in Aberdeen.
Are you really interested in buying it?
The philosopher said:
I will think about it.
The next day he came and said:
No, I don't want to purchase that car.
The whole night I couldn't sleep.
I remained awake thinking and thinking and thinking,
and I could not find any reason

why I should like to be in Aberdeen
at three o'clock in the morning.

Whenever you read a book, ask, inquire,
for what reason you would like to be in Aberdeen
at three o'clock in the morning.

You read a book.
You read something about God,
you read something about *moksha,*
you read something about the soul,
you read something about bliss –
you become fascinated.
Words of those who know are really fascinating.
But you forget completely for what reason
you would like to encounter God.
Just by reading a book, just by reading a man –
for example, reading Jesus –
you will become fascinated,
because this man is drunk with God,
his every word is alcoholic.
If you hear him, you will feel drunk.

But close the Bible,
escape from this Jesus,
brood over whether this is your inquiry
or whether this man has sold his inquiry to you.
With another's inquiry your own search becomes false.

The first thing to remember is –
your question must be yours.
Then the second thing to remember is –
the answer must be yours.
Books supply both.
That's why I said:
Burn the books and be authentic.
Come out of the jungle of words
and feel what you want, what your desire is,
and follow it wheresoever it leads.
Sooner or later you will come to the Divine.
It may take a little longer,

but the search will be real.

If all books were burnt,
the world would be more religious.
There are so many books and ready-made answers
that everybody knows the question, the answer.
It has become a game; it is not your life.

The world should be freed of books,
should be freed of all ideals,
should be freed of all borrowed inquiries.
Every man should start feeling
his own heartbeat, his own pulse –
where it leads, what it desires,
what his question is.
If you can find your question,
the answer is waiting just nearby.
It may be that in finding the question
you have already found the answer,
because the answer lies in authenticity.
If the question is authentic,
if you have become authentic in questioning,
fifty percent of the problem is already solved.
Just a little more effort, going a little deeper,
and the question always hides the answer behind it.

Questioning is just one aspect of the coin.
The other aspect is the answer.
Just behind questioning,
the answer is lying, waiting for you.
But if you have not come to your question,
how can you come to your answer?
And only the answer that is yours will free you,
will make you free.

Jesus says truth liberates.
Yes, truth liberates,
but never borrowed truth.
Jesus' truth will not liberate you.
But Christians believe

that Jesus' truth will liberate them.
Not only that,
they think that just by Jesus' crucifixion
humanity is already liberated.

This is being blind, absolutely blind.
Nothing is liberated; nobody is liberated.
Salvation has not happened.
Jesus was crucified, that's okay,
but through Jesus' crucifixion,
Jesus was liberated, not you.
The whole thing seems to be a trick.
Jesus died on the cross
and humanity, particularly Christianity,
is liberated;
one who is a Christian is already liberated.

This is how the mind thinks.
It goes on throwing responsibility
onto somebody else.
If you are a sinner,
you are a sinner because Adam sinned
and was thrown out of heaven.
And now you are liberated

because Jesus has again entered the kingdom of God.
So Adam and Jesus are the authentic persons.
You are just shadows.
Adam sins, and you have become a sinner.
So who are you?
You are a shadow.
Adam is thrown out of heaven,
therefore you are thrown out.
This can happen only to a shadow,
not to a real person.
If I am thrown out of this house,
only my shadow will be thrown with me,
nothing else.
And if I enter the kingdom of God,
only my shadow will enter with me.

You cannot enter.

Jesus solved everything.
He entered the kingdom of God,
and all humanity entered with him.
Nobody has entered,
nobody can enter in such an easy way.
You have to pay the cost,
you have to carry your own cross,
you have to be crucified through suffering –
your suffering, remember.
Neither Jesus' suffering, nor anybody else's
will open the doors.
They are closed,
and you cannot enter just following Jesus.
Nobody can enter that way.
The doors open for the individual,
because the individual is the authentic reality.

The disciple said:
I have already entered, master,
so why are you giving this map to me?
A map is needed for one who is lost
but I have reached the goal.
So why this map?
And the master said:
The map is very precious.
All the paths are indicated on it.

Would the disciple hesitate for a single moment?
The master's penetrating eyes
were searching his heart
to see if he would hesitate,
if he would say:
Okay, maybe the master is right
and the map is precious.

But what does a man need a map for
when he has reached the goal?
So he threw the book in the fire.
He threw away the map.

I have heard:
A man, driving his car on a lonely road,
suspected that he had missed the path,
suspected that he was moving in a wrong direction.
He saw a beggar walking,
so he stopped the car and asked the beggar:
Does this road lead to Delhi?
The beggar said:
I don't know.
So the man asked:
Does this road lead to Agra?
The beggar said:
I don't know.
The man, who was already irritated,
became more irritated,
and said to the beggar in anger:
So you don't know much.
The beggar laughed and said:
But I am not lost.

So the question is not of knowledge.
The question is whether you are lost or not.
The beggar said:
But I am not lost.
Whether I know or not is not the point.

When you are lost a map is needed,
knowledge is needed, a book is needed.
When you are not lost,
what is the point of carrying a book, a map?
And an enlightened person is at the goal everywhere.
Wherever he is, is the goal.
Once you become aware that you are the goal,
you cannot be lost.

The beggar is not lost.
Why?
Because he is not going to Delhi,
he is not going to Agra,
he is not going anywhere.

Wherever he reaches, that is the goal.
He is not lost
because he is not moving in any direction;
he is not lost
because there is no desired goal.

This disciple threw away the map
because there is no goal.
He is the goal now.
Wherever he is,
he is at peace, at home.
There is no desire and no motivation.
The future has disappeared.
This moment is enough.

Throw away all the maps
because you are the goal.
Maps can help if the goal is somewhere else;
maps cannot help if you are the goal.
They may even distract you,
because when you look at a map
you cannot look at yourself.
Books cannot help,
because you are the truth
and there is no book in which you are written.
The book is you, no other book.
Here you are, written in this book, which is you.

You have to be deciphered,
and if you are wrong,
all books that you carry will go wrong.
All maps that you carry will be wrong
and will indicate wrongly,
because who will read those books
and who will follow the instructions
indicated in the map?

I have heard:
A man was driving
and his wife was looking at the map.

Suddenly the wife cried out in panic and said:
We are lost, because this map is upside down.
The map is upside down.
We are lost!

The map can be put right side up;
no map is upside down by itself.
But the wife must have been upside down.
If you are upside down,
all the books you read will turn upside down.
If you are disturbed,
it will be reflected in your Koran, in your Bible,
in your Gita;
if you are mad,
your interpretations of the Vedas will be mad;
if you are afraid
you will meet fear wherever you go.
Whatsoever you do,
your doing will come out of you.
Your interpretations will come out of you
and you will be wrong.

So a master is not interested
in giving you a right book.
There are none.
No right book exists,
only right people and wrong people,
right persons and wrong persons.
A real master
is interested in putting you right side up.
A master is interested in changing you, the person.
He is not interested in giving you a book.

That's why the disciple said:
What are you saying?
Such a nonsensical thing you have never said before.
You have gone mad saying:
Keep, preserve the book,
it is precious.

No book is precious.
Only the person is precious.
But when you don't know your value
you think the book is precious.
When you don't know the precious value
of your being,
then every type of theory becomes valuable.
Words are valuable
because you have not known
the value of the being.

Anything more?

Bhagwan,

There will be a precious value to this book
when it comes out,
because it can tell people
that there is a Buddha available now,
and that he has methods
suitable to the time and to us.

But one of the questions which has arisen here
and will certainly arise in the West is:
How do I know I need a master?

Yes,
this book is going to be very precious.
Keep, preserve it.
Seven generations of masters have given it to me
and I have given it to you.

Now it depends on what you do.
I have added my understanding to it,
but as far as I'm concerned,
I am giving you this book
just to throw in the fire.
The day you can throw it in the fire
will be the day you have understood it.
If you go on preserving it, you have missed.

But the book is needed,
because if it is not there
what will you throw in the fire?
It is needed.
Try to preserve it.
It is very precious.
And when you understand,
you will throw it in the fire.

So I am not saying
give only the Koran to the fire,
give my books to the fire also,
because they can be more dangerous
than the Koran and Gita and Bible
which have become out of date in a sense.

You are very, very far away from Mohammed,
even further away from Krishna.
Their voices have become very, very distant,
dim things.
My voice is nearer to you.
It is immediate; it is direct.
It may become a greater prison for you,
because it is more alive right now.
It can capture you;
it can become more of a burden.
If a living master can free you,
a living master can become more of a prison also.
It depends.

There are directions in the book.
It is a map,

a map into the world of consciousness,
a map of how to get roots into the earth,
a map of how to get wings into the sky.

But trees don't need it.
If I tell them how to get roots into the earth,
they will say:
Don't disturb us.
We have already got roots into the earth.
If I tell them how to get wings into the sky,
they will say:
Don't disturb the silence.
We are always standing in the sky,
swaying in the sky.
And if I tell them to preserve this book,
they will laugh;
and if they can find a fire,
they will throw the book in it.

So what am I saying?
I am saying to you:
Get roots and throw away the maps;
get wings and throw away the maps.
Don't get fixed on what I say;
don't be obsessed with what I say.
Put the words aside and look at me.
And what I hope is that one day, if I say:
Preserve this book,
you will be able to shout at me and say:
What are you saying?
Have you gone mad?!

You can say that
without reaching the point where it becomes meaningful –
but you cannot deceive me.
You can throw the book into the fire
without throwing the attachment.
Then you are imitating.
Imitation won't help.

Buddhas have existed on the earth;

disciples have existed.
Everything has happened that can happen
and everything is written.
You may decide you can imitate,
but imitation won't help.

It happened once that a man came to a Zen master.
He had read all the scriptures, memorized them,
and had become a great philosopher
because he was very efficient
at using words, logic.
And this Zen master was just a villager,
just like the beggar who said: I am not lost.
He had never read the Lotus Sutra,
one of the greatest Buddhist scriptures,
worth preserving, always keeping near.
Just as there are bedside books,
so the Lotus Sutra is a heartside book.
It is concerned with the heart.
The lotus is the symbol for the heart.
Fully bloomed, in full bloom, it is the heart.
And Buddhists think there is nothing comparable
to the Lotus Sutra.

This man had memorized the whole Lotus Sutra.
He could repeat it from anywhere.
Ask any question and immediately
he would answer —
like a computer, very efficiently.
So he asked the Zen master:
Have you read the Lotus Sutra?
The Zen master said:
Lotus Sutra?
Never heard of it.
The man, the pundit, the scholar, said:
Never heard of it?
And people think you are enlightened.
The Zen master said:
People must be wrong.
I am an ignorant man.

How can I be enlightened?

The scholar was at ease now, so he said:
Now I will repeat the Lotus Sutra.
Can you read?
The monk said:
I can't read.
So he said:
Okay, then listen to me and I will explain
anything you want to ask.
He had come to seek a master
but now he had become a master.
The ego never wants to be a disciple,
it is always in search of being a master.
How the Buddhas must have laughed at the situation.

The master became the disciple,
and the disciple became the master and said:
Listen.
The master started listening.
The disciple said:
Okay.
He began to repeat the Lotus Sutra.

In the Lotus Sutra,
it is said everything is emptiness –
this world is empty, hell is empty,
heaven is empty, God is empty,
everything is emptiness.
Emptiness is the nature of all things,
nothingness,
so be attuned to nothingness and you will achieve.

Suddenly the master jumped
and hit the pundit on the head.
The pundit became mad.
He started shouting and said:
Not only are you not enlightened,
not only are you ignorant,
you seem to be neurotic also.
What are you doing?

The master sat again and said:
If everything is nothingness,
From where does this anger come?
The world is emptiness,
heaven is emptiness, hell is emptiness,
the nature of things is nothingness.
From where does this anger come?

The pundit was puzzled.
He said:
It is not written in the Lotus Sutra.
You ask foolish questions.
It is not written in the Lotus Sutra.
The whole Sutra I have memorized,
and this is no way of asking a question.
Hitting me is no way of asking a question.

But this is the only way.
Theories are not of much help.
You can say that everything is nothingness,
but just a little hit,
and anger arises out of nothingness.
A woman passes and sex arises out of nothingness;
you look at a beautiful house,
and the desire to possess arises out of nothingness.
When Buddha said everything is nothingness,
he was saying:
If you can understand this, nothing will arise.
How can anything arise out of nothingness?
Nothingness is a meditation, not a theory.
It is a falling into the abyss.
Then anger cannot arise and sex cannot arise.
How can they?

There are two types of persons –
one, those who are in search of theories,
and please don't be that type,
because that is the most stupid type;
and the other type is the wise type,
those in search of experience, not of theories.

This book and whatsoever I say
can become a theory for you.
Then you miss.
It can become a thirst, a hunger,
a deep urge to experience.
Then you have got the point,
but don't be addicted to the words.
Don't carry the container, remember the content.
When the disciple threw the book into the fire,
he was throwing away the container.
The content was preserved in his heart.
And the master was happy
that this man had understood.

The container has to be thrown away
and the content preserved.
Whatsoever I say, throw it in the fire.
But whatsoever happens to you in my presence,
that is the content.
Preserve it, it is precious.
But there is no need to preserve it.
If it happens, you will preserve it.
If you know, it is preserved,
and then there is no way to throw it in the fire.
Only books can be thrown in the fire,
truth cannot.

That's why the disciple shouted:
What are you saying?
Can a precious thing be thrown into the fire?
Can a precious thing be burned in the fire?
If the fire can burn your book,
what type of preciousness is it?
What type of truth is this?
If the fire can burn the truth,
it is not worth preserving.

That which cannot be burned,
that which cannot be dead,
even through fire it becomes more alive, more pure –

that is the truth.
That's why I said throw the Bible into the fire.
Not that I am against the Bible,
I am against the container.
The content cannot be thrown.

The container is the Lotus Sutra.
The content is in your lotus,
and that is your heart.

Anything more?

Bhagwan,

A lot of people say
they can't really let themselves go in meditation
because of the physical pain,
because of bumping into each other
and falling down.
They feel this may be some sort of excuse
for not really letting go.

Could you talk to us about this physical aspect?

A child can fall but he will not feel hurt.
A drunkard, walking in the street, falls,
but his body is preserved,
his bones are not fractured.
What is happening?
The real thing is not the other bumping into you,
the real thing is your resistance.
You are afraid the other may bump into you,

so you are resisting the whole time.
Somebody may not bump into you,
but you are afraid.
Fear closes you.
You become stiff.
And if somebody then bumps into you,
that stiffness is hurt, not you.
But you feel that you are hurt,
and then your mind says:
You were right to be afraid from the very beginning,
and it was good to be alert
so that nobody would bump into you.

The mind is a vicious circle.
It gives you an idea,
and because of that idea certain things happen.
Then that idea becomes more fixed.
You become more afraid,
and then you are constantly in fear.
How will you do meditation?

In Japan they have a science of wrestling.
They call it judo or ju-jitsu,
and the whole science consists
of a very meditative thing –
the judo wrestler learns how not to resist.
When somebody attacks you,
you have to absorb his energy, not resist,
as if he is giving energy to you.
Absorb his energy; don't resist.
He is not the enemy,
he is the friend coming to you;
and when he hits you with his hand or his fist
much energy is released.
Soon he will be exhausted,
so absorb the energy that is released from his fist.
When he is exhausted,
just by absorbing his energy you will feel stronger,
stronger than ever.

But you resist, you shrink,
you become stiff so that you may not be hurt.
Then his energy and your energy clash,
and in that clash, pain happens.
It is you.

In meditation, remember this –
if somebody bumps into you, absorb his energy.
And here is a meditative person bumping into you.
You are lucky.
He is releasing beautiful energy.
A meditative energy is coming out of him.
Absorb it.
Feel happy, feel thankful,
and start jumping again.
Don't be stiff, don't resist,
because he was sharing his energy with you,
unknowingly.
Share it, and soon you will come to know
a different quality, that of non-resistance.
The whole body and mind
then behaves in a different way.
You know a secret.

You fall on the ground suddenly.
Fall as if the ground, the earth, is your mother.
Make it a rest, not a clash.
Fall down but don't be stiff.
If you are stiff you may get a fracture.
The fracture will happen because you were stiff
and there was a fight between you and the earth.
And the earth is, of course, greater than you,
so you will be a loser.
Fall down just like a drunkard.
You see them falling every day on the street,
but by the morning they are back, completely okay.
Every night they fall down,
and their bones are never fractured.
These drunkards know a certain secret
that you don't know.

What do they know?
They fall without any consciousness on their part,
without any ego there.
They just fall.
There is nobody to fight with the earth.
The earth absorbs them
and they absorb the earth.

Be a drunkard.
Fall without the ego.
Enjoy the fall,
and feel friendly, intimate, with the earth.
Soon you will be back on your feet
with more energy than ever.
And once you know the knack
there will be no disturbance.

You are hurt because you are in a fight,
a continuous fight;
you are hurt because you are always resisting.
Consciously, unconsciously,
you are always ready to resist.
And when so many people are doing meditation,
you become afraid that somebody may hit you.
But if there is this fear,
how will you meditate?

Rather than being in fear, be in love.
With so many persons meditating,
much divine energy is released.
This is a celebration, so why be in fear?
Be in love.
Enjoy this group consciousness,
so many people dancing.
Become part, lose your ego,
be one with this collective force and energy.

It will be difficult in the beginning
because many lives have been lived
with a fixed attitude of resistance.

But someday you will become aware;
someday a gap will be cleared and you will see.
One experience will do.
If you someday fall on the earth,
and there is no hurt and you feel beautiful,
you have come to know a secret,
you have stumbled upon the key.
Now this key can be used on many locks.
It is a master key.

Whenever someone comes to fight you, absorb him;
when someone insults you, absorb him, and see –
his insult becomes a flower.
He is releasing energy.
When someone insults you,
he is giving away energy.
He is foolish, stupid,
so you absorb his energy, thank him,
and go back and see what happens.
When someone is ready to fight,
simply allow him to hit you.
Be as if you are not there
and he is fighting an emptiness.
Allow him.
Don't resist and you will come to know.
There is no other way.
Just listening to me will not do.
This is an art; it is not a science.
Science can be explained; art has to be experienced.

It is just like swimming.
If you tell a non-swimmer:
There is nothing to it.
You just take a jump
and start throwing your arms around,
he will say:
What are you saying?
This will be suicide.

How can you explain to a non-swimmer

that swimming is beautiful,
the most beautiful experience
of any that the body can give to you?
It is such a flowing experience,
such a oneness with the river.
The whole body, every fibre of it, every cell,
is alive.
The water is life,
because all life arises out of the water.
Water is vital.
In your body you are eighty-five percent water,
so eighty-five percent water, liquid,
is meeting with a big river, or the ocean.
You have come to the original source of vitality.

But you cannot explain to anyone
who is a non-swimmer.
It is not a science.
You have to take him step by step –
in the beginning,
shallow water so he becomes confident,
then by and by, deeper and deeper water.
In the beginning he will be awkward,
he will be afraid,
he will be fighting with the river,
afraid that it might drown him.

He will feel the river as being antagonistic,
but soon he will realize
that the river is not antagonistic,
that it enjoys him swimming there,
that it feels happy
that one of its parts has come back.
It is a celebrating moment for the river.
A river with no one swimming in it is sad,
but where many people dance and swim and enjoy,
the river is happy.

Soon he will feel that the river is helping him,
that he is unnecessarily fighting,

and by and by,
he will drop his movements and activity.
When a swimmer becomes perfect,
he simply floats on the river.
No activity is needed; the river does everything
and the swimmer simply floats on the river.

In old yoga traditions
there is a particular meditation –
just float on the river and feel one with it.
Don't make any movement, don't move the body,
let the river do the work.
And if the river is doing the work
and you are simply floating, non-doing,
you will have the feeling of the whole existence.
This is how existence floats.
You are unnecessarily fighting.

In meditation
you are entering a river of consciousness.
So many people around you
creates a tremendous force, a stream.
Enter into it like a swimmer,
not fighting, just floating,
and see what happens.
It is an art.

I cannot tell you.
I can just indicate,
and you have to experience.
You have to wait
until the experience happens to you,
a single moment of experience
that nobody is against you,
nobody is going to harm you.
The existence is whole, there will be no hurt.
And I say:
Even if your bone is broken,
there will be no pain, there will be no hurt.
If you fall down and you die,

even then there will be no pain.
If you are just falling back to mother earth
there will be no pain.
You are simply absorbed.

And who knows?
In meditation, just someone bumping into you
may become your first glimpse of an enlightenment,
because it is a shock –
a sudden awareness comes to you.
Who knows?
Just falling on the ground
and breaking a bone,
may become your first satori,
your first enlightenment.
Nobody knows.
Life is mysterious.
Enlightenment has happened in such different ways.
Nobody knows.

Do it in love.
Feel at home and allow things.
If somebody bumps into you, let him bump.
And let him pass through you.
Don't be a wall; don't come in his way.
Allow him to pass.
Be porous.

Ninth Talk

18th June 1974

Bhagwan,

Nansen found two groups of monks
squabbling over the ownership of a cat.

Nansen went to the kitchen
and brought back a chopper.
He picked up the cat and said to the monks:
If any of you can say a good word,
you can save the cat.

Not a word was said,
so Nansen cut the cat in two
and gave half to each group.

When Joshu returned that evening,
Nansen told him what had happened.
Joshu said nothing.
He just put his sandals on his head
and walked out.

Nansen said:
If you had been there,
you could have saved the cat.

Nothing is saved by the mind,
by thinking, by logic,
and if you try to save by logic
you will lose.
Life can be saved only through an irrational jump,
through something that is not intellectual,
but total.

But the whole story seems to be too cruel.
Nansen's disciples were struggling over a cat.
Nansen had a big monastery,
and the monastery had two wings.
This cat was moving from one wing to another,
and both wings claimed that the cat belonged to them.
And the cat was a beautiful one.

The first thing to be understood is
a real *sannyasi* cannot claim any ownership.
A *sannyasi* means one who has left all possessions,
or all possessiveness,
which is deeper and more basic.
You can leave possessions,
that is easy.
But to leave possessiveness is difficult,
because it goes deeper in the mind.
You can leave the world,
but the mind goes on clinging to it.

These monks, Nansen's disciples,
had left the world behind –
their homes, their wives, their children –
but now they were fighting
over the ownership of a cat.

This is how the mind works.
You leave one thing
and the mind claims another.
But the basic thing remains the same,
and it makes no difference
if the object of ownership changes.
It makes no difference.
The difference, the revolution, the real change,
comes only when the subjectivity changes,
when the owner changes.

This is the first thing to be understood.
Monks claiming ownership of a cat looks foolish,
but this is how monks have been acting
all over the world.
They leave their houses,
then they claim ownership of the temple,
of the church.
They leave everything,
but they can't leave their minds,
and the mind creates new worlds for them,
continuously.
So it is not a question of possessing a kingdom.
Even a cat will do.

And wherever possession comes in,
fighting, violence and aggression
are bound to be there.
Whenever you possess, you are fighting,
because that which you possess
belongs to the whole.
You cannot possess anything;
you can use it, that's all.
How can we possess the sky,

and how can we possess the earth?
But we possess.
And that possession
creates all types of conflict, struggle,
wars, violence and so on.

Man has been fighting and fighting and fighting
continuously.
Historians say
that within the last three thousand years
there have been wars almost continuously
somewhere or other on the earth.
In three thousand years,
we have fought at least fourteen thousand wars.

Why so much fighting?
It is because of possession.
If you possess,
you have started a war with the whole.

Buddha, Mahavir or Jesus, all said:
If you possess, you can't enter the kingdom of God.
Jesus said:
It is easier
for a camel to pass through the eye of a needle,
than for a rich man to enter the kingdom of heaven.

It is impossible,
because when you possess
you are constantly fighting with God.
When you claim ownership,
from whom are you claiming ownership?
The whole belongs to the whole.
The part cannot claim the whole.
The part cannot even claim the part.
Every claim is aggression.
So those who possess
cannot be in deep contact with the Divine.

Non-possessiveness doesn't mean
you should not live in a house.

Live in a house,
but be thankful to the whole, to the Divine.
Use it, but don't possess it.
If you can use things without being possessive,
you have become a *sannyasi.*

These followers of Nansen have left the world,
but their minds have followed them like shadows.
Now they claim ownership of a cat.
The whole thing is foolish.

But the mind is foolish.
The mind always goes on searching
for excuses to fight.
If you have a mind,
you have a potential fighter within you
who is always in search of a fight with somebody.
Why is the mind always in search of a fight?
By fighting, ego is accumulated, becomes stronger.
Through fighting your ego grows;
if you don't fight, ego disappears.

Mahavir insisted
and Buddha insisted on non-violence.
The basic reason for not fighting is
once you stop fighting, the ego cannot exist.
Ego exists in fight.
It is a consequence of fight.
The more you fight, the more ego exists.

If you alone remained on the earth,
nobody to fight with,
would you have an ego?
You would not have an ego.
The other is needed to create it;
the other is a must.
Ego is a relationship.
It is not in you.
Remember, the ego is not in you.
It is not located within you.

It is always located within you and the other –
somewhere in between, where fight exists.

There are two types of relationship.
One is of fight, fear, hatred.
This creates ego.
The other is of love, compassion, sympathy.
These are the two types of relationship.

Wherever love is, fight ceases, ego drops.
This is why you cannot love.
It is difficult,
because to love means to drop the ego,
to drop yourself.
Love means not to be.

So look at the strange phenomenon –
lovers go on fighting.
How can lovers fight?
If there is love, fight should drop
and the ego will disappear.
Your whole being thirsts for love;
your whole mind thirsts for ego.
So you make a compromise –
you love and you fight.
The lover becomes an intimate enemy,
but the enmity remains.

All lovers go on fighting and go on loving.
They have made a compromise.
In some moments they are loving.
Then they drop the ego.
But the mind feels uneasy,
and again the mind starts fighting.
So in the morning they fight,
in the evening they make love,
and the next morning they fight again.
Then a rhythm of fight and love is created.

True love means the fight has disappeared,
the two have become one.

Their bodies exist separately
but their being has mingled.
The boundaries are lost; there is no division.
There is no 'I' and no 'thou'.
No one exists.

These monks of Nansen had left everything,
but the mind was there.
It wanted to possess.
It wanted to create a fight.
It wanted to be egoistic.
A cat became just an excuse.

Nansen called all the monks, all the disciples,
caught hold of the cat, and he said:
Say something which can save this cat.

What did he mean when he said:
Say something which can save this cat?
He meant: Say something Zen-like,
say something meditative,
say something of the other world,
say something of ecstasy,
say something which doesn't belong to the mind.
This cat can be saved if you say something
which comes from no-mind,
which comes from your inner silence.

He demanded the impossible.
If there had been inner silence,
these monks would not have been claiming possession;
if there had been inner silence,
it would have been impossible for them to fight.

The monks were at a loss.
They knew if they said something
it would come from the mind
and the cat would be killed.
So they remained silent.
But that silence was not real silence,
otherwise the cat would have been saved.

They remained silent not because they were silent.
They remained silent
because they couldn't find anything to say
which came from no-mind,
which came from an inner source,
from the very being, from the centre.
They remained silent as a strategy.
It was tactics:
It is better to remain silent,
because the master may be deceived
that this silence is our response –
this is what they were saying.
But you cannot deceive a master.
And if you can deceive a master,
then that master is not a master at all.

Their silence was false.
Inside there was turmoil,
inside there was continuous chattering.
They were thinking and thinking,
in search of one answer
so that this cat might be saved.
They were very troubled inside.
The whole mind was functioning fast.
The master must have looked at them.
Their minds were not inactive;
they were not inactive.
There was no meditation;
there was no silence.
Their silence was just a false facade.

You can sit silently without being silent,
and you can talk and be silent.
You can walk and be inactive,
and you can sit statue-like and be active.
The mind is complex.
You can walk, run, move,
and inside, deep at the centre, nothing happens,
you are inactive.

I am talking to you and I am silent.
You are not talking to me and you are not silent.
The mind continues.
The inner chattering goes on and on and on.
The mind is a monkey.
It cannot sit silently.

Darwin discovered that man comes from the monkeys,
but in the East meditators have always been aware
that whether man comes from monkeys or not,
the mind definitely comes from monkeys.
It is monkeyish –
jumping, chattering, doing something or other,
never silent.

What Nansen said to his disciples was:
If you stop behaving like monkeys,
this cat can be saved.

But they couldn't help it.
You cannot help it.
If the mind is there what can you do?
If you try to hold it still, it becomes more active;
if you force it to be silent, it talks more;
if you suppress it, it rebels.
You cannot suppress it, you cannot persuade it.
You cannot do anything about it,
because the moment you do something,
it is the mind which is doing.
This is the problem.

They all wanted to save the cat;
they all wanted to possess the cat.
The cat was really beautiful.
But how can a mind which is possessive be silent?
And how can a mind which is possessive save anybody?
It can only kill.

Remember, it was not Nansen who killed the cat.
It was these monks who killed it.

This is the secret key in the story.
Nansen gave an opportunity.
He said:
You can save this cat.
Say something which comes from no-mind,
from your very being.
And if you don't say anything,
I am going to cut this cat and divide it in two,
so both parties can possess it.

It was not Nansen who killed the cat.
It seemed as though he killed it,
but in fact the monks killed the cat.

Whenever you possess a live thing,
you have already killed it.
Whenever you claim that you possess a live person,
you have murdered,
because life cannot be possessed.

The cat was moving from this wing to that.
The cat was alive, fully alive,
more alive than these monks.
She had no home.
She didn't belong to anybody.
She was just like a breeze –
sometimes passing through the left wing,
sometimes passing through the right.
And the cat never claimed
that these monks belonged to her,
or those monks belonged to her.
She never possessed.

Animals are non-possessive.
Trees are non-possessive.
Only man is possessive.
And with possessiveness,
man has missed all that is alive.
You can possess only a dead thing.
The moment you possess
you are making something dead.

You love a woman,
and then you try to possess her.
You kill her.
A wife is a thing, not a person;
a husband is a thing, not a person.

This is the misery –
you love a person and then you start possessing.
Unknowingly you are poisoning.
And sooner or later the day will come
when you have poisoned the person completely.
Now you possess,
but how can you love a thing?
The love happened in the first place
because the person was alive.
Now the flow has stopped,
now life doesn't move,
now all the doors of freedom are closed.
Now it has become a frozen thing.
The river is frozen,
now there is no movement.
Certainly, now, this person cannot go to another.
You possess him completely.
But how can you love a dead person?

This is the misery of love.
You cannot love a dead person,
yet whenever you love you start possessing.
All possession creates death.
Only things can be possessed.

These monks had already killed the cat.
Nansen was not going to kill it.
He was only going to make manifest
what had already happened.

This story has been used against Zen monks,
Zen masters,
to show that these people are violent.
Think of a Christian theologian reading this story.
He will say:

What type of religious man is this Nansen?
He killed the cat, a poor cat.
Those monks who claimed it were better.
At least they were not killing.
What type of master is this?
What manner of man?

If Jains, not Mahavir, if Jains read this story,
they will throw Nansen into hell.
He has killed a cat.
Nansen is violent in appearance
only to those who cannot understand.
To those who can understand,
he is simply manifesting
a thing which has already happened.
The cat was dead the moment it was possessed,
the moment people started claiming it.

He gave them one more opportunity,
but they couldn't use that opportunity.
They remained silent.
But if the silence had been real,
the cat would have been alive.
The silence was false,
the silence was only on the surface,
on the faces, skin-deep.
Inside, the mad mind was functioning fast.
It was whirling, spinning.
Many answers must have come to those monks,
but not the answer.

So Nansen had to kill.
He chopped the cat in two,
gave one part to the left-wing claimers,
another part to the right-wing claimers.
Those monks must have been happy, happy in the sense
that at least they possessed half the cat.

That is what is happening to you all.
Whenever you fight, life goes dead and is divided.

A father and mother fight over a son.
There is continuous fighting over children.
The father says that the son belongs to him,
that he should follow him,
and the mother thinks the son belongs to her,
that he should follow her.
Claiming, they are killing.
Sooner or later,
the son will be divided in two halves, chopped.
Half of the son will belong to the father,
half to the mother.

And his whole life is destroyed,
because now it will be very difficult
for him to be whole.
Half of his heart will always belong to the mother,
and half always to the father.
And one half will be against the mother,
and one half will be against the father.
Now he is divided.
Now this division is going to follow him
his whole life.
He is chopped in two.

This is what Nansen was saying
by chopping the cat in two:
Don't fight over a person.
Don't try to possess a person,
because you will chop him.
Visibly he may seem one,
but deep down in his heart he has become two,
and now there will be constant conflict.

The mother and father were fighting over the son.
Now the mother may be dead
and the father may be dead,
but they will go on fighting within the son –
sometimes the voice of the mother,
sometimes the voice of the father,
and the son will always be at a loss whom to follow.

And he cannot be whole.

You come to me in search of being whole,
and I always say:
To be whole is to be holy.
There is no other way to be holy.
Just be whole.
Divisions within you must fall,
you must become a unity.

But you are a conflict.
Your father is fighting,
your mother is fighting,
your brothers are fighting,
your teachers are fighting,
your gurus are fighting –
everybody is fighting to possess you.
There are many claimants.
They have fragmented you;
they have chopped you into many parts.
You have become many.
You are not one, you are a crowd.

Neurosis comes out of it,
madness comes out of it,
insanity comes out of it.
Have you ever observed how many souls you have,
how many selves you have?
You are not one, that is certain.

In my university days I used to live with a boy.
He would never get up in the morning at five,
but every day he would set the alarm.
So I asked him:
Why do you set it?
Why do you bother, because you never get up?
You always turn the alarm off and go to sleep again.
So why bother and why be disturbed every morning?

He laughed, but his laugh was hollow.
He knew himself that he would not get up.

But in the evening another self said:
No, tomorrow morning I am going to get up.
I said:
Okay, try.
And at the time he was setting the alarm
he was confident, absolutely confident
that he would get up in the morning at five.
There was no suspicion.

But this was only one fragment who said:
Absolutely, you have to get up.
You have slept enough.
No more time is left.
The exam is coming near.

At five I was waiting for him.
He looked at me when the alarm went off.
He looked at me.
I was aware.
I was sitting on my bed.
He smiled, put off the alarm,
changed sides and went to sleep again.

Later in the morning,
at eight o'clock when he used to get up,
I asked him about it.
He said:
I thought just for a few minutes . . .
And what is wrong
in just sleeping for a few minutes more?
I was feeling so sleepy,
and the night was so cold.
But tomorrow you will see,
I will get up.

These are two different fragments.
And he was not aware
that the one who said: Get up at five,
was a different part,
completely unaware of the part who would say:
Go to sleep.

The night is very cold.

You are doing the same.
You decide a thing and the next moment
you have simply forgotten what you decided.

You say you are not going to be angry again,
and even the next moment is very far away.
If someone starts arguing with you, saying no,
you will become angry.
You may become angry because he is arguing.
Immediately anger can come to you,
and you have decided not to be angry.

A divided house you are.
There are many rooms in your house,
not connected with each other.
The connections are broken;
the bridges have dropped.
You exist as a poly-psychic being,
with many minds.
So whatsoever you possess,
you will chop it.
You are already chopped.

Those monks could not save the cat
because they were divided.
Nansen was saying:
Do something, say something, in a whole way,
in a holy way, undivided.
Act as a unity and this cat can be saved.
Not a single one could act,
and the cat was chopped.

A question arises.
How could Nansen cut the cat?
Is it just a parable, a symbolic story,
or did he really chop the cat?

There are people who would like to save Nansen.
I am not one of them.

He really did cut the cat.
It is not a parable,
it is not an anecdote, symbolic, metaphorical.
No.
Literally, it happened
exactly the way it is said.
He cut the cat in two.

Could a saintly man do that?
I say to you:
Only a saintly man can do that.

That's what Krishna said to Arjuna in the Gita:
Then don't bother!
Chop these fellows.
These who are standing against you, cut them down.
Kill them, but remember only one thing –
that which is hidden in them cannot be destroyed.
Only the body can be destroyed,
because the body is already dead.
Only what is dead can be destroyed.
What is alive remains alive;
it is eternal,
nothing can be done to it.
Fire cannot burn it,
weapons cannot cut it.
Nainam chhindanti shastrani –
no weapon can cut it.
No fire can burn it, only the form.
But don't bother about the form,
because form is unreal.
It is part of illusion.

This Nansen must have been
in the same state of mind as Krishna,
in the same state of consciousness as Krishna.
He chopped the cat.
He knows the soul of the cat cannot be destroyed.
He knows that only the form can be changed.

And one thing more
which is very difficult to understand,
because moralists have created
so much confusion and smoke around it –
when a cat is chopped by a Nansen,
it is a beneficial to the cat,
it is a blessing to the cat,

This cat must have been rare.
And now this cat will not be reborn as a cat,
she will be reborn as a man.
To be chopped by Nansen is a rare opportunity,
and the cat
must have been wandering around the monastery,
waiting for this moment.

Nansen changed the form.
The cat will be reborn as a higher being,
just because Nansen has chopped her.
In that moment,
the cat was more silent than the monks,
and the cat was more ecstatic than the monks.
And being chopped by Nansen
is not an act of aggression,
it is an act of love.
Nansen freed the cat from the form,
from the form of cat.
She will be reborn as a higher being.

But this is difficult to follow,
and I am not telling you
to go and free people from their forms
so they will be reborn as higher beings.
Don't chop anybody –
you would like to,
you would enjoy it.

For Nansen, it was an act of deep prayer.
He must have been watching this cat.
This cat was no ordinary cat.
There are animals who are crying out

to be freed from their forms.

It happened at a camp in Matheran.
I was staying very far away
from the campus ground.
The first evening, when I was going to my bungalow,
a dog followed, really a rare dog.
And then the dog remained continuously.
Three times I would go to conduct the camp,
and three times I would return.
It was half an hour's journey.
Three times I was asleep,
and he would sit just on the veranda.
Even when he went to eat something,
he never left me.
For the whole camp this was his routine.

He would follow me to the camp,
and when others were meditating,
he would sit more silently, more deeply,
than those who were attending the camp.
And then he would go back with me.

The last day, when I left Matheran by train,
he followed the train.
He was running by the side of the train.
Many people may be here who were witnesses there.
He was running by the side of the train,
and the guard took compassion on him
and he took him in.

Up to Neral he came.
This train was a slow train, a toy train,
coming from Matheran to Neral,
just seven miles travelling for two hours,
and the dog could follow.
But from Neral it is a fast train,
and when I took the train from Neral to Bombay,
others were standing there on the platform,
weeping and crying,

and the dog was also standing there in tears.

I know that cat must have been extraordinary,
otherwise Nansen would not have taken
such trouble to chop it.
He created an opportunity for his disciples,
and he used that opportunity for the cat also.
He hit two targets with one stone.

This is possible.
If you are ready, then your form can be destroyed
and you will receive a higher form,
because your higher form depends
on the moment when you die.

The cat died in the hands of Nansen.
A very rare opportunity.
Such a silent man was Nansen,
the cat must have caught the silence;
such an ecstatic being,
the cat must have been filled with his ecstasy.
And then he chopped it.
The cat was not afraid,
she must have enjoyed the game.
It was a surgical act.
The cat must be born in the next life
as a very much higher soul.
But that is an inner story
and cannot be understood by ordinary morality.
And persons like Nansen
don't follow ordinary morality,
they follow the inner rules, the inner laws.
Ordinary morality is for ordinary men.

And then by the evening
another monk came in from outside,
another disciple who had not been in the monastery.
Nansen told the story to him:
This has happened, and I had to cut the cat.
I had to divide it in two because there was no way.

These foolish fellows couldn't save the cat.
They couldn't save the cat.
They couldn't utter a single word,
they couldn't act in a Zen-like way,
they couldn't prove their Zen.
Only Zen could have saved the cat, nothing else.

The disciple listened to the story,
put his shoes on his head and walked out.
Nansen called him and said:
If you had been here, the cat would have been saved.

This was the right man.
What did he do?
He took his shoes off, put them on his head,
and walked out.
He said many things without speaking.

The first thing.
He listened to the story and didn't comment on it.
The monkey was silent; the mind was not chattering.
He didn't try to think out an answer,
he simply acted.
That action was not from the mind,
the action was from his total being.

And what did he do?
He put his shoes on his head.
Absurd!
But he said that the mind, the head,
is no more valuable than the shoes.
Shoes, the meanest thing,
he put them on his head.

He said by this act:
The mind is nothing but shoes.
The mind is valueless.
Thinking cannot help.
The mind has to be thrown to the shoes.
Even shoes are more worthy
and command more respect than the mind.

That's what he said.
And then he simply walked out.

And Nansen said:
Had you been here this morning,
you could have saved the cat.
The cat would have been saved.

Here was a man who didn't believe in the mind,
who didn't believe in answers.
Here was a man who could act spontaneously.
Life can be saved only if you can act spontaneously –
not only the cat's life, your life also.

Throw the mind to the shoes.
It is not more worthy in any way.
And shoes have not troubled you so much.
Sometimes they may pinch, but only sometimes,
and if they are the right size, they are always okay,
but the mind has been pinching you
for many, many lives,
and it is never the right size.
It is always the wrong size.
The mind is never the right size.
Shoes can be the right size,
but the mind is always the wrong size.
It goes on pinching.

The mind is the wrong size.
You cannot make a good mind.
There is no possibility.
You cannot make a beautiful ugliness;
you cannot make a healthy disease.
That is impossible.
The mind is always wrong.
It goes on pinching.

And whether you think or whether you pray,
if the mind is there, everything goes wrong.
The mind is the factor which creates wrongness in life.
This is the source of error, perversion, neurosis.

Life can be saved only when you drop the mind.

What did this disciple do?
It was difficult to drop the head,
it was easier to put the shoes on the head.
But it was symbolic.
He was saying:
I have dropped the head.
Don't ask me foolish questions.

And he acted.
That's the thing.
Meditation is not contemplation, it is action –
action of the whole, of the total being.

In the West particularly,
Christianity has created a false impression,
and meditation looks like contemplation.
It is not.
Because of Christianity,
the West has missed many things,
and one of them is meditation,
the rarest flowering of a human being,
because they have made it equivalent to contemplation.
Contemplation is thinking.
Meditation is no-thinking.

For *dhyan,* Zen, there exists no equivalent
in the English language,
because meditation itself means thinking –
to meditate upon.
Some object is there.

Remember, *dhyan* is the original word.
Dhyan travelled to China with Bodhidharma,
and in the Chinese language it became 'Ch'an'.
And then from China it travelled to Japan,
and in Japanese it became first 'Zan',
and then 'Zen';
but the original root is *dhyan*–Ch'an, Zan, Zen.

In English there is no word equivalent to it.
Meditation also means thinking,
a consistent thinking.
Contemplation means thinking too.
It may be thinking about God, but it is thinking,
and *dhyan* or Zen is a no-thinking state.
It is action, without thought.
Thought needs time.

In the morning the monks were sitting
thinking what to do.
They thought and thought and couldn't find.
Thought will never find the right answer.
The cat had to be chopped.
Life became death because thought is poisonous.
Thinking leads to death, not to more life.
The cat had to be chopped.
Nansen couldn't help.
Those monks killed the cat.

This man, this disciple who came in the evening,
listened to the story without commenting,
without saying anything.
He simply took off his shoes,
put them on his head and walked out.
He acted.
He said something through his action,
not through his mind.
He didn't use words, he used himself.
And he didn't wait, he didn't contemplate,
he didn't try to find the answer
to how the cat should have been saved.

If you had been there in the evening
and you were told the story,
you would surely have started to think:
How?
When the 'how' comes, mind has come.
This disciple acted without the 'how'.
He simply acted,

and the act was spontaneous, very symbolic.
Putting the shoes on his head, he said something –
he said the head is valueless.

This Nansen, the master, used to ask people:
What is the most valueless thing in the world?
He used to give it as a meditation to his disciples.
Think, what is the most valueless thing in the world?
His master also gave this *koan* to him.
He meditated, meditated,
then one day he came and told his master:
The head.
The master asked:
Why?
So Nansen said:
Cut a head and go to the market and try to sell it.
Nobody will purchase it.

This is what Nansen's disciple did.
By putting shoes on his head, he said:
Worthless head.
And you go on insisting, asking head-questions.
There is no answer.
How can the shoes answer?

He walked out,
and Nansen said:
You could have saved the cat.
Had you been there this morning
the cat would have been alive and kicking.

Some absurd act was needed –
absurd, spontaneous.
Rational?
No, something irrational was needed,
because 'ir-reason' is deeper than reason.

That's why if you are too much head-fixed,
you cannot fall in love,
because love is irrational, absurd.
The head goes on saying:

This is useless.
What will you gain out of it?
There is no profit.
You may even get into trouble.
Think about it.

It is said of Emmanuel Kant,
one of the greatest systematizers,
that one girl proposed to him.
In the first place,
it is bad that the girl should propose,
it is always the boy who proposes.
But the girl must have waited and waited
and Kant wouldn't propose.
The idea never occurred to him.
He was so much rooted in his head,
the heart was denied.
So the girl,
feeling too much time had been lost, proposed.
Kant said:
I will think it over.

How can you think about love?
Either it is there or not.
It is not a question to be solved,
it is a situation to respond to.
Either your heart says yes or your heart says no,
and it is finished.
What will you think?
It is not a business proposal.

But it was a business proposal to Kant.
Too much head-orientation
makes everything business-like.
So he thought;
he not only thought, he went to the library
and concentrated on the books about love, marriage.
Then he noted down in his notebook
all that was in favour of marriage
and all that was against.

And he thought and thought and thought,
and it is said that weighing the pros and cons,
he decided in favour of marriage,
because a few points were more in favour than against,
So it was a logical decision.
Then he went and knocked at the girl's door,
and the father said:
She is already married and a mother of three children.
So much time passed.
You come a little late.

Time is needed for the mind.
The mind is always late because time will be needed,
and the situation will be lost.
And when you knock at the door, the girl has moved.
She is already a mother of three children.

And this is happening every moment.
Remember, a situation is there,
so act, don't think,
because if you think,
the situation will not wait for you.
The girl will have moved.
And when you are ready to respond,
there will be nothing to respond to.

Kant was ready, but the mind takes time,
and situations are moving.
Life is a flow, a flux.
It is not static,
otherwise the mind would have found the answer.
If the girl had remained . . .
But the girl was getting old,
she was missing life.
She could not wait,
she had to move, make a decision.

Life is not static.
If life were static,
there would be no need for meditation.
The mind would do.

Then you could think,
and whenever, after many lives,
you knocked at the door,
the girl would be waiting for you.
But life is a flux, a movement.
Every moment it is changing and becoming new.
If you miss a moment, you have missed.

This disciple didn't miss a single moment.
He heard the story, took off his shoes,
put them on his head and walked out.
If he had waited a single moment to think,
Nansen would have beaten him.
I tell you, he would have been beaten.
Because the cat was not there any more,
he might have chopped this disciple.
But he acted.

Action without the mind
is the most beautiful thing possible.
But you are afraid,
because you think if you act without the mind
you may do something wrong.
Because this fear exists, the mind exploits it –
think first, then act.
But you go on missing the train.
Leave this fear,
otherwise you will never be meditative.
Act!

In the beginning,
there will be a deep shaking and trembling,
because you have always been acting out of thinking.
It is just like a man who has been living in a prison,
in a dark cell, for many years.
His eyes have become attuned to darkness.
If he is suddenly brought out of the cell,
he will not be able to open his eyes.
The sun will be too much,
the light will be too much.

His whole being will tremble, and he will say:
Let me go back to my cell.

This is what has happened to you,
to everybody.
We have lived in the mind for many, many lives,
and we have become attuned to its darkness,
its ugliness, futility.
When you act without the mind,
your whole being trembles.
You are moving on a dangerous path.

The mind says:
Be alert!
Think first, then act.
But if you think first, and then do something,
your doing will always be dead, stale.
It will be out of thought,
it will not be real and authentic.
Then you cannot love,
then you cannot meditate,
then you cannot really live and you cannot die.
You become a phantom, a phony existence.
Love knocks at your heart and you say:
Wait!
I will think about it.
Life goes on knocking at your gates and you say:
Wait!
I will think about it.

This disciple must have been deep in meditation.
He acted, he simply acted.
He could have saved the cat.
This means he has already saved it.
He has already saved all that is alive.
Don't think about this story,
otherwise I will have to chop the cat.
You can save it,
otherwise the cat will have to be chopped again,
and you will be responsible.
Act!

But the story won't help you.
Don't try to put your shoes on your head.
That won't help.
It helped that disciple,
but it won't help you.
The cat will have to be chopped
if you put the shoes on your head and walk out,
because that will be false again.
That will be from the mind.
You know the story.
The mind cannot give you the real.
Whatsoever you do, don't imitate.

I have heard that in a Chinese town,
there was one big restaurant, very rich,
the most beautiful, rich restaurant in the town.
And just near that restaurant lived a poor Chinese.
He couldn't go in the restaurant.
It was too costly.
But the smell of the food, the aroma . . .
He used to sniff it,
and when he took his lunch or dinner,
he took a chair out of his house
and went as near to the restaurant as he dared.
And he would sit there and sniff the aroma,
the smell that was coming from the restaurant,
and eat his food.
He enjoyed it.
He ran a small laundry.

But one day he was surprised.
There came a man, the owner of the restaurant,
with a bill for the smell of the food.
That poor man ran into his house,
brought his tiny money box,
rattled it in the ears of the owner,
and said:
Hereby I pay for the smell of your food,
by the sound of my money.

The mind is just smell and sound, nothing real.
Whatsoever you do, the mind is smell and sound,
nothing authentic.
It is the source of all falsity.

So you have heard the story.
Don't try now to imitate it.
You can do it easily now.
Now the secret is known.
You can put the shoes on your head and walk,
but the cat will be chopped.
It will not save it, it will not help it.

Act spontaneously.
Put aside the mind and do something.
And doing it,
you will come to know the cat has never been chopped,
because the cat cannot die.
Putting aside the mind,
you will come to know your own eternity,
and the very same moment
you know the eternity of the cat also.
The mind is mortal, not you.
You are immortal.
The mind has a death waiting for it, not you.
You are deathless.
Putting aside the mind, you will laugh,
and you will say this Nansen played a trick.
The cat cannot be killed.

That's what Krishna went on saying to Arjuna:
Don't you be worried.
You chop these fellows,
because nobody can be killed.

The Gita is very dangerous.
Nowhere on the earth
does such a dangerous book exist,
so nobody has followed it.
People recite it, but nobody follows it.

It is dangerous.
And even people who love it very much,
and respect it very much,
never listen to what it says.
Even a man like Mahatma Gandhi,
who called Gita his mother, wouldn't listen to it.
How could Mahatma Gandhi listen to it?
He believed in non-violence and this Krishna said;
Chop these fellows!
Nothing exists;
it is like a dream.
And I tell you, nobody is killed,
so don't bother about it.

How could Gandhi believe?
So he had to play a trick.
This is how the mind plays tricks.
He said:
This is a parable,
this is metaphorical;
don't take it literally,
the fight is not real.
Kauravas and *Pandavas,* these two groups of warriors,
are just a story.
Kauravas represent evil and *Pandavas* represent good.
It is the fight between good and evil,
between God and the Devil,
it is not a real fight.
But this was Gandhi's mind playing tricks.

There have been Buddhist interpreters of Nansen also.
They said:
This is just a parable.
There was no real cat,
and this never happened.

But I tell you this happened.
The cat was real, as real as Nansen,
and the cat was chopped.
Nansen could do it.

Nansen was a Krishna.
He knew nothing is destroyed.

This word, the English word 'destruction',
is very beautiful, meaningful.
the word 'destruction' means de-structuring –
nothing is destroyed, only the structure changes.
A new structure arises.
The old structure goes out of existence,
and a new structure arises.
Destruction means de-structuring.
Only the form changes.

The cat may be sitting here.
It is more possible than anywhere else.
When you go back home, look in the mirror.
You may be the cat,
and you have come here again.
Do something, otherwise I will chop you again.

And remember,
now nobody can save you.
That time the monks could have saved you.
This time you are a monk,
so nobody can save you except yourself.
Action out of immediacy, spontaneous action, saves life.
That is the only saviour.
There exists no other saviour.

Anything more?

Bhagwan,

In place of the ten commandments,
with which I was brought up,
I have given myself a new set of rules –

be alert,
be patient,
be spontaneous,
accept myself.

All questions are mind questions.
No question comes out of no-mind.
And all answers are no-mind answers.
So questions and answers never meet.
You ask a question and I give you an answer.
They never meet.
They cannot meet,
because your question runs on the track of the mind
and my answer runs on the track of no-mind.
They may run parallel, but they never meet.

Either I should drop my no-mind –
then there can be a meeting –
or you should drop the mind.
Then there can be a meeting.

And remember,
I am not going to drop my no-mind.
It cannot be dropped,
because how can you drop a no-thing?
You can drop a thing,
but you cannot drop a no-thing.
So you have to drop the mind.
Then the answer will be heard, understood.
Then it will penetrate you.

And the mind is a deeper source of new questions,
new puzzles, new riddles,
so you can change the ten commandments.
You can create another ten.
That will not do,

because if they are created by the mind,
nothing changes.

Now the ten commandments have become very old,
out of date.
They speak in a language of the past.
At that time, that language was relevant,
but now they don't look relevant.
You can change,
you can make new commandments,
but those new commandments,
if they are put together by the mind,
will not be of any use.
Your mind can think
and put them together,
and they may look beautiful,
but they will be false.
You can make let-go a commandment,
total acceptability a commandment,
but if they are put by the mind,
they are meaningless.
Why?
It is because the mind cannot allow itself
to be in a total let-go.
It can pretend,
but it cannot really allow itself to let go.

And the mind cannot accept,
because the mind exists through rejection.
That is why the mind
always likes to say no rather than yes.
Whenever you say no, you feel the ego;
whenever you say yes, you don't feel the ego.
That's why people go on saying no more than yes.
They say yes
only when it becomes absolutely necessary,
otherwise they say no.
Whenever something is asked,
the first thing that arises in your mind is no —
because when you reject, you are,

and when you accept, you are not there.

Yes-saying will create a no-mind.
So a theist is a yes-sayer,
and an atheist is a no-sayer.
He says no.
And when you say there is no God,
then you feel a tremendous energy in the ego.
Then you are.

Nietzsche has said:
If God is, then I won't like to be,
and if I am, then I won't allow God to be,
because both cannot exist.

And he is right.
How can both exist, you and God together?
If you are there, then you are the God.
God cannot exist.
If he exists, then how can you exist?
The ultimate no comes to the mind –
no God.

The mind rejects, cannot accept.
So you can change, you can think about it,
you can change the old ten commandments
and create a new ten,
but if they come out of the mind,
they are useless.
And if they do not come out of the mind,
what is the need?
If the no-mind has happened and you feel it,
what is the need of commandments?
Commandments are for the mind.
They are from the mind and for the mind.
Rules exists for the mind,
because the mind cannot exist without rules.

This is one of the most basic things.
Rules exist for the false, not for the real.
The real can exist without rules,

but the false cannot exist.
It has to be propped, helped,
supported by the rules.

You play a game,
you play cards—
can you play cards without rules?
There can be no possibility.
If you say:
I will follow my rules and you follow your rules
and we play the game,
there will be no game.
We have to follow the rules.
And we both know that rules are just rules,
nothing real in them.
We have agreed on the rules.
That's why they exist.

A game cannot continue if rules are not followed,
but life will continue without rules.
What rules are these trees following?
What rules does the sun follow?
What rules does the sky follow?
The human mind is such that the human mind
thinks they are also following rules,
moving according to rules.
The sun moves, it follows a rule,
so there is a ruler, the God who controls everything.
He is like a great super-manager.
He goes spying on everybody —
who is following, who is not following.
This is a mind creation.

Life exists without rules;
games cannot exist without rules.
So real religion is always without rules.
Only false religion has rules,
because false religion is a game.

I have heard that one young woman

came to a barber's shop with her young boy.
The boy was dressed like a soldier,
looked very dangerous,
and he had a toy six-shooter.
Immediately he jumped on the chair and said:
Bang! Bang!
He just made noise.
And the lady said to the barber:
I am going to leave my son here for half an hour.
I have some shopping to do.
The barber became uneasy and he said:
If this young man becomes too restless,
what am I supposed to do?
And that young boy
was standing with his six-shooter on the chair,
looking very dangerous, soldier-like.
The young lady said:
If he gets too restless,
you will simply have to drop dead a few times,
that's all.
If he says:
Bang!—
you drop dead.
Follow the rule.
That's the rule.
Then he will not be restless.
So you have to drop dead a few times,
and then he will be happy
and there will be no trouble.

All the commandments are:
Bang!
Drop dead!
For real life there is no commandment.
You flow in it, without any rules.
You simply be.
Why follow rules?
Out of your being, everything will happen.

These things you say

will happen if you are simply there,
without any rules.
Then acceptance will come, let-go will come.
Then the mind will drop.
So these rules cannot be made rules.
They are consequences of being spontaneous and total.

If somebody follows them,
and he has made a commandment
that he has to accept everything, and then accepts,
it is false,
because in accepting he has already rejected.
And if you have to accept something
because of the commandment,
you have already rejected.
Your mind says:
Accept!
Why accept?
Before it has said: Reject.
Then rejection has come before the acceptance.
But if there is no rejection,
how will you be aware of acceptance?
You will simply accept and flow.

Become river-like.
Become a white cloud floating in the sky,
and let the winds take you wheresoever they take.
Don't, don't follow any rules.
This is what I mean when I say:
Be a *sannyasi.*

Just be.
Your ochre robes, your *mala* –
these are rules.
This is a game.
This is not what I mean by real *sannyas.*
But you are so accustomed to games,
that before I lead you to a rule-less life,
in the transitory period, you will need rules.
Moving from this world of rules, of games,

to that world without rules and games,
a bridge has to be passed.
Your orange clothes, your *mala,*
are just for that transitory period.
You cannot drop rules immediately,
so I give you new rules.

But be fully alert
that your robes are not your sannyas,
your mala is not your sannyas,
your new name is not your sannyas.
Sannyas will be there when there is no name,
when you become nameless.
Then there will be no rules.
Then you will be so ordinary,
you will not be recognized.
Only then . . .

But don't think that now it is okay,
so no need to take sannyas
and no need to take an orange robe.
That is again a trick.
You have to pass through this,
you have to go through this.
You cannot by-pass it.
And if you try to by-pass,
you will never reach to the other shore.

Rules of the world,
then rules of sannyas,
and then comes a no-rule state.

No, commandments are needed.
Don't change the old commandments.
They are okay as they are.
You be.
Simply be.
And follow
and flow into the being.

Tenth Talk

19th June 1974

Bhagwan,

Buddha was to give a special talk one day,
and thousands of followers
had come from miles around.

When Buddha appeared he was holding a flower.
Time passed, but Buddha said nothing.
He just looked at the flower.
The crowd grew restless,
but Maha-Kashyap,
who could restrain himself no longer,
laughed.

Buddha beckoned him over,
handed him the flower,
and said to the crowd:
I have the eye of the true teaching.
All that can be given with words
I have given to you;
but with this flower, I give to Maha-Kashyap
the key to this teaching.

To all teachings,
not only for a Buddha, but for all masters,
Jesus, Mahavir, Lao-Tse,
the key cannot be given through verbal communication,
the key cannot be delivered through the mind.
Nothing can be said about it.
The more you say
the more difficult it becomes to deliver,
because a Buddha and you
live in such different dimensions –
not only different but diametrically opposite –
that whatsoever a Buddha says will be misunderstood.

I have heard that one evening
three slightly deaf women met on the road.
The day was very windy, so one woman said:
Windy, isn't it?
The other said:
Wednesday?
No, it's Thursday.
And the third said:
Thirsty?
I am also,
so let's go to the restaurant and have a cup of tea.

This is what happens
when a Buddha says something to you.

He says:
Windy?
You say:
Wednesday?
No, it's Thursday.

The physical ear is okay;
the spiritual ear is missing.
A Buddha can talk only to another Buddha.
This is the problem.
And with another Buddha, there is no need to talk.
Buddha has to talk with those who are not enlightened.
With them exists the need to talk and communicate,
but then communication is impossible.

It is reported of one Mohammedan saint, Farid,
that he was passing near Benares
where Kabir lived.
Followers of Farid said:
It would be just wonderful if you and Kabir met.
For us it would be a blessing.

The same thing happened to Kabir and his followers.
They heard that Farid was passing,
so they said to Kabir
that it would be good if he would ask Farid
to stay a few days in the ashram.

Farid's disciples said:
You both talking would be a great opportunity for us,
we would like to hear
what two enlightened persons say to each other.
Farid laughed when they said this and replied:
There will be a meeting,
but I don't think there is going to be any talking.
But let us see.

Kabir said:
Ask Farid.
Let him come and stay –

but whosoever speaks first
will prove that he is not enlightened.

Farid came; Kabir received him.
They laughed and embraced each other.
Then they sat in silence.
Two days Farid was there,
and for many hours they sat together,
with the disciples restless,
waiting for them to say something, utter something.
But not a single word was communicated.

The third day Farid left
and Kabir came to see him off.
They again laughed, embraced each other, parted.
The moment they parted,
Farid's disciples gathered around him and said:
What nonsense!
What wastage of time.
We were hoping that something was going to happen.
Nothing happened.
Why did you suddenly become so dumb?
You talk too much to us.

Farid replied:
All that I know, he knows also.
Nothing is to be said.
I looked into his eyes,
and he is there, where I am.
Whatsoever he has seen, I have seen;
whatsoever he has realized, I have realized.
Nothing is to be said.

Two ignorant persons can talk.
They talk much;
they do nothing except talk.
Two enlightened persons cannot talk.
It would be absurd.
Two ignorant persons talking is meaningless
because there is nothing to convey.

They don't know anything that can be said,
that should be said,
but they go on talking.
They are chattering.
They cannot help it.
It's just a mad catharsis, a release.

Two enlightened persons cannot talk
because they know the same.
Nothing is to be said.
Only one enlightened person
and one unenlightened person
can have a meaningful communication,
because one knows
and the other is yet in ignorance.

A meaningful communication, I said.
I don't say that the truth can be conveyed,
but some hints, some indications,
some gestures can,
so that the other becomes ready to take the jump.

The truth cannot be conveyed,
but the thirst can be given.
No teaching worth the name
can give the key through words.

Buddha talked.
It's difficult to find another person
who talked so much.
Scholars have been studying
all the scriptures in existence
that are in the name of Buddha,
and it seems an impossible accomplishment
because after his enlightenment
he lived only forty years,
walking from one village to another.

He walked all over Bihar,
and the name 'Bihar' comes because Buddha walked there.
Bihar means the walking paths of Buddha.

The whole province is called Bihar
because this is the boundary where Buddha walked –
his Bihar, his wanderings.

He continuously walked.
Only in the rainy season did he rest.
So much time was wasted in walking,
and then, also, he had to sleep,
so scholars have been calculating.
They say: This seems impossible.
Sleeping, walking, doing other daily routines,
there are so many scriptures,
how could he have talked so much?
If he was continuously talking for forty years,
without a gap of a single moment,
only then could this much have been talked.
He must have talked too much, continuously,
yet still he says
the key cannot be conveyed through words.

This story is one of the most significant ones,
because from this was passed the tradition of Zen.
Buddha was the source,
and Maha-Kashyap was the first,
the original master of Zen.
Buddha was the source,
Maha-Kashyap was the first master,
and this story is the source
from where the whole tradition –
one of the most beautiful and alive
that exists on earth,
the tradition of Zen –
started.

Try to understand this story.
Buddha came one morning,
and as usual a crowd had gathered.
Many people were waiting to listen to him.
But one thing was unusual –
he was carrying a flower in his hand.

Never before had he carried anything in his hand.
People thought that someone must have presented it.

Buddha came; he sat under the tree.
The crowd waited and waited and he would not speak.
He wouldn't even look at them.
He just went on looking at the flower.
Minutes passed, then hours,
and the people became very much restless.

It is said that Maha-Kashyap couldn't contain himself.
He laughed loudly.
Buddha called him,
gave him the flower
and said to the gathered crowd:
Whatsoever can be said through words,
I have said to you,
and that which cannot be said through words,
I give to Maha-Kashyap.
The key cannot be communicated verbally.
I hand over the key to Maha-Kashyap.

This is what Zen masters call
transference of the key without scripture –
beyond scripture, beyond words, beyond mind.
He gave the flower to Maha-Kashyap,
and nobody could understand what happened.
Neither Maha-Kashyap nor Buddha
ever commented upon it again.
The whole chapter was closed.

Since then, in China, in Tibet, in Thailand,
in Burma, in Japan, in Ceylon –
everywhere Buddhists have been asking
for these twenty-five centuries:
What was given to Maha-Kashyap?
What was the key?

The whole story seems to be very esoteric.
Buddha was not secretive.
This was the only incident . . .

Buddha was a very rational being.
He talked rationally, he was not a mad ecstatic,
he argued rationally, and his logic was perfect –
you could not find a loophole in it.
This was the only incident where he behaved illogically,
where he did something which was mysterious.
He was not a mysterious man at all.
You cannot find another master who was less mysterious.

Jesus was very mysterious.
Lao-Tse was absolutely mysterious.
Buddha was plain, transparent.
No mystery surrounds him, no smoke is allowed.
His flame burns clear and bright,
absolutely transparent, smokeless.
This was the thing that seemed mysterious,
hence many Buddhist scriptures never relate this anecdote.
They have simply dropped it.
It seemed as if someone had invented it.
It didn't make any sense with Buddha's life and teaching.

But for Zen this is the origin.
Maha-Kashyap became the first holder of the key.
Then six holders in succession existed in India,
up to Bodhidharma.
He was the sixth holder of the key,
and then he searched and searched all over India,
but he couldn't find a man
of the capability of Maha-Kashyap –
a man who could understand silence.
He had to leave India
just in search of a man to whom the key could be given;
otherwise the key would be lost.

Buddhism entered China with Bodhidharma
in search of a man to whom the key could be given,
a man who could understand silence,
who could talk heart to heart
without being obsessed in the mind,
who had no head.

A man with no head was difficult to find in India,
because India is a country of pundits and scholars,
and they have the biggest heads possible.
A pundit, by and large,
forgets everything about the heart,
and he becomes the head.
His whole personality becomes lopsided
as if only the head exists,
and the whole body shrinks and disappears.

This communication beyond words
is possible only from heart to heart.
So, for nine years, Bodhidharma searched in China,
and then he could find only one man.

For nine years Bodhidharma was sitting in China,
not facing people.
He would always sit facing the wall.
If you had gone to hear him,
he would have been facing the wall,
his back towards you.
People used to ask him:
We have come to listen to you,
why do you sit in such a peculiar way?

And Bodhidharma would reply:
I am waiting for the man who can listen to me.
I will not look at you; I will not waste my time.
I will look only at the person who can listen to me.

Then came a man.
He stood behind Bodhidharma, cut off his right hand,
threw it at Bodhidharma and said:
Turn towards this side,
otherwise I am going to cut off my head.
Bodhidharma immediately turned and said:
Right — so you have come.
Take this key and relieve me of the work.

The key that was passed from Buddha to Maha-Kashyap,
Bodhidharma delivered to this man;

a Chinese became the seventh master.
And up to now it has been travelling.
The key is still there;
somebody is still holding it.
The river has not dried.

To me, if all the scriptures of Buddha disappear,
nothing is lost.
Only this anecdote should not disappear.
This is the most precious,
and scholars have dropped it from Buddha's biography.
They say:
This is irrelevant; it doesn't fit with Buddha.

But I say to you:
All that Buddha did was just ordinary –
anybody could do that –
but this is extraordinary, this is exceptional.
Only a Buddha can do this.

What happened that morning?
Let us start to penetrate into it.
Buddha came, sat, and started looking at the flower.
He would not look at the people.
The flower became the wall.
That's what Bodhidharma did.
He would look at the wall;
he would not look at the people –
he would not waste his look.
The flower became the wall
and the crowd disappeared.

Buddha looked and looked at the flower.
What was he doing?
When Buddha looks at anything,
the quality of his consciousness is transferred.
And a flower is one of the most receptive things in the world.
Hence, Hindus and Buddhists go with flowers
to put at their master's feet or in the temple,
because a flower can carry something of your consciousness.

A flower is a very receptive thing,
and if you are aware of the new research in the West,
you will understand it.
Now they say plants are more sensitive than you, than man.
A flower is the heart of the plant;
the whole being comes into it.

Much research is going on in Soviet Russia,
in the USA, in England,
about the sensitivity of plants,
and something wonderful has been discovered.
One man, a scientist, was working on plants –
how they feel, whether they feel anything or not,
whether they have emotions or not.
He was sitting with a plant with electrodes fixed to it
to detect any movement in its inner being,
any sensation, any emotions.

He thought:
If I cut this plant,
if I tear down a branch or cut it from the earth,
what will happen?
Suddenly, the needle making the graph jumped.
He had not done anything;
he had just had a thought:
If I cut this plant . . .
The plant became afraid of death
and the needle jumped,
recording that the plant was trembling.
Even the scientist became scared
because he had not done anything –
just a thought and the plant received it.
Plants are telepathic.

Then he worked much.
He worked on long distances.
The plant was removed one thousand miles.
His plant,
the plant he had helped to grow, had watered, loved,
was removed one thousand miles away.

Here he thought against the plant
and there, one thousand miles away,
the plant became disturbed.
So now, scientifically, it could be seen
that the plant's emotions were disturbed.

Not only this,
but if you think of cutting one plant,
all the other plants surrounding the area
become emotionally disturbed.
Also, if someone has cut a plant,
and he comes into the garden,
all the plants become disturbed
because this man is not good.
And they carry the memory.
Whenever this man enters the garden,
the whole garden feels
that an evil person is coming in.

Now a few scientists think
that plants can be used
for telepathic communication,
because they are more sensitive than the human mind.
And a few scientists think
that plants can be used
to receive communications from other planets,
because our instruments are not so refined.

In the East it has always been known
that a flower is the most receptive thing.
When Buddha looked at the flower
and continued to look at the flower,
something of him was transferred to that flower.
Buddha entered the flower.
The quality of his being,
the alertness, the awareness, the peace, the ecstasy,
the inner dance, touched the flower.
With Buddha looking at the flower,
so at ease, at home, without any desire,
it must have danced in its inner being.

He looked, to transfer something to the flower.
One thing to be understood
is that only the flower and he existed
for a long period of time.
The whole world dropped.
Only Buddha and the flower were there.
The flower entered Buddha's being,
and Buddha entered the flower's being.

Then the flower was given to Maha-Kashyap.
It was not just a flower now.
It carried Buddhahood.
It carried the inner quality of Buddha's being.

And why to Maha-Kashyap?
There were other great scholars, ten great disciples;
Maha-Kashyap was only one.
And he was included in the ten only because of this story,
otherwise he would never have been included;
nothing much is known about Maha-Kashyap.
There were great scholars like Sariputra there –
you could not find a more keen intellect –
and Modgalayan was also there, a very great scholar.
He had all the Vedas in his memory,
and nothing that had ever been written
was unknown to him.
A great logician in his own right,
he had thousands of disciples.
And there were others.
Ananda was there, Buddha's cousin-brother,
who for forty years was continuously moving with him.

But no.
Someone who was unknown before, Maha-Kashyap,
suddenly became most important.
The whole gestalt changed.
Whenever Buddha was speaking,
Sariputra was the significant man
because he could understand words more than anybody else;
and when Buddha was arguing,

Modgalayan was the significant man.
Nobody thought about Maha-Kashyap very much.
He remained in the crowd, was part of the crowd.

But when Buddha became silent,
the whole gestalt changed.
Now Modgalayan and Sariputra were not significant.
They simply dropped out of existence,
as if they were not there.
They just became a part of the crowd.
A new man, Maha-Kashyap, became the most important.
A new dimension opened.

Everybody was restless, thinking:
Why is Buddha not speaking?
Why is he keeping silent?
What is going to happen?
When will it end?
They became uncomfortable, restless.

But Maha-Kashyap was not uncomfortable or restless.
Really, for the first time he was at ease with Buddha;
for the first time he was at home with Buddha.
When Buddha was talking he may have been restless.
He may have thought:
Why this nonsense?
Why go on talking?
Nothing is conveyed; nothing is understood.
Why go on knocking your head against the wall?
People are deaf.
They cannot understand.
He must have been restless when Buddha was talking.
And now for the first time he was at home.
He could understand what silence was.

Thousands were there and everybody was restless.
He couldn't contain himself,
looking at the foolishness of the crowd.
They were at ease when Buddha was talking;
now they were restless when he was silent.
When something could be delivered,

they were not open;
when nothing could be delivered, they were waiting.
Now, through silence,
Buddha could give something which is immortal,
but they could not understand.
So he couldn't contain himself and laughed loudly.
He laughed at the whole situation,
the whole absurdity.

We require even a Buddha to talk,
because that's all we understand.
This is foolish.
You should learn to be silent with a Buddha,
because only then can he enter you.
Through words he can knock at your door,
but can never enter;
through silence he can enter you,
and unless he enters, nothing will happen to you.
His entry will bring a new element to your world;
his entry into the heart
will give you a new beat and a new pulse,
a new release of life,
but only his entry.

Maha-Kashyap laughed at the foolishness of man.
They were restless and thinking:
When will Buddha stand up
and drop this whole silence
so that we can go home?
He laughed.

Laughter started with Maha-Kashyap,
and has been going on and on in Zen tradition.
There is no other tradition which can laugh.
Laughter looks so irreligious, profane,
that you cannot think of Jesus laughing,
you cannot think of Mahavir laughing.
It's difficult even to conceive
of Mahavir having a belly laugh,
or of Jesus laughing uproariously.

No, laughter has been denied.
Sadness, somehow, has become religious.

One of the famous German thinkers, Count Keyserling,
has written that health is irreligious.
Illness has a religiousness about it
because an ill person is sad, desireless,
not because he has become desireless
but because he is weak.
A healthy person will laugh,
would like to enjoy, will be merry –
he cannot be sad.
So religious persons have tried in many ways
to make you ill –
go on a fast, suppress your body, torture yourself.
You will become sad, suicidal,
crucified on your own.

How can you laugh?
Laughter comes out of health.
It's an overflowing energy.
That's why children can laugh
and their laughter is total.
Their whole body is involved in it.
When they laugh, you can see their toes laughing.
The whole body,
every cell, every fibre of the body,
is laughing and vibrating.
They are so full of health, so vital.
Everything is flowing.

A sad child means an ill child,
and a laughing old man means he is still young.
Even death cannot make him old.
Nothing can make him old.
His energy is still flowing and overflowing.
He is always flooded.
Laughter is a flooding of energy.

In Zen monasteries,
they have been laughing and laughing and laughing.

Laughter became prayer only in Zen,
because Maha-Kashyap started it.
Twenty-five centuries before,
on a morning just like this,
Maha-Kashyap started a new trend, absolutely new,
unknown to the religious mind before –
he laughed.
He laughed at the whole foolishness, the whole stupidity.
And Buddha didn't condemn.
Rather, on the contrary,
he called him near,
gave him the flower
and spoke to the crowd.

And when the crowd heard the laughter,
they must have thought:
This man has gone mad.
This man is disrespectful to Buddha,
because how can you laugh before a Buddha?
When a Buddha is sitting silently,
how can you laugh?
This man is not paying respect.

The mind will say that this is disrespect.
The mind has its own rules,
but the heart does not know them;
the heart has its own rules,
but the mind has never heard about them.
The heart can laugh and be respectful;
the mind cannot laugh,
it can only be sad and then be respectful.
But what kind of respect is this which cannot laugh?

A very new trend entered with Maha-Kashyap's laughter,
and down the centuries the laughter has continued.
Only Zen masters, Zen disciples, laugh.

All over the world, all religions have become ill
because sadness has become so prominent,
and temples and churches look like graveyards.
They don't look festive;

they don't give a sense of celebration.
If you enter a church, what do you see there?
Not life, but death.
Jesus crucified on the cross
completes the whole sadness there.

Can you laugh in a church, dance in a church,
sing in a church?
Yes, singing is there, but that is sad,
and people sit with long faces.
No wonder nobody wants to go to church –
it's just a social duty to be fulfilled;
no wonder nobody is attracted to the church –
it is a formality.
Religion has become a Sunday thing.
For one hour you can tolerate being sad.

Maha-Kashyap laughed before Buddha,
and since then, saints, monks, *sannyasis,* masters,
have been doing such things which religious minds,
so-called religious minds,
cannot even conceive of.

If you have seen any Zen book,
you may have seen Zen masters depicted, painted.
No painting is true.
If you look at Bodhidharma's painting
or Maha-Kashyap's painting,
they are not true to their faces,
but just looking at them
you will have a feeling of laughter.
They are hilarious; they are ridiculous.

Look at Bodhidharma's painting.
He must have been one of the most beautiful men.
That he was otherwise is not possible,
because whenever a man becomes enlightened,
a beauty descends,
a beauty which comes from the beyond.
A blessing comes to his whole being.

But look at Bodhidharma's painting.
He looks ferocious and dangerous.
He looks so dangerous that you will become scared
if he comes to visit you in the night –
never again in your life will you be able to sleep.
He looks so dangerous,
as if he is going to kill you.
It was just disciples laughing at the master,
creating a ridiculous portrait.
It looks like a cartoon.

All Zen masters are depicted in a ridiculous way.
Disciples enjoy it.
But those portraits carry a quality
that Bodhidharma is dangerous,
that if you go to him he will kill you,
that you cannot escape him,
that he will follow you and haunt you,
that wherever you go, he will be there,
that unless he kills you, he cannot leave you.
That is the thing depicted
with all Zen masters, even Buddha.

If you look at Japanese and Chinese paintings of Buddha,
they don't look like the Indian Buddha.
They have changed him totally.
If you look at Indian paintings of Buddha,
his body is proportionate, as it should be.
He was a prince, then a Buddha,
a beautiful man, perfect, proportionate.

A big-bellied Buddha?
He never had a big belly,
but in Japan,
in his paintings, his scriptures,
he is painted with a big belly,
because a man who laughs must have a big belly.
Belly laughter –
how can you do it with a small belly?
You cannot do it.

They are joking with Buddha,
and they have said such things about Buddha.
Only very deep love can do that,
otherwise it looks insulting.

Bankei always insisted
on having a painting of Buddha just behind him,
and talking to his disciples he would say:
Look at this fellow.
Whenever you meet him, kill him immediately,
don't give him a chance.
While meditating he will come to disturb you.
Whenever you see his face in meditation,
just kill him then and there,
otherwise he will follow you.

And he used to say:
Look at this fellow;
if you repeat his name –
because Buddhists go on repeating:
Namo Buddhaya, Namo Buddhaya –
if you repeat his name,
then go and wash your mouth.
It looks insulting.
It is Buddha's name and this man says:
If you repeat it,
the first thing to do is wash your mouth.
Your mouth has become dirty.

And he is right because words are words.
Whether it is the name of Buddha or not
makes no difference.
Whenever a word crosses your mind,
your mind has become dirty.
Wash out even Buddha's name.

And this man,
keeping the portrait of Buddha always behind him,
would bow down to it every morning.
So his disciples asked:

What are you doing?
You go on telling us:
Kill this man.
Don't allow him to stand in the way.
And you say:
Don't take his name; don't repeat it.
If it comes, wash your mouth.
And now we see you bowing down.

So Bankei said:
All this has been taught to me by this man,
this fellow,
so I have to pay respect.

Maha-Kashyap laughed,
and this laughter carried many dimensions in it.
One dimension was at the foolishness of the whole situation,
at a Buddha silent and nobody understanding him,
everybody expecting him to speak.
His whole life Buddha had been saying
that the truth cannot be spoken,
and still everybody expected him to speak.

The second dimension –
he laughed at Buddha also,
at the whole dramatic situation he had created,
sitting there with a flower in his hand,
looking at the flower,
creating so much uneasiness, restlessness,
in everybody.
At this dramatic gesture of Buddha,
he laughed and he laughed.

The third dimension –
he laughed at his own self.
Why couldn't he understand up to now?
The whole thing was easy and simple.
And the day you understand, you will laugh,
because there is nothing to be understood.
There is no difficulty to be solved.

Everything has always been simple and clear.
How could you miss it?

With Buddha sitting silent,
the birds singing in the trees,
the breeze passing through the trees,
and everybody restless,
Maha-Kashyap understood.

What did he understand?
He understood
that there is nothing to be understood,
there is nothing to be said,
there is nothing to be explained.
The whole situation is simple and transparent.
Nothing is hidden in it.
There is no need to search,
because all that is, is here and now,
within you.

He laughed at his own self also,
at the whole absurd effort of many lives
just to understand this silence –
at so much thinking.

Buddha called him,
gave him the flower and said:
Hereby, I give you the key.

What is the key?
Silence and laughter is the key –
silence within, laughter without.
And when laughter comes out of silence,
it is not of this world,
it is divine.

When laughter comes out of thinking,
it is ugly.
It belongs to this ordinary, mundane world;
it is not cosmic.
Then you are laughing at somebody else,

at somebody else's cost,
and it's ugly and violent.

When laughter comes out of silence
you are not laughing at anybody's cost.
You are simply laughing at the whole cosmic joke.
And it really is a joke.
That's why I go on telling jokes to you,
because jokes carry more than any scriptures.
It is a joke
because inside you you have everything,
and you are searching everywhere.
What else should a joke be?

You are a king, and acting
like a beggar in the streets;
not only acting, not only deceiving others,
but deceiving yourself that you are a beggar.
You have the source of all knowledge
and are asking questions;
you have the knowing self
and think that you are ignorant;
you have the deathless within you
and are afraid and fearful of death and disease.
This really is a joke,
and if Maha-Kashyap laughed, he did well.

But except for Buddha, nobody understood.
He accepted the laughter,
and immediately realized Maha-Kashyap had attained.
The quality of that laugh was cosmic.
He understood the whole joke of the situation.
There was nothing else to it.
The whole thing is as if the Divine
is playing hide-and-seek with you.

Others thought Maha-Kashyap was a fool,
laughing in front of Buddha.
But Buddha thought this man had become wise.
Fools always have a subtle wisdom in them,
and the wise always act like fools.

In the old days all great emperors
always had one fool in their court.
They had many wise men, counsellors,
ministers and prime ministers,
but always one fool.
Although intelligent and wise,
emperors, all over the world,
in the East and the West,
had a court joker, a fool.

Why?
Because there are things
so-called wise men will not be able to understand,
that only a foolish man can understand,
because the so-called wise are so foolish
that their cunningness and cleverness closes their minds.

A fool is simple and was needed,
because many times
the so-called wise would not say something
because they were afraid of the emperor.
A fool is not afraid of anybody else.
He will speak, whatsoever the consequences.
A fool is a man who will not think of the consequences.

That's what Krishna was saying to Arjuna:
Be a fool.
Don't think of the consequences, the result.
Act!

This is how fools act —
simply, without thinking what is going to happen,
what the result will be.
A clever man always thinks first of the result,
then he acts.
Thought comes first, then action.
A foolish man acts.
Thought never comes first.

Whenever someone realizes the ultimate,
he is not like your wise men.

He cannot be.
He may be like your fools,
but he cannot be like your wise men.

When Saint Francis became enlightened,
he used to call himself God's fool.
The Pope was a wise man,
and when Saint Francis came to see him
even he thought this man had gone mad.
He was intelligent, calculating, clever.
Otherwise how could he be a Pope?

To become a Pope,
one has to pass through much politics.
To become a Pope, saintliness is not needed.
Cunningness is needed, cleverness is needed,
diplomacy is needed,
a competitive aggression is needed
to put others aside,
to force your way,
to use others as ladders and then throw them.
It is politics because a Pope is a political head.
Religion is secondary or nothing at all.
He may be a theologian, but he is not religious
because how can a religious man compete?
How can a religious man fight and be aggressive
for a post?
They are only politicians.

Saint Francis came to see the Pope,
and the Pope thought this man a fool.
But trees and birds and fishes
thought in a different way.
When Saint Francis went to the river,
the fishes would jump in celebration
that Francis had come.
Thousands witnessed this phenomenon.
Millions of fishes would jump simultaneously;
the whole river would be lost in jumping fishes.
Saint Francis had come and the fishes were happy.

And wherever he would go, birds would follow.
They would come and sit on his leg,
on his body, in his lap.
They understood this fool better than the Pope.
Even trees which had become dry
and were going to die,
would become green and blossom again
if Saint Francis came near.
These trees understood well
that this fool was no ordinary fool –
he was God's fool.

When Maha-Kashyap laughed, he was a God's fool
and Buddha understood him
because Buddha was not a Pope.
Later on, Buddhist priests didn't understand him,
so they dropped the whole anecdote.

I was talking in a Buddhist community once,
the Neo-Buddhists,
so I told them this anecdote.
The priest came to me later on and said:
From where have you got this? –
because this is not written in the scriptures.
It is false.
A man like you shouldn't say things
which are not written in the scriptures,
because people believe you.

So I told him:
You bring your scripture.
I'll add this anecdote
and sign it on my own account.
I said:
This happened.
I was a witness there.

The priest looked at me.
He must have thought:
This man is mad the way he is talking.

I told that priest:
I have no power but I have authority.

Power belongs to the politicians;
authority to the religious man.
Power depends on others –
they give it to you –
but authority comes from within.

So I told him:
I was a witness.
I can give you
in writing with my sign
that I was a witness.
This happened.
You have somehow missed in the scriptures,
but I am not at fault for that.
I'm not responsible
if you have missed in your scriptures.

The man, the priest, used to come to me before.
He stopped coming; he never came again.
A dead scripture is more important to a priest
than a live person.
Even if I say I am a witness, I cannot be believed.

This anecdote has been dropped
from Buddhist scriptures
because it is sacrilegious to laugh before Buddha.
To make it the original source of a great religion
is not good.
This is not a good precedent
that a man laughed before Buddha,
and also not a good thing
that Buddha gave the key to this man,
not to Sariputra, Ananda, Modgalayan,
and others who were more important, significant.
And finally, it was they,
Sariputra, Ananda and Modgalayan,
who recorded the scriptures.

Maha-Kashyap was never asked.
Even if they had asked, he would not have answered.
Maha-Kashyap was never consulted
if he had something to say to be recorded.
When Buddha died all the monks gathered
and started recording what happened and what not.
Nobody asked Maha-Kashyap.

This man must have been discarded by the *sangha,*
by the community.
The whole community must have felt jealous.
The key had been given to this man
who was not known at all,
who was not a great scholar or pundit.
Nobody knew him before,
and suddenly, that morning,
he became the most significant man,
because of the laughter, because of the silence.

And in a way they were right,
because how can you record silence?
You can record words,
you can record what happened in the visible.
How can you record
what has not happened in the visible?
They knew the flower had been given to Maha-Kashyap.
Nothing else.

But the flower was just a container.
It had something in it –
Buddhahood, the touch of Buddha's inner being,
the fragrance that cannot be seen,
that cannot be recorded.
The whole thing seems as if it never happened,
or as if it happened in a dream.

Those who were the recorders were the men of words,
proficient in verbal communication,
in talking, discussing, arguing.
But Maha-Kashyap is never heard of again.
This is the only thing known about him,

such a small thing that the scriptures must have missed it.

Maha-Kashyap has remained silent,
and silently the inner river has been flowing.
To others the key has been given,
and the key is still alive, still opens the door.

These two are the parts.
The inner silence –
the silence so deep
that there is no vibration in your being;
you are, but there are no waves;
you are just a pool, without waves,
not a single wave arises;
the whole being silent, still;
inside, at the centre, silence –
and on the periphery, celebration and laughter.
And only silence can laugh,
because only silence can understand the cosmic joke.

So your life becomes a vital celebration;
your relationship becomes a festive thing.
Whatsoever you do, every moment is a festival.
You eat, and eating becomes a celebration;
you take a bath, and bathing becomes a celebration;
you talk, and talking becomes a celebration.
Relationship becomes a celebration.
Your outer life becomes festive.
There is no sadness in it.
How can sadness exist with silence?

But ordinarily you think otherwise.
You think if you are silent you will be sad.
Ordinarily you think how you can avoid sadness
if you are silent.
I tell you,
the silence that exists with sadness cannot be true.
Something has gone wrong.
You have missed the path; you are off the track.
Only celebration can give proof

that the real silence has happened.

What is the difference
between a real silence and a false silence?
A false silence is always forced.
Through effort it is achieved.
It is not spontaneous,
it has not happened to you.
You have made it happen.

You are sitting silently
and there is much inner turmoil.
You suppress it
and then you cannot laugh.
You will become sad
because laughter will be dangerous –
if you laugh you will lose silence,
because in laughter you cannot suppress.
Laughter is against suppression.
If you want to suppress, you should not laugh;
if you laugh, everything will come out.
The real will come out in laughter,
and the unreal will be lost.

So whenever you see a saint sad,
know well the silence is false.
He cannot laugh, he cannot enjoy,
because he is afraid.
If he laughs, everything will be broken,
the suppression will come out,
and then he will not be able to suppress.

Look at small children.
Guests come to your home and you tell them:
Don't laugh.
What do they do?
They close their mouths and suppress their breath,
because if they don't suppress their breath,
then laughter will come out.
It will be difficult.

They don't look anywhere,
because if they look at something, they forget.
So they close their eyes,
or almost close their eyes,
and they suppress their breath.

If you suppress, your breath cannot be deep.
Laughter needs a deep breath;
if you laugh, a deep breath will be released.
That's why nobody is breathing deeply,
just shallow breathing,
because much has been suppressed in your childhood
and after it.
You cannot breathe deeply.
If you go deeper you will become afraid.

Sex has been suppressed through breath,
laughter has been suppressed through breath,
anger has been suppressed through breath.
Breath is a mechanism to suppress or release —
hence my insistence on chaotic breathing,
because if you breathe chaotically,
then laughter, screaming,
everything will come up
and all your suppressions will be thrown out.
They cannot be thrown out in another way,
because breathing, breath,
is the way you have suppressed them.

Try to suppress anything.
What will you do?
You will not breathe deeply.
You will breathe shallowly;
you will breathe
just from the upper part of the lungs.
You will not go deeper
because deeper it is suppressed.
In the belly, everything is suppressed.
So when you really laugh, the belly vibrates —
hence, Buddha's big-bellied portraits.

The belly is relaxed,
and then the stomach is not a suppressed reservoir.

If you see a saint sad, sadness is there,
but the saint is not there.
He has stilled himself somehow
and is every moment afraid.
Anything can disturb him.

Nothing can disturb if real silence has happened.
Then everything helps it to grow.
If you are really silent you can sit in a market,
and even the market cannot disturb it.
Rather, you feed on the noise of the market
and that noise becomes more silence in you.

Really, to feel silence a market is needed –
if you have real silence,
because then the market becomes the background
and the silence becomes perfect in contrast.
You can feel the inner silence bubbling
against the market.

There is no need to go to the Himalayas.
And if you go, what will you see?
Against the silence of the Himalayas
your mind will be chattering.
Then you will feel more chattering,
because the background is in silence.
The background is the silence,
and you will feel more chattering.

If the real happens to you and you are unafraid,
it cannot be taken away.
Nothing can disturb it.
And when I say nothing, I mean nothing –
nothing can disturb it.
And if something does,
it is forced, it is cultivated.
Somehow you have managed it.
But a managed silence is not silence,

it is just like a managed love.

The world is so mad.
The parents, the teachers and the moralists
are so mad and insane
that they teach children to love.
Mothers say to their children:
I am your mother, love me –
as if the child can do something to love.
What can the child do?

The husband goes on saying to the wife:
I am your husband, love me,
as if love is a duty,
as if love is something which can be done.
Nothing can be done.
Only one thing can be done –
you can pretend.
And once you learn how to pretend love,
you have missed.
Your whole life will go wrong.
Then you will go on pretending that you love.
Then you will smile and pretend;
then you will laugh and pretend.
Then everything is false.
Then you will sit silently and pretend;
then you will meditate and pretend.
Pretension becomes the style of your life.

Don't pretend.
Let the real come out.
If you can wait and be patient enough,
when the pretensions have dropped
the real will be waiting there to explode.
Catharsis is to drop the pretences.

Don't look at what the other is saying
because that is how you have pretended,
how you have been pretending.

You cannot love –

either it is there or not –
but the mother says:
Because I am your mother . . .
and the father says:
I am your father . . .
and the teacher says:
I am your teacher, therefore love me –
as if love is a logical thing.

I am your mother, therefore love me.
What will the child do?
You are creating such problems for the child
that he cannot conceive of what to do.
He can pretend.
He can say:
Yes, I love you.
And once the child loves his mother as a duty,
he will become incapable of loving any woman.

Then the wife will come and it will be a duty;
then the children will come and it will be a duty.
Then the whole life will become a duty.
It cannot be a celebration.
You cannot laugh; you cannot enjoy.
It is a burden to be carried.

This is what has happened to you.
It is a misfortune.
But if you understand it,
you can drop it.

This is the key –
the inner part of it is silence,
and the outer part of the key is celebration,
laughter.
Be festive and silent.
Create more and more possibility around you –
don't force the inner to be silent,
just create more and more possibility around you
so that the inner silence can flower in it.

That's all we can do.

We can put the seed in the soil,
but we cannot force the plant to come out.
We can create the situation.
We can protect,
we can give fertilizer to the soil,
we can water,
we can see whether the sun-rays reach or not,
or how much sun-rays are needed,
whether more or less.
We can avoid dangers,
and wait in a prayerful mood.
We cannot do anything else.
Only the situation can be created.

That's what I mean
when I tell you to meditate.
Meditation is just a situation.
Silence is not going to be the consequence of it.
No, meditation is just creating the soil,
the surrounding, preparing the ground.
The seed is there.
It is always there.
You need not put in the seed,
the seed has always been with you.
That seed is Brahma; that seed is Atma.
That seed is you.

Just create the situation
and the seed will become alive.
It will sprout and a plant will be born,
and you will start growing.

Meditation doesn't lead you to silence.
Meditation only creates the situation
in which the silence happens.
And this should be the criterion –
that whenever silence happens,
laughter will come into your life.
A vital celebration will happen all around.

You will not become sad,
you will not become depressed,
you will not escape from the world.
You will be here, in this world –
but taking the whole thing as a game,
enjoying the whole thing as a beautiful game,
a big drama,
no longer serious about it.
Seriousness is a disease.

Buddha must have known Maha-Kashyap.
He must have known
when he was looking at the flower silently
and everybody was restless,
he must have known only one being was there,
Maha-Kashyap, who was not restless.
Buddha must have felt the silence
coming from Maha-Kashyap,
but he would not call.
When he laughed,
then he called him and gave him the flower.
Why?

Silence is only the half of it.
Maha-Kashyap would have missed
if he had been innocently silent and didn't laugh.
Then the key would not have been given to him.
He was only half grown,
not yet a fully grown tree, not blossoming.
The tree was there, but flowers had not yet come.
Buddha waited.

Now, I'll tell you
why Buddha waited for so many minutes,
why for one or two or three hours he waited.
Maha-Kashyap was silent,
but he was trying to contain laughter,
he was trying to control laughter.
He was trying not to laugh,
because it would be so unmannerly:

What would Buddha think?
What would the others think?

But then, the story says,
he couldn't contain himself any more.
It had to come out as a laugh.
The flood became too much,
and he couldn't contain it any more.
When silence is too much, it becomes laughter.
It becomes so overflooded
that it starts overflowing in all directions.
He laughed.
It must have been a mad laughter,
and in that laughter there was no Maha-Kashyap.
Silence was laughing.
Silence had come to a blossoming.

Then immediately Buddha called Maha-Kashyap:
Take this flower.
This is the key.
I have given to all others
what can be given in words,
but to you I give that which cannot be given in words.
The message beyond words, the most essential,
I give to you.
Buddha waited for those hours
so that Maha-Kashyap's silence became overflooded,
it became laughter.

Your enlightenment is perfect
only when silence has come to be a celebration.
Hence my insistence that after you meditate,
you must celebrate.
After you have been silent, you must enjoy it,
you must have a thanksgiving.
A deep gratitude must be shown towards the whole
just for the opportunity that you are,
that you can meditate,
that you can be silent,
that you can laugh.

Anything More?

Bhagwan,

Buddha had many enlightened people around him,
yet he felt something special
for this one enlightened person.

Is there something different in enlightenments?

Yes, Buddha had many enlightened persons around,
but the key can be given only to such a person
who can become a master in his own right,
because the key is to be delivered on and on.
It has to be kept alive.
It was not going to become a treasure
for Maha-Kashyap,
it was a great responsibility,
it had to be given to somebody else.

There were other enlightened persons,
but the key couldn't be given to them.
The key would be lost with them.
Really, Buddha chose the right person,
because the key is still alive.
Maha-Kashyap did well.
He could find another person
who would transfer it to somebody else.

The question is to find the right person.
Just enlightened is not enough.
Not all enlightened persons are masters.
A distinction has to be made.

Jains have a beautiful distinction.
They have two types of enlightened persons.

One enlightened person is known as *Kaivali,*
one who has attained to absolute loneliness.
He has become perfect but he cannot be a teacher.
He cannot give this perfection to somebody else.
He is not a master; he cannot guide.
He himself has become an ultimate peak,
but whatsoever he knows,
he cannot transmit in any way.

The other type of enlightened person
is called *Teerthankara,*
one who becomes a vehicle for others.
He is enlightened,
but he is also a master of a certain art
of communicating through words
and communicating through silence.
He can deliver the message.
Others can be enlightened through him.

Buddha said:
Whatever can be said by words
I have told you.
That which cannot be said by words
I give to Maha-Kashyap.

Maha-Kashyap was the master of silence.
Through his silence he could teach.
Others were masters of words,
and through their words they could teach
and carry on the work.
It was not so essential; it was on the periphery.
But that too was needed
because Buddha's words had to be recorded.
What Buddha did had to be recorded
and transferred from generation to generation.
This, too, was essential,
but it existed on the periphery.

His scholars, Modgalayan, Sariputra, Ananda,
would record everything.
That is a treasure, because Buddha was really happy.

All should be recorded,
and not a single word should be left,
because, who knows,
that single word may become enlightenment to someone.
But the silence also had to be carried.

So two traditions exist –
the tradition of the scripture
and the tradition of silence.
Then many can become enlightened.
And the moment they become enlightened,
they become so silent, so content,
that not even the desire to help others
arises in them.
But Jains say that the Teerthankara
is a person who has gathered some karma –
and this is strange –
and has to fulfill this karma
by conveying the message to others.

It is not a very good thing.
Karma is not a very good thing.
In his past life,
he has gathered karma to be a master.
It is not a good thing,
because something has to be done,
something has to be completed.
And he must do it,
then his karmas are fulfilled;
then he is relieved completely.

The desire to help others is still a desire.
Compassion towards others
is still energy moving towards others.
All desires have disappeared but one,
to help others.
That, too, is a desire,
and unless this desire also disappears
this man will have to come back.

So a master is one who has become enlightened,

but one desire is left.
That desire is not a trouble in becoming enlightened.
To help others helps to become enlightened.
But you will still be attached to the body.
Only one stream, all sources cut,
but one bridge is there.

There were other enlightened persons,
but the key could not be given to them.
It had to be given to Maha-Kashyap,
because he had an inner desire to help –
his past karmas.
He could become a Teerthankara;
he could become a perfect master.
And he did well.
Buddha's choice was perfectly right –
because there was one other of Buddha's disciples
who could have been given the key.
His name was Subhuti.

He was as silent as Maha-Kashyap, even more.
It will be difficult for you –
how silence, how perfection, can be more –
but it is possible.
It is beyond ordinary arithmetic.
You can be perfect,
and you can be even still more perfect
because perfection has growth.
It goes on growing infinitely.

Subhuti was the most silent man around Buddha,
even more than Maha-Kashyap.
But the key could not be given to him
because he was so silent.

It will be difficult now.
You are entering a very complex phenomenon.
In the first place, he would not laugh.
And the key could not be given to him
because he would not laugh.

He was not there.
He was so silent, he was not there to laugh.
He was not there to contain or not to contain.
Even if Buddha had called:
Subhuti, come!
he would not have come.
Buddha would have had to go to him.

It is related of Subhuti
that one day he was sitting under a tree,
when suddenly, out of season,
flowers started falling on him.
So he opened his eyes.
What was the matter?
The tree was not in blossom.
The season was not there.
Then from where, suddenly, these millions of flowers?
He looked and he saw many deities all around,
over the tree, in the sky,
dropping flowers.
He would not even ask the deities
what was the matter.
He closed his eyes again.

Then those deities said to Subhuti:
We are thanking you
for the sermon you have given on emptiness.
And Subhuti said:
But I haven't said a single word.
And you say you are thanking me
for the sermon that I have given on emptiness.
I have not spoken a single word.
The deities said:
You have not spoken and we have not heard.
That is the perfect sermon on emptiness.

He was so empty
that the whole cosmos felt it,
and gods had to come to shower flowers on him.

This Subhuti was there,
but he was so silent that he was not there.
He was not even bothered
why Buddha was sitting with the flower.
Maha-Kashyap was –
not like the others, but still in a way.
He looked at Buddha,
he felt the silence, he felt the absurdity,
but there was one who was feeling.

Subhuti must have been there somewhere, sitting.
There arose no idea
why Buddha was sitting silently today,
why he was looking at the flower.
Then there was no effort to contain it.
Then there was no explosion.
Subhuti was there as if absolutely absent.
He would not laugh,
and if Buddha had called, he would not have come.
Buddha would have had to go to him.
And no one knows –
if the key had been given to him,
he might have thrown it away.

He was not a man meant to be a Teerthankara;
he was not a man meant to be a teacher or a master.
He had no past karmas.
He was perfect, so perfect.
And whenever something is so perfect,
it becomes useless.
Remember, a person so perfect is useless,
because you cannot use him for any purpose.

Maha-Kashyap was not so perfect.
Something was lacking and he could be used,
so in that gap the key could be put.
The key was delivered to Maha-Kashyap
because he could be relied upon to deliver it
to somebody else.
Subhuti was not reliable.

Perfection, when absolute, just disappears.
It is not there in the world.
You can shower flowers on it but you cannot use it.

That's why many enlightened persons were there,
but only one in particular, Maha-Kashyap, was chosen.
He was a man who could be used
for this great responsibility.

This is strange.
That's why I say ordinary arithmetic won't help,
because you will think
that the key should be given to the most perfect.
But the most perfect will forget
where he has put the key.
The key should be given to one who is almost perfect,
just on the brink where one disappears.
And before he disappears,
he will hand over the key to somebody else.

To the ignorant the key cannot be given;
to the most perfect the key cannot be given.
Someone has to be found
who is just on the boundary,
who is passing from this world of ignorance
to that world of knowing,
just on the boundary.
Before he crosses the boundary,
this time can be used and the key delivered.
To find a successor is very difficult,
because the most perfect is useless.

I will tell you one event
that happened just recently:
Ramakrishna was working on many disciples.
Many attained, but nobody knows about them.
People know about Vivekananda, who never attained.
And the key was given to Vivekananda
who was not the most perfect.
Not only was he not the most perfect,

but Ramakrishna wouldn't allow him to be perfect.
And when Ramakrishna felt
that Vivekananda was going to enter
into the perfect *samadhi,*
he called him and said:
Stop!
Now I will keep the key with me
for this final entry,
and only before your death, three days before,
the key will be returned to you.

And only three days
before Vivekananda died,
he had a first taste of ecstasy,
never before.

Vivekananda started crying and weeping and said:
Why are you so cruel to me?
Ramakrishna replied:
Something has to be done through you.
You have to go to the West, to the world.
You have to give my message to people,
otherwise it will be lost.

There were others, but they were already in.
He could not call them out.
They would not be interested in going to the West
or around the world.
They would say that this was nonsense.
They were just like Ramakrishna.

Why would he not go himself?
He was already in,
and somebody had to be used who was out.
Those who are far out cannot be used;
those who are almost in, just near the door,
can be used.
And before they enter,
they deliver the key to somebody else.

Maha-Kashyap was just near the door, fresh,

entering into silence.
Silence became celebration,
and he had a desire to help.
That desire has been used.
But Subhuti was impossible.
He was the most Buddha-like, the most perfect,
but when somebody is Buddha-like, he is useless.
He can give himself the secret key;
there is no need to give it to him.

Subhuti never made anybody a disciple.
He lived in perfect emptiness,
and gods had to serve him many times.
And he never made a disciple.
He never said anything to anybody,
everything was so perfect.
Why bother?
Why say anything?

A master is fulfilling his past karmas.
He has to fulfill them.
And when I have to find a successor,
many will be there who will be like Subhutis.
They cannot be given the key.
Many will be there who are like Sariputras.
Only words can be given to them.
Somebody has to be found
who is entering silence, celebrating,
and has been caught just near the door.
That is why.

Eleventh Talk

20th June 1974

Bhagwan,

The monk Zuigan used to start every day
by saying out loud to himself:
Master, are you there?
And he would answer:
Yes, sir, I am.

Then he would say:
Better sober up.
And he would reply:
Yes, sir, I'll do that.

Then he would say:
Look out now, don't let them fool you.
And he would answer:
Oh no, sir, I won't, I won't.

Meditation cannot be a fragmented thing.
It should be a continuous effort.
Every moment,
one has to be alert, aware and meditative,
but the mind has played a trick.
You meditate in the morning,
and then you put it aside;
or you pray in the temple, and then forget it.
Then you come back to the world,
completely unmeditative, unconscious,
as if walking in a hypnotic sleep.

This fragmented effort won't do much.
How can you meditate for one hour
when you have been non-meditative
for twenty-three hours of the day?
It is impossible.
Suddenly becoming meditative for one hour
is not possible.
You can simply deceive yourself.

Consciousness is a continuum.
It is like a river, flowing constantly.
If you are meditative the whole day,
every moment of it,
and only when you are meditative the whole day,

the flowering will come to you.
Nothing will come before.

This Zen anecdote looks absurd,
but it is very meaningful.
The master, the monk, used to call himself.
This is what meditation means –
calling yourself.
He used to call his own name.
He would say:
Are you there?
And he himself would reply:
Yes, sir, I am here.

This is an effort, a peak effort, to be alert.
You can use this; it will be very helpful.
Suddenly, walking on the street, you call yourself:
Teertha, are you there?
Suddenly thinking stops, and you have to answer:
Yes, sir, I am here.
It brings you to a focus.

When thinking stops, you are meditative, alert.
This calling to oneself is a technique.
Going to sleep, putting off the light in the night,
suddenly you call:
Are you there?
And in that darkness alertness comes.
You become a flame and inside you answer:
Yes, I am here.

And then this monk used to say:
Sober up!
Be sincere; be authentic.
Don't play the game.
He used to call to himself:
Sober up!
And he would reply:
Yes, I will make every effort that I can.

Our whole life is a fooling around.
You can do it
because you are not aware of how you waste time,
how you waste energy.
How life is wasted you are not aware.
It is going down the drain.
Everything is going down the drain.

Only when death comes to you,
you may become aware, alert:
What have I been doing?
What have I done with life?
A great opportunity has been lost.
What was I doing fooling around?
I was not sober.
I never reflected upon what I was doing.

Life is not just to pass,
it is to reach somewhere deep within you.
Life is not on the surface,
it is not the circumference,
it is the centre.
And you have not reached to the centre yet.
Sober up!
Enough time is already wasted.
Be alert and see what you are doing.

And what are you doing?
Searching for money?
It is finally, ultimately useless.
It is again a game, the money game.
You have more than others, you feel good;
others have more than you, you feel bad.
It is a game.

But what is the meaning of it?
What do you gain from it?
Even if you have all the money the world contains,
at the moment of death, you will die as a beggar.
So the whole wealth of the world
cannot make you rich.

Games cannot make you rich.
Sober up!

Somebody is after power, prestige,
somebody is after sex,
and somebody after something else.
All is a game.

Unless you touch the centre of your being,
all is a game.
On the surface only games exist,
and on the surface are only waves,
and in those waves you will only suffer and drift.
You cannot be anchored into your self.

This is why he had to call:
Sober up!
He was saying:
Don't play games.
Enough, you have played enough.
Don't be foolish any more.
Use life for anchoring,
use life to gain roots,
use life as an opportunity to reach the Divine.

You are sitting just outside the temple,
sitting just on the steps, playing games,
and the ultimate is waiting just behind you.
Knock and the door shall be opened unto you.
But you have no time left from the games.

Sober up means
remember what you are doing
and why you are doing it.
But even if you succeed, where can you reach?
This is the paradox –
whenever a man succeeds in these foolish games,
for the first time he becomes aware
that the whole thing has been nonsense.
Only those who never succeed go on playing the game;
those who succeed suddenly become aware

that nothing has been reached.
Ask an Alexander,
ask a Napoleon what he has reached.

It is reported of Alexander
that before he was going to die,
he told his court:
When you carry my dead body in the streets
let both my hands hang out.
Don't cover them.

This was rare.
Nobody was carried that way.
The court couldn't understand, so they asked:
What do you mean?
This is not the usual way.
The whole body is hidden.
Why do you want both your hands hanging out?

Alexander replied:
I want it to be known
that I am dying with empty hands.
Everybody must see it,
and nobody should try to be an Alexander again.
I have gained much and still gained nothing;
my kingdom is great but I am still poor.

You die a beggar,
even if you are an emperor.
Then the whole thing seems like a dream.
Just as in the morning the dream is broken
and all emperorhoods disappear,
all kingdoms disappear,
so death is an awakening.
That which remains in death is real;
that which disappears was a dream.
This is the criterion.
And when this monk used to call: Sober up!
he meant this –
remember death and don't fool around.

You go on in such a way
as if you are not going to die, ever.
Your mind says:
Death always happens to others, never to me;
it is always a phenomenon happening to others,
never to me.
Even if you see a man dying,
you never think that you are dying in him.
His death is symbolic.
The same is going to happen to you.
If you can see that you are going to die,
will you be able to play these games so seriously,
putting your whole life at stake for nothing?
The monk was right to call in the morning:
Sober up!
Whenever you start playing a game again,
with your wife, in the shop, in the market,
in politics,
close your eyes, call yourself and say:
Sober up!
And the monk used to reply:
Yes, sir, I will make every effort that I can.

Another thing is that
he used to remember in the morning.
And why the morning?
The morning sets the pattern;
the first thought in the morning becomes the door.
Hence all religions insist on at least two prayers.
If you can be prayerful, it is the right thing,
but if not, then say at least two prayers –
one in the morning, one in the night.

In the morning,
when you are fresh and sleep has left you,
and consciousness is rising again,
the first thought,
the prayer, the meditation, the remembrance,
will set the pattern for the whole day.

That will become the door,
because things move in a chain.

If you are angry in the morning,
the whole day you will become more and more angry.
The first anger creates the chain,
the second anger follows easily,
the third becomes automatic,
and then you are in it.
Then whatsoever happens around you creates anger.
To be prayerful in the morning,
or to be alert,
to call yourself, to be mindful,
sets the pattern.

In the night also, when you go to sleep,
the last thought
becomes the pattern for the whole sleep.
If the last thought is meditative,
the whole sleep will become meditation;
if the last thought is of sex,
then the whole sleep will be disturbed
by sexual dreams;
if the last thought is of money,
then the whole night you will be in the market,
purchasing and selling.
A thought is not an accident.
It creates a chain.
Then things follow and similar things follow.

So, pray at least twice a day.
Mohammedans pray at least five times.
It is beautiful,
because if a man is to pray five times a day,
then it is almost a continuous thing.
He has to remember:
Now the morning has come,
now the afternoon,
now the evening prayer,
now the night has come . . .

There are gaps,
but two prayers are so near
that they become joined together.

Look at Mohammedans praying.
They are the most beautiful people for prayer.
Hindus don't look so prayerful.
They will do it in the morning,
but a Mohammedan has to pray five times.
Only then is he a Mohammedan.

It is a simple rule,
and five times, continuously remembering,
sets the pattern.
It becomes an inner flow;
you have to come again and again to it.
Between two prayers
it will be difficult to be angry;
between two prayers
it will be difficult to be greedy;
between two prayers
it will be difficult to be aggressive and violent.
The fundamental thing
is that if what one does is continuous,
there is no need for five prayers.
For still there will be gaps,
and you are so cunning
that you can fill the gaps with something wrong
and then your prayer will be affected.
Then it will not be real prayer.
You will be praying,
but inside, deep down,
the wrong current will go on and on and on.

In the morning, this monk used to call himself,
because Buddhists don't believe in prayer,
they believe in meditation.
And the distinction has to be understood.

I, myself, don't believe in prayer.

My emphasis is also on meditation.
There are two types of religious people –
one, the praying type,
and the other, the meditating type.

Buddhists say there is no need to pray,
but just to be alert, aware,
because alertness will give you the prayerful mood.
There is also no need to pray to a God.
How can you pray to a God you don't know?
Your prayer is in the dark;
you don't know the Divine.
If you knew him, there would be no need to pray.
So your prayer is just groping in the dark.
You are addressing someone you don't know,
so how can your address be authentic and real,
how can it come from the heart?
It is just a belief and deep down there is doubt.
Deep down,
you are not certain whether God exists or not;
deep down, you are not certain
whether this prayer is a monologue or a dialogue,
whether there is someone who is listening
and will answer,
or whether you are alone, talking to yourself.
This uncertainty will destroy the whole thing.

Buddha emphasized meditation.
He said:
There is no need for the other;
know well that you are alone.

At least that much is certain –
that you are alone.
Base your life
on something which is absolutely certain,
because how can you base your life
on something which is uncertain, doubtful,
which exists only as a belief, not as a knowing?

But what is certain in life?

Only one thing is certain, and that is you.
Everything can be doubted.

I am here, talking to you;
you may not be there, it may be just a dream.
You are here, listening to me;
I may not be here, it may be just a dream,
because many times in dreams you have listened to me.
And when the dream is on, it looks real.

How can you make the distinction
whether this is a dream or not?
How can you make the distinction
between the real and the dream?
There is no way.
About the other you can never be certain.
There is no way to be certain about the other.
About yourself only, you can be certain.
The only certainty that is there, is you.
Why?
Because even to doubt yourself, you have to be there.

The father of modern western philosophy, Descartes,
started by doubt.
He doubted everything,
because he was in search of something
which could not be doubted.
Only that can become the base of real life,
authentic life –
that which can be doubted.
That which has to be believed
cannot become the real foundation.
This foundation is sinking,
and you are building a house on the sands.

So he doubted everything.
The gods can be doubted easily,
the world can be doubted, it may be just a dream;
the others . . .
He doubted everything.

Then suddenly he became aware
that he could not doubt himself.
That is contradictory.
If you say that you doubt yourself,
it means you have to believe you are there to doubt.
You can say that you may be deceived about yourself,
but there is somebody
who has to be there to be deceived.
The self cannot be doubted.

Hence Mahavir didn't believe in God.
He believed only in the self,
because that is the only certainty.
You can grow out of certainty;
you cannot grow out of uncertainty.
When there is certainty, there is trust;
when there is uncertainty, there may be belief,
but the belief is always hiding the doubt.

So many people come to me who are theists.
They believe in God,
but their belief is just skin-deep.
Poke them a little,
push them a little, shake them a little –
they become doubtful
and they become afraid.
What type of religion is possible
if you are so much in doubt?
Something indubitable is needed.

Mahavir and Buddha both emphasized meditation.
They cancelled prayer.
They said:
How can you pray?
You don't know the Divine,
so you cannot really believe.
You can force a belief,
but a forced belief is a false belief.
And you can argue and convince yourself,
but that won't help,

because your arguments, your convictions, are always yours;
and the mind goes on wavering.

So Buddha and Mahavir both emphasized meditation.
Meditation is a totally different technique.
There is no need to believe,
no need to move to the other.
You are alone there.
But you have to wake yourself.
That is what that monk is doing.
He is not calling the name of Ram,
he is not calling the name of Allah,
he is calling the name of himself,
and only himself,
because nothing else is certain.
He calls his whole name:
Are you there?
And he doesn't wait for any God to reply.
He replies to himself:
Yes, sir, I am here.

This is the Buddhist attitude,
that you are alone there.
If you are asleep,
you have to call yourself, you have to answer.
It is a monologue.
Don't wait for any God to answer you.
There is no one to answer you.
Your questions will be lost in the empty sky.
Your prayers will not be heard.
There is nobody else to hear them.

So this monk seems foolish.
But really, all those who are in prayer
may be more foolish than this monk.
This monk is doing a more certain thing,
calling himself and answering himself.

You can make yourself alert.
I tell you, your name is the mantra.

Don't call Ram, don't call Allah,
call your own name.
Many times a day, whenever you feel sleepy,
whenever you feel that the game is taking over,
and you are losing yourself in it,
call yourself:
Are you there?
And answer yourself.
Don't wait for anybody's answer.
There is no one to answer you.
Answer:
Yes, sir, I am here.
And don't answer verbally.
Feel the answer:
I am here.
And be there, alert.

In that alertness, thoughts stop.
In that alertness, the mind disappears,
even for a moment.
And when there is no mind, there is meditation.
When the mind has stopped,
meditation comes into being.

Remember, meditation is not something
that is done by the mind,
it is the absence of the mind.
When the mind stops, meditation happens.
It is not something out of the mind,
it is something beyond the mind.
And whenever you are alert, the mind is not.

So, we can conclude, your sleepiness is your mind,
your unawareness is your mind,
your somnambulism is your mind.
You move as if drunk, not knowing who you are,
not knowing where you are going,
not knowing why you are going.

And the third thing the monk says

is to remember not to be fooled by others.
Others are fooling you continuously.
Not only are you fooling yourself,
others are also fooling you.

How are the others fooling you?
The whole society, culture, civilization,
is a collective conspiracy.
That's why no society allows rebellious people.
Every society requires obedience, conformity.
No society allows rebellious thoughts.
Why?
Rebellious thoughts make people aware
that the whole thing is just a game.
and when people become aware
that the whole thing is just a game,
they become dangerous,
they start going beyond the society.

Society exists as a hypnotic state,
and the crowd is a hypnotizing factor.
You are born,
but when you are born,
you are neither a Hindu nor a Parsee,
because consciousness cannot belong to any sect.
Consciousness belongs to the whole.
It cannot be sectarian.

A child simply is,
innocent of all nonsense of Hindus, Buddhists, Jains.
A child is pure mirror,
but immediately society starts working on the child.
A mould has to be given.
A child is born as a freedom,
but immediately society starts killing his freedom.
A mould has to be given, a pattern.

If you are born in a Hindu family,
your parents will start teaching you
that you are a Hindu.
Now they are creating a hypnotic state.

Nobody is a Hindu.
But this child is innocent; he can be befooled.
This child is simple.
He will believe the parents,
that he is a Hindu –
not only a Hindu, but a Brahmin,
not only a Brahmin, but a *Deshastha* Brahmin.

Sects within sects.
Just like Chinese boxes –
boxes within boxes.
And the more he becomes narrowed,
the more he becomes a prisoner.
The box goes on getting smaller and smaller.
He was just like the sky when he was born.
Then he became a Hindu, a smaller box;
then he became a Brahmin – a smaller box;
then he became a Deshastha – an even smaller box.

This goes on and on.
Society goes on forcing him into smaller boxes,
and then he will have to live as a Deshastha Brahmin.
His whole life he will be with this box.
He will carry this box around him.
This box is a grave.
He must come out of these boxes.
Only then will he know what real consciousness is.

Then society gives concepts;
then society gives prejudices,
and systems and religions.
And then he will never be able to look directly.
Always society will be there to interpret.

You are not aware when you say something is good.
Are you there, looking?
Is this your feeling,
that something is good,
or just an interpretation of the society?
Something is bad.

Have you looked into it,
and come to the conclusion
that something is bad,
or has society simply taught you
that this is bad?

Look!
A Hindu looking at cow dung thinks
that this is the purest thing possible in the world.
Nobody in the world will think of cow dung
as the purest thing in the world –
cow dung is dung, excreta –
but a Hindu thinks of cow dung
as the purest thing in the world.
He will eat it happily.
He eats it.
Nobody in the world can believe
how Hindus can be befooled in this.
But they are befooled.
When the Hindu child is initiated,
panchamrita is given to him –
a particular combination of five things.
In these five things cow dung is one,
and the urine of the cow is another.
It is difficult.
Nobody can believe that this is right.
But they have their own prejudices.

Put down all prejudices and look directly.
But no society allows you to look directly.
It always comes in and interprets,
and you are befooled by it.

This monk in the morning used to call:
Don't be fooled by others.
And he would reply:
Yes, sir.
Yes, sir, I will not be befooled by others.

This has to be constantly remembered,
because the others are all around,

and they are befooling you in such subtle manners.

And now the others have more power than ever.
Through advertisement, through radio,
through newspapers, through television,
the others are manipulating you.

In America, the whole market depends
on how you can befool the customer,
how you can create an idea in the minds of others.
Now, a two-car garage is a must
if you want to be happy.
In America, a two-car garage is a must.
Nobody asks why.
If you are not happy with one car,
how can you be happy with two cars?
If there is fifty percent happiness with one car,
how can you be happy with two cars?
With one car you are unhappy;
with two cars
you will be doubly unhappy, that's all.
The mathematics is simple,
but there is advertisement, propaganda.
The whole society exists by manipulating others.

Happiness is something
like a commodity in the market –
you go and purchase it.
It has to be purchased.
How can happiness be purchased?
Happiness is not a commodity, it is not a thing,
it is a quality of living,
a consequence of another life.
You cannot purchase it.
There is no way.

Look at American newspapers
and you will see that you are missing.
Just through money, happiness can be purchased.
They create a feeling that you are missing something –

then you start working for it,
then you earn money,
then you purchase it.
And then you feel that you have been deceived.
But that feeling is not very deep,
because before you feel that you have been deceived
some new deceptions have entered the mind,
and now they are pulling you ahead:
You must have a hill station house,
or you must have a summer resort,
or you must have a yacht.
Something is always there to be achieved.
Only then will you be happy.
They will go on pulling you up to your death.
Until you die, those advertisements, that propaganda,
will go on pulling you.

This monk was right.
This must be part of your alertness –
that you should not be befooled by others.
The whole society exists on exploitation,
exploiting the other.
Everybody is exploiting,
and this exploitation is not only in the market,
it is in the temple, in the church, in the synagogue.
It is everywhere,
because the priest is also a businessman,
and the Pope is a super-businessman.

Because you need peace, you ask for peace,
so there are people who say:
Come to us, we will give you peace.
You ask for bliss,
and there are people
who are ready to sell bliss to you.
If people like Maharishi Mahesh Yogi succeed in the West,
they don't succeed in the East.
Nobody listens to them in India.
Nobody is bothered.
But America listens to every type of nonsense.

Once you get on to the right channel of propaganda,
once you get all the right advertising people,
then there is no problem.

Maharishi Mahesh Yogi talks
as if the inner silence can be purchased immediately,
as if within a week you can find meditation.
Just by sitting for fifteen minutes
and repeating a mantra,
you will be happy forever and ever.
And the American mind,
which has been poisoned by advertisements,
is attracted and a crowd gathers.
It goes on changing, but it is always a crowd,
and it appears as if things are happening.
Even temples and churches have become shops.

Meditation cannot be purchased
and no one can give it to you.
You have to achieve it.
It is not something outer,
it is a something inner, a growth,
and that growth comes through awareness.

Call your own name,
in the morning, in the night, in the afternoon.
Whenever you feel sleepy, call your own name.
And not only call it,
answer it and say it loudly.
Don't be afraid of others.
You have been afraid of others enough.
They have already murdered you through fear.
Don't be afraid.
Even in the market place you must remember.
Call your own name:
Teertha, are you here?
And answer:
Yes, sir.

Let people laugh.

Don't be befooled by them.
The only thing to be achieved is alertness,
not respect, not respectability from people.
Because that is one of their tricks –
they make you obedient through respectability.
They say:
We will respect you.
You bow down and be obedient.
Don't be there at all.

Just follow the society
and the society will pay you much respect.
This is a mutual arrangement.
The more dead you are,
the more society will pay you respect;
the more alive you are,
the more society will create trouble for you.
Why?
A Jesus had to be crucified
because he was an alive man.
He must have called in his childhood:
Jesus, don't be befooled by others.
And he was not befooled,
so others had to crucify him,
because he was not part of the game.
Socrates had to be poisoned and killed,
Mansoor had to be murdered.
These are people who have escaped from the prison,
and whatsoever you say,
you cannot persuade them to come back.
They will not come into the prison.
They have known the freedom of the open sky.

Remember.
Be mindful and alert.
If you are alert,
if your actions become more and more aware,
whatsoever you do will not be done sleepily.

The whole effort of society

is to make you automatic,
is to make you like an automaton,
is to make you a perfect efficient mechanism.

When you start learning to drive,
you are alert, but not efficient,
because alertness takes energy,
and you have to be alert to many things –
the gears, the wheel, the brake, accelerator, clutch.
There are so many things you have to be aware of,
that you cannot be efficient, you cannot go fast.
But by and by, when you become efficient,
you need not be aware.
You can go on humming a song,
or thinking inside or solving a puzzle,
and the car goes by itself.
The body takes it automatically.
The more automatic you become,
the more efficient.

Society needs efficiency,
so it makes you more and more automatic:
In everything you do, be automatic.
Society doesn't bother about your awareness.
Your awareness is a problem for society.
You are asked to be more efficient, more productive.
Machines are more productive than you.
The society doesn't want you to be as men,
it needs you as mechanical devices,
so it makes you more efficient and less aware.
This is automatization.
This is how the society fools you.
You become efficient, but your soul is lost.

If you can understand me,
then the whole effort of meditative techniques
is to de-automatize you, to make you again alert,
to make you again a man, not a machine.

In the beginning you will become less efficient,
but don't be bothered by it

because everything has settled as an automaton.
In the beginning everything will become a mess.
You will not be able to do anything efficiently.
You will feel difficulty,
because you have become fixed
with unconscious efficiency.
To be consciously efficient,
long effort will be needed,
but, by and by, you will be aware and efficient.

If there exists in the future,
any possibility of a real human society,
the first thing,
the basic thing that will have to be done is this –
don't make children automatic.
Even if it takes a little longer
to make them efficient,
make them efficient with awareness.
Don't make them machines.
It will take longer,
because two things have to be learned –
the efficiency and awareness.
A human society will give you awareness,
even with less efficiency,
but efficiency will come by and by.
Then when you are alert,
you will be able to be efficient with alertness.

Meditation is de-automatization in the beginning.
Then you'll start working with a new awareness –
efficiency remains in the body,
and consciousness remains alert.
You don't become a machine, you remain a man.
If you become a machine,
you have lost humanity.

This monk was doing this de-automatization.
From the very morning he called himself –
said: Be alert!
said: Don't fool yourself!

said: Don't be befooled by others!
These three layers of mindfulness
have to be achieved.

I have heard
once it happened that a young man
belonging to a very rich and aristocratic family,
came to a Zen master.
He had known everything, indulged in every desire.
He had enough money, so there was no problem,
but then he got fed up –
fed up with sex, fed up with women,
fed up with wine.
He came to the Zen master and said:
Now I am fed up with the world.
Is there some way that I can know myself,
who I am?

The young man said:
But before you say anything,
let me tell you something about myself.
I am indecisive,
and cannot continue anything for long,
so if you give me some technique,
or if you tell me to meditate,
I may do it for a few days and then I will escape,
knowing well that there is nothing in the world,
knowing well that only misery awaits there, death.
But this is my type of mind.
I cannot continue, I cannot persist in anything,
so before you choose something, remember this.

The master said:
Then it will be very difficult if you cannot persist,
because long effort will be needed
to undo all that you have done in the past.
You will have to travel back.
It will have to be a regression.
You will have to reach back
to the moment when you were born, when fresh, young.

Again, that freshness will have to be achieved.
It is not ahead, but back you will have to go,
to become a child again.
But if you say you cannot persist,
and within days you will escape,
it will be difficult.
But let me ask you one question.
Have you ever been interested in something so deeply
that you were absorbed completely?

The young man thought and he said:
Yes, only in chess, the game of chess,
I have been very much interested.
I love it,
and that's the only thing that is saving me.
Everything has fallen.
Only chess is with me,
and I can, somehow, pass my time.

The master said:
Then something can be done.
You wait.
He called the attendant and told him
to bring one monk who had been meditating
for twelve years in the monastery,
and to tell the monk to bring a chess board.

The chess board was brought.
The monk came.
He was acquainted a little with chess,
but for twelve years
he had been meditating in a cell.
He had forgotten the world and chess and everything.

The master said to him:
Listen, monk! –
this is going to be a dangerous game.
If you are defeated by this young man,
the sword is here,
and I will cut off your head,
because I wouldn't like a meditative monk,

who has been meditating for twelve years,
to be defeated by an ordinary young man.
But I promise you, if you die by my hand,
then you will reach the highest heaven.
So don't be disturbed.

The young man became also a little uneasy,
and then the master turned to him and said:
Look, you say that you get absorbed in chess,
so, get totally absorbed
because this is a question of life and death.
If you are defeated, I will cut off your head,
and remember, I cannot promise heaven for you.
This man is okay.
He will go anyhow.
But I cannot promise any heaven for you.
If you die, hell is the place.
Immediately you will go to the seventh hell.

For a moment, the young man thought to escape.
This was going to be a dangerous game,
and he had not come here for this.
But then, it looked dishonourable.
He was a samurai, a son of a warrior,
and just because of death, imminent death,
to escape was not in his blood.
So he said:
Okay.

The game started.
The young man started trembling
as a leaf in a strong wind,
the whole body trembling.
He started perspiring,
and cold perspiration came to his body.
He started sweating
from his head to the soles of his feet.
It was a question of life and death,
and thinking stopped,
because whenever there is such emergency,

you cannot afford thought.
Thought is for leisure.
When there is no problem, you can think;
when there is really a problem, thinking stops
because the mind needs time.
And when there is emergency, there is no time.
You have to do something immediately.

Every moment, death was coming nearer.
The monk started,
and he looked so serene and calm
that the young man thought:
Well, death is certain.

But when the thoughts disappeared,
he became totally absorbed in the moment.
When thoughts disappeared,
he also forgot that death was awaiting –
because death, too, is a thought.
He forgot about death, he forgot about life,
he became just a part of the game,
absorbed, totally immersed in it.

By and by, as the mind disappeared completely,
he started playing beautifully.
He had never played that way.
In the beginning the monk was winning,
but within minutes the young man got absorbed,
started beautiful movements,
and the monk started losing.

Only the moment existed, only the present.
There was no problem then.
The body became okay.
Trembling stopped; perspiration evaporated.
He was light like a feather, weightless.
The perspiration even helped.
He became weightless.
His whole body felt as if it could fly.
His mind was no more there.
Perception became clear, absolutely clear,

and he could see ahead, five movements ahead.
He had never played so beautifully.
The other's game started crumbling.
Within minutes the other would be defeated.
His victory was certain.

Then suddenly,
when his eyes were clear, mirror-like,
when perception was profound, deep,
he looked at the monk.
He was so innocent.
Twelve years of meditation –
he had become like a flower;
twelve years of austerity –
he had become absolutely pure.
No desire, no thought, no goal,
no purpose existed for him.
He was as innocent as possible.
Not even a child is so innocent.
His beautiful face, his clear, blue-sky eyes . . .

This young man started feeling compassion for him –
sooner or later his head would be cut off.
The moment he felt this compassion,
unknown doors opened,
and something absolutely unknown
started filling his heart.
He felt so blissful.
All over his inner being, flowers started falling.
He felt so blissful.
He had never known this bliss,
this beatitude, this benediction.

Then he started making wrong moves knowingly,
because the thought came to his mind:
If I am killed, nothing is disturbed.
I have nothing of worth,
but if this monk is killed,
something beautiful will be destroyed;
but for me, just a useless existence.

He started making wrong movements consciously,
to make the monk win.
At that moment the master upturned the table,
started laughing and said:
Nobody is going to be defeated here.
You both have won.

This monk was already in heaven; he was rich.
No need to cut off his head.
He was not troubled at all when the master said:
Your head is to be cut off.
Not a single thought arose in his mind.
There was no question of choice.
If the master says it is going to be so,
it is okay.
He said yes with his whole heart.
That was why there was no perspiration, no trembling.
He was playing chess; death was not a problem.

And the master said:
You have won,
and your victory has been greater than this monk's.
Now I will initiate you.
You can be here,
and soon you will be enlightened.

Both basic things had happened –
meditation and compassion.
Buddha has called these two the basic –
pragya and *karuna,* meditation and compassion.

The young man said:
Explain it to me.
Something has happened I don't know.
I am already transformed.
I am not the same young man
who came to you a few hours before.
That man is already dead.
Something has happened.
You have done a miracle.

The master said:
Because death was so imminent, you couldn't think,
thoughts stopped.
Death was so much on you,
thinking was impossible to do.
Death was so near,
there was no gap between you and death,
and thoughts need space to move.
There was no space, so thinking stopped.
Meditation happened spontaneously.

But that was not enough,
because that type of meditation
which happens because of emergency will be lost.
When the emergency is gone,
that meditation will be lost.
So I couldn't throw the board at that moment,
I had to wait.
If meditation really happens, whatsoever the cause,
compassion has to follow.
Compassion is the flowering of meditation.
If compassion is not coming,
your meditation is, somewhere, wrong.

Then I looked at your face.
You were filled with bliss
and your eyes became Buddha-like.
You looked at the monk,
and you felt and you thought:
It is better to sacrifice myself than this monk.
This monk is more valuable than me.
This is compassion,
when the other becomes more valuable than you.
This is love,
when you can sacrifice yourself for the other.
When you become the means
and the other becomes the end,
this is love.
When you are the end
and the other is used as a means,

this is lust.
Lust is always cunning,
and love is always compassionate.

Then, I saw in your eyes the compassion arising.
And then you started to make wrong movements,
just to be defeated,
so that you would be killed and this monk saved.
At that moment, I had to throw the board.
You had won.
Now you can be here.
I have taught you both meditation and compassion.
Now follow this track,
and let them become spontaneous in you —
not situational, not depending on any emergency,
but just a quality of your being.

Carry this story within you, in your heart.
Let it become the beat of your heart.

Rooted in meditation,
you will have wings of compassion.
That's why I say
that I would like to give you two things:
roots into this earth and wings into that heaven.
Meditation is this earth; it is here and now.
The very moment you can spread your roots, do it.
And once roots are there,
your wings will reach to the highest sky possible.
Compassion is the sky; meditation is the earth.
And when meditation and compassion meet,
a Buddha is born.

Go deeper and deeper into meditation
so you can go higher and higher in compassion.
The deeper the roots of a tree reach,
the higher the peak.
You can see the tree;
you cannot see the roots,
but they are always in proportion.

If the tree is reaching to the sky,
the roots must be reaching
to the very end of the earth.
The proportion is the same.
As deep as your meditation is,
the same depth will be achieved in compassion.

So compassion is the criterion.
If you think you are meditative,
and there is no compassion,
then you are deceiving yourself.
Compassion must happen,
because that is the flowering of the tree.
Meditation is just a means towards compassion.
Compassion is the goal.

Make yourself more and more alert.
Call your name and answer,
just to create more awareness.
When you really become aware,
you will feel a new upsurge of energy.
Compassion will happen to you,
and with compassion, bliss;
with compassion, beatitude;
with compassion, conviction.

Anything more?

Bhagwan,

At the start of the camp you said
you were moving into a new phase of your work.
We've felt it in meditation,
but most important,
you've changed the way you speak to us.
At one time, for example,

you never admitted to being an enlightened master,
and now you do.

Could you tell us more
about this new phase of your work?

I can only say things
which you have become capable of hearing.
It depends on you.
If you have become a disciple,
then I can easily say that I am a master,
but if you are not a disciple,
it will be just meaningless
saying to you that I am a master.
If somebody comes who is just curious about me,
I will not say this to him.
It would be pointless.
He will not understand,
rather, he will misunderstand.

When you are ready to receive,
only then can I give.
And now that you are ready,
I can say many things
which cannot be said to casual visitors.
They are curious.
Their curiosity is shallow;
they have not come to receive something.
Their mind functions in a childish way.
They just want to know everything,
and they are not going to penetrate deeper into it.

Now I can say many things to you,
because I know that you will not misunderstand.
Even if you don't understand,

this much is certain –
you will not misunderstand.

This will be a new phase.
It has already started.
I will be working
only with those who are sober, not fooling around.
I will be working
only with those who have really come to a point
where they need transformation –
who are really sincere, authentic seekers
and are ready to do whatsoever I say.
To them I can say:
I am enlightened.
To them I can say:
I am a master.
To them I can say:
Come to me and drink out of me,
and you will not be thirsty, ever.

But this cannot be said to everybody.
This cannot be said to somebody who is just passing,
who you meet on the street.
The more you get ready,
the more I can pour myself into you.
Before, your pots were there, but upside down.
Even if I had poured, it would have been a wastage.

Now many of you are in a situation,
where now, your pots are not upside down.
Now they are right side up.
Now I can pour.
Now I can trust that you will take it as a treasure,
that you will hide it,
that you will share it
only with those who are sincere,
who are in search.
Many more secrets will be following,
but they will only follow
as you get more ready.

The phase, a new phase, has started.
I will not be working with the masses now,
and I will be dropping all those
who are just hanging around for other reasons,
and not for their spiritual growth.
There are many types of people,
and even they are not aware
why they are hanging around.
But I know.
I will be dropping them.

Fewer and fewer will be accepted now.
If I drop you, you will not be able to know
that I have dropped you,
because you will go on thinking that you dropped me.
That's how the ignorant mind always consoles itself.

Now I will be working only with few, a chosen few,
and as you get ready,
many more secrets can be given to you,
and I will be able to talk easily.
Then I can be true.
I need not say a lie to you then.
I will not say what you want to hear.
No, I will say what is really to be said to you.

And don't wait for the future,
because no one knows about the future.
This very moment,
open yourself as much as you can
so you can receive me.

I will tell you one anecdote.
It happened to the head
of one of the most famous
European banking families,
the Rothschilds.
Baron Rothschild was standing in his garden one day,
and a man looking like a beggar, a pedlar,
came to him and told him

to purchase a lottery ticket.
He said:
Come on, take a chance.

The Baron wanted to get rid of him.
He said:
What should I do with the lottery ticket?
I don't need it, I have got enough.
The beggar said:
No one has got enough.
Take a chance.
Who knows, you may win it.
So, just to get rid of the nuisance,
he purchased the ticket.

Next morning, the man knocked again and said:
Look, you have won one million dollars.
The Baron was very much pleased and said:
I suppose I must reward you.
Then the Baron thought and said:
What will you choose?
I can give you twenty-five thousand dollars
right this moment,
or ten thousand dollars a year for your whole life.

The man was not more than thirty or thirty-five.
He was perfect in his health;
he was going to live at least thirty, forty years,
even more.
Forty years at ten thousand dollars a year
comes to four hundred thousand dollars –
or right now, twenty-five thousand dollars.

The beggar thought for a single moment and said:
You please give me twenty-five thousand dollars
right now.
Even the Baron was puzzled.
He said:
You think over what you are doing.
Your whole life, I say –
ten thousand dollars per year.

The man said:
I will choose twenty-five thousand right now,
because looking at the luck you Rothschilds have,
I will not be alive six months.
Looking at the luck you Rothschilds have,
I will not live for six months more.
You give me right now.
The next moment is uncertain.
Don't waste time.

That's what I say to you.
Right this moment, I am here, available.
Don't wait for the future, because nobody knows.
Open your heart, become more receptive, get attuned.
Everything is possible.
At this very moment I can give you the key.

A new phase has started.
Now get ready for it,
because it is not a question concerning me,
it is a question concerning you.
How much you can get, you will get.
Your capacity will be the limit.
If you are open totally, there is no limit.
The whole ocean is ready to fall into the drop,
but the drop is afraid.
It is trying to protect itself.

Kabir, one of the greatest mystics ever born,
has said two things.
He has said:
In the beginning, when I was in search of God,
I was thinking my drop of water
would drop into the ocean of the Divine.
But when it really happened,
it happened quite otherwise –
the ocean dropped into my small drop.

It always happens otherwise.
You are not going to meet God,

God is going to meet you.
How can you seek him?
You don't know his whereabouts;
you don't know his address.
He is in search of you constantly,
and whenever you are ready,
the ocean drops into you.

Meditation will make you ready;
compassion will make you perfect.
So, carry these two mantras –
pragya, meditation; *karuna,* compassion.
Let these two be the goals.
Let your whole life revolve around them,
and very soon you will be attuned.
Then I can pour myself into you.

Anything more?

Bhagwan,

You've said meditation is a flowering.
And for us,
the perfume of the flower is gratitude.

Is there anything we can do for you?

Yes –
meditation, compassion and gratitude.
Whenever you are meditative, you feel blissful;
whenever you are in compassion, you feel ecstatic.
And then gratitude arises,

not towards anyone in particular,
gratitude just arises.
It is not towards me or towards Jesus,
or Zarathustra or Buddha,
it is simply gratitude.
You feel so grateful just for being here,
just for being alive,
just for being able to be meditative,
just for being able to be in compassion.
You feel simply grateful.
That gratefulness is not towards anybody,
it is towards the whole.

If you feel grateful towards me,
it is a gratitude of the mind.
If you meditate and if you flower in compassion,
you will feel simply grateful,
not grateful towards me.
Then there is no 'towards' –
you feel simply grateful,
towards all.
And when you feel grateful towards all,
that is really gratefulness towards me,
never before it.

When it is a choice, you choose me.
Then your master becomes a point, not the whole.
That's what is happening everywhere.
Disciples get fixed with the master,
and masters help them to be fixed.
That's not good, it's ugly.

When you really flower,
then your perfume is not addressed to anybody;
when you really flower,
the perfume goes in all directions.
It simply moves in all directions,
and whosoever passes near you
is filled with your fragrance,
he carries your fragrance.

And if nobody passes you,
then on that silent, lonely path
your fragrance goes on spreading,
but it is not addressed.

Remember, the mind is always addressed;
being is never addressed.
The mind is always moving towards something;
being is simply moving towards all.
It is a movement without any goal.

A goal exists because of motive.
You move towards something because there is desire.
When there is no desire, how can you move?
Movement is there, but no motivation.
Then you move in all directions.
Then you overflow.

Then your master is everywhere.
Then I am everywhere.
And only when this point comes,
are you free from the master also.
Then you are freed of all relationship;
you are freed of all presence, of all bondage.
And if a master cannot free you from himself,
he is not a master at all.

So you need not do anything for me.
You do something for you.
Meditation, compassion –
that is doing for me.
Then the presence will come,
and not thought by the mind.

Right now, you think and you feel:
What shall we do?
Then it is the mind.
How to pay the master?
He has done so much for you, what should you do?
This is the mind,
thinking in terms of giving and taking.

No, this mind won't help.

One thing you can do for me –
drop this mind.
Allow your being to flower.
Then you will be fragrant.
Then in all dimensions and directions,
the whole will be happy.
You will be a bliss,
and your gratitude will not be narrow.
It will not be towards a point,
it will be moving all over, everywhere.
Only then do you achieve prayer.
This gratitude is prayer.

When you go in a temple and do a prayer,
it is not prayer;
but when, after compassion, gratitude arises,
the whole existence becomes the temple.
Whatsoever you touch, it becomes a prayer;
whatsoever you do, it becomes prayerful.
You cannot be otherwise.
Deeply rooted, anchored in meditation,
deeply flowing into compassion,
you cannot be otherwise.
You become prayer,
you become gratitude.

But remember, the mind is always addressed.
It has a goal, a desire to achieve.
Being is unaddressed.
It has no goal; it has nothing to achieve.
The kingdom of being is already achieved,
the emperor is already there on the throne.
You move because movement is life,
but don't move towards any goal,
because when there is no goal, there is no tension.
Then movement is beautiful, graceful.

RAJNEESH MEDITATION CENTRES

INDIA

Shree Rajneesh Ashram, 17 Koregaon Park, Poona 411 001, Tel: 28127.

Sagar Deep, 52 Ridge Road, Malabar Hill, Bombay 400 006, Tel: 814783

Rajyoga, C5/44 Safdarjang Development Area, Opp, I.I.T., Palam Road, New Delhi 16, Tel: 654533

Manisha, 'Jupiter', 33 Landons Rd., P.B. 1019, Madras 600 010, Tel: 663118

NEPAL

Asheesh, P.O. Box 278, Tahachal, Kathmandu, Tel: 14504

JAPAN

Asheesh, Gohchi-machi 794, Akishima-shi, Tokyo 196, Tel: 0425-43-2321

AUSTRALIA

Sahajam, 17 Saleham Street, Victoria Park, W.A. 6100

Devayan, 25 Martyn Street, Cairns, Queensland 4870

NEW ZEALAND

Shanti Niketan, 9 Edenvale Road, Mount Eden, Auckland, Tel: 686-528

U.S.A.

Dhyanataru, 375a Huron Ave., Cambridge, Mass. 02138, Tel: 617-491-2671

Shantiduta, 1703 Banks, Houston, Texas 77098

Sarvam, 6412 Luzon Avenue, Washington D.C. 20012, Tel: 202-726-1712

Geetam, Box 576, Highway 18, Lucerne Valley, California 92356, Tel: 714-248-6163

Paras, 4301 24th Street, San Francisco, California 94114, Tel: 415-285-2122

Devadip, 2350 South Dahlia, Denver, Colorado 80222, Tel: (303) 757-4461

Premsagar, P.O. Box 2862, Chapel Hill, North Carolina 27514, Tel: 919-929-2433

Satgit, 415 Central Park West, New York 10025

CANADA

Arvind, 1721 Wallace, Vancouver, B.C., VGR 4J1

Unmada, 156 Central Avenue, London, Ontario N6A IM5, Tel: 519-432-7434

MEXICO

Prem Niketan, Tata Vasco 16, Coyoacan 21 DF

COSTA RICA

Mouna, Apartado 10165, San Jose

BRAZIL

Purnam, Caixa Postale 1946, Porto Alegre 90000, RG do Sul, Tel: 240673

ENGLAND

Kalptaru, Top Floor, 10A Belmont Street, London NW1, Tel: 01-485-3216

Nirvana, 82 Bell Street, London NW1, Tel: 01-262-0991

Suryodaya, The Old Rectory, Gislingham-by-Diss, Nr. Eye, Suffolk

Tushita, Wallingford Road, North Moreton, Nr. Didcot, Oxon 119BA, Tel: Didcot 813256

Anurodha, 122 Billesley Lane, Mosely, Birmingham 13 9DR, Tel: 021-449-7363

SCOTLAND

Prasthan, 21 Wilmot Road, Glasgow G13 1XL, Tel: 041-959-6237

FRANCE

Prempath, Place de la Mairie, 45-390 Desmonts, Tel: (38) 33-65-92

Shantidweep, c/o Mme Depre, 17 Cite Malesherbes, 75009 Paris

SPAIN

Palash, Can Bonet, Sta. Gertrudis, Ibiza, Baleares

HOLLAND

Amitabh, Post Box 3280, 1001 AB, Amsterdam, Tel: 020-221296

Darshan, Provenierstraat 15b, 3033 CE Rotterdam, Tel: 010-661361

Nishant, Rodenbachlaan 30, Eindhoven, Tel: 040-446007

DENMARK

Anand Niketan, Skindergade 3, DK-1159 Copenhagen K, Tel: 01-1179-09

ITALY

Arihant, Via Mancinelli 19, Milan, Tel: (02) 3282687

SWITZERLAND

Satyam, Schilberg, 16 Rue Richemont, 1202 Geneva

WEST GERMANY

Purvodaya, D-8051 Margarethenried, Fongi-hof, Tel: 087-64426

Shreyas, 8 Munich 60, Raucheneggerstr. 4/11, Tel: 089-8888-177

Anandlok, 1 Berlin 61, Mehringdamm 61, Tel: 030-693-2901

Satdharma, 8000 Munich 40, Amalienstr. 38, Tel: 089-282-113

BELGIUM

Mansarovar, 75 Ave. Edmond Mesens, 1040 Brussels

EAST AFRICA

Anand Need, Kitisuru Estate, P.O. Box 72424, Nairobi, Kenya

SOUTH AFRICA

Bodhisattva, P.O. Box 1, New Germany, Natal, Tel: 72-6065

Majida, 356 Oak Ave., Ferndale, Randburg, Tvl.